COSMIC TRIGGER III

MY LIFE AFTER DEATH

WHAT Critics Have Said ABOUT
ROBERT ANTON WILSON's Books

A very funny man ....readers with open minds will like his books
    —Robin Robertson, *Psychological Perspectives*

Does for quantum mechanics what Durrell's *Alexandria Quartet* did for Relativity, but *Wilson is funnier*
    —John Gribbin, physicist

While pretending to amuse, Wilson actually rids the reader of important fictions necessary to the conduct of life as we know it. A *very dangerous* book!
    —Dr. Nick Herbert, physicist

A profound book that reveals with raw humor the intrinsic inconsistencies in the thought systems underlying much of the craziness in our society.
    —Peter Russell, author of *The Global Brain*

The most important philospher of this century...
    —Timothy Leary, Ph.D.

A master satirist who views history as an open question
    —Brad Linaweaver, *Atlanta Constitution*

Like swallowing a hand grenade coated with LSD: it will either expand your mind or blow it to Kingdom Come.
    —Victor Koman, author of *The Jehovah Contract*

One of the most important writers working in English today... Courageous, compassionate, optimistic and original.
    —Elwyn Chamberling, author of *Gates of Fire*

Robert Anton Wilson is a dazzling barker, hawking tickets to the most thrilling tilt-a-whirls and daring loop-o-planes on the midway of higher consciousness.
    —Tom Robbins, author of Even Cowgirls Get the Blues

Intellectually *challenging and stimulating*....surreal fantasy, satire and a carefully constructed chaos
    —*Chicago Reader*

Deliberately annoying
    —Jay Kinney

Malicious, misguided fanaticism
    —Robert Sheaffer, CSICOP

Stupid
    —Andrea Antonoff

COSMIC TRIGGER III

MY LIFE AFTER DEATH

BY

Robert Anton Wilson

1995
NEW FALCON PUBLICATIONS
TEMPE, ARIZONA U.S.A.

International Standard Book Number: 0-56184-112-9

First Edition 1995

Cover by S. Jason Black

The paper used in this publication meets the minimum requirements of the American National Standard for Permanence of Paper for Printed Library Materials Z39.48-1984

Address all inquiries to:
NEW FALCON PUBLICATIONS
1739 East Broadway Road Suite 1-277
Tempe, AZ 85282 U.S.A.
(or)
1605 East Charleston Blvd.
Las Vegas, NV 89104 U.S.A.

Other Titles From New Falcon Publications

Sex and Drugs
Prometheus Rising
The New Inquisition
    By Robert Anton Wilson
Rebels and Devils
    Edited by C. S. Hyatt; with William S. Burroughs, et. al.
Undoing Yourself With Energized Meditation
Secrets of Western Tantra
The Tree of Lies
    By Christopher S. Hyatt, Ph.D.
Pacts With The Devil
    By S. J. Black and Christopher. S. Hyatt, Ph.D.
Urban Voodoo
    By Christopher. S. Hyatt, Ph.D. and S. J. Black
Eight Lectures on Yoga
Gems From the Equinox
    By Aleister Crowley
Neuropolitique
Info-Psychology
Game of Life
    By Timothy Leary, Ph.D.
Zen Without Zen Masters
    By Camden Benares
The Complete Golden Dawn System of Magic
What You Should Know About the Golden Dawn
    By Israel Regardie
Metaskills: The Feeling Art of Therapy
    By Amy Mindell, Ph.D.
Astrology and Consciousness: The Wheel of Light
    By Rio Olesky
Carl Sagan and Immanuel Velikovsky
    By Charles Ginenthal
Soul Magic: Understanding Your Journey
    By Katherine Torres, Ph.D.

And to get your free catalog of *all* of our titles, write to:

NEW FALCON PUBLICATIONS
Catalog Dept.
1739 East Broadway Road, Suite 1-277
Tempe, AZ 85282 U.S.A.

Other Books by Robert Anton Wilson

Chaos and Beyond
*Coincidance: A Head Test
*Cosmic Trigger I: The Final Secret of the Illuminati
*Cosmic Trigger II: Down to Earth
*Cosmic Trigger III: My Life After Death
*Ishtar Rising
Masks of the Illuminati
Natural Law, or Don't Put a Rubber on Your Willy
Nature's God
*Neuropolitics (with Timothy Leary and George Koopman)
PLAYBOY'S Book of Forbidden Words
*Prometheus Rising
*Quantum Psychology
*Reality Is What You Can Get Away With
Right Where You Are Sitting Now
*Sex and Drugs: A Journey Beyond Limits
The Earth Will Shake
The Illuminati Papers
The Illuminatus trilogy (with Robert Shea)
    The Eye in the Pyramid
    The Golden Apple
    Leviathan
*The New Inquisition
The Schroedinger's Cat trilogy
    The Universe Next Door
    The Trick Top Hat
    The Homing Pigeons
The Sex Magicians
The Widow's Son
*Wilhelm Reich in Hell

*Published by New Falcon Publications

TABLE OF CONTENTS

Part Two—The Reality of Masks

PROLOGUE

Future events like these will affect you in the future!
—Plan 9 From Outer Space

There are many arguments to the contrary,
but you wouldn't understand them.
—The Trial

I did not write this book *entirely* to vex those unfortunate librarians who will soon have the irksome duty of trying to fit it into the Dewey Decimal System. I have other, more subversive amusements in mind. (You have had warning.)

This book revels in mysteries, wallows in puzzles and ambiguities. We will, so to speak, peer at wiggling things that look like rattlesnakes from one side and look much more like the middle of next week from a different but equally plausible angle of view. Those with tired or rigidly dogmatic minds will find these perceptual relativities distressing. True Believers of all sorts should certainly avoid this book "as the Devil flees holy water." I warn you. You have had warning. Don't complain later if this book seems like a bloody abattoir for your own favorite Sacred Cows and you get a bit uneasy about things that formerly looked simple and honest.

Those bold bad folk who pass that warning will soon read, for instance, about a mysterious Hungarian who may have produced a large number of the canonical classics of modern painting, and another most extraordinary artist crawling about the jungles of Uganda, intent upon dressing gorillas in clown suits. We will explore the rantings of Femigoguery to study the decline and fall

9

of Shakespeare, and the sexual horror hidden in Beethoven's music, with comments on other amazing innovations of the Politically Correct.

I will also reveal my life after death, and discuss the real/ surreal paradoxes of the 18.5 camera lens. We will study a secret society that may have superhuman origins, a group of intelligent Europeans who regularly receive instructions from an alleged extraterrestrial correspondence school named UMMO, and the latest scoop on the infamous Illuminati of Bavaria. We will wander in the murk of Aristotle's excluded middle and fuzzy logic. You'll learn of an unsuccessful effort to find the normal or average, and see multi-culturalist Heresy invading the calendar. We will even examine a mathematician who produced more important theorems than anyone of our time, and did it all without the necessity of even having a body—

Our paradigm: One day in 1986, I browsed, reverently, through the Long Room at Trinity College Library, in Dublin, where they keep their precious first editions. I felt eerie, "mystical," trans-time sensations looking at such items as the first printings of works by Locke, Hume, Newton, Buffon, Tom Paine; even more weird feelings stirred as I looked at *The Book of Kells*, hand-printed and hand-illustrated in the 8th Century. But nothing moved me so strangely and deeply as the book called *Travels in Remote Parts of the World,* published in 1726 by one Lemuel Gulliver of Nottinghamshire. Journeying in my Poetic Imagination (another name for the Divine, according to Blake) I shared what the first readers must have felt, as they turned those plausible pages...

My present audience may even, at times, feel like 1726 fans of travel books (a fad at the time) who rushed out to buy Mr. Gulliver's volume and suffered increasing bouts of perplexity and Heisenberg's Syndrome—terminal Uncertainty—as they read about dwarfs smaller than any in Europe, giants bigger than any in Europe and intellects "vast, cool and unsympathetic" floating above them in a space-city. (The publisher could not alleviate readers' doubts: the manuscript had arrived in the middle of the night, amid deliberate mystification). The *Travels'* veracity soon became as much a matter of debate as anything in post-modernist art, or even post-modernist criticism. Some 1720s readers experienced painful, proto-Foucoultian doubts about Mr.

Gulliver, a "scientific modern observer" who described every fabulous kingdom with finicky detail and exact mathematics. It didn't really aid puzzled readers to note that Mr. Gulliver also tried to write like an intelligent horse, because he had learned to love horses better than people.

The artist, Aristotle says, imitates Nature. The trickster, practical joker and counterfeiter also imitate Nature, if you think about it. Certain insects imitate Nature so successfully that they become invisible, except to those who look at all things with suspicious eyes; and Philip K. Dick has memorably suggested that we may share space-time with "Zebra," a hypothetical giant intelligence that we can't see because it disguises itself as the whole environment. Lemuel Gulliver merely imitated the Royal Scientific Society, but some of the people we will meet in this book seem to imitate all sorts of things, in Nature and beyond Nature.

Who, except the card-carrying paranoid, looks closely enough to see all the masks that hide—well, whatever masks hide?... But we don't want to become paranoids. We merely want to look at certain masks that shed light on those urgent problems of the real and the counterfeit that currently bedevil, not just the "mentally ill", but those who pass as linguistic philosophers, art/literature critics, and earnest students of Controversial Science (called Pseudo-Science by those panicky souls who wish to end the controversy in a hurry.) And although I can't promise to tie all this mystery and mummery into one neat bundle, I will include in the new, improved Big Picture many elements left unclear in the first two volumes of this trilogy.

I would like to acknowledge the Usual Sources, who here, as in earlier books, have vastly influenced my perceptions/conceptions—R. Buckminster Fuller, Timothy Leary, Barbara Marx Hubbard, Alfred Korzybski, Marshall McLuhan. I would also like to acknowledge specially a few who played a major role in shaping and inspiring the present work—Moses Horowtiz, Orson Welles, James Joyce, Jean Cocteau, Harold Garfinkle and the man who called himself Elmyr.

CSICON (The Committee for Surrealist Investigation of Claims of the Normal) does not bear any responsibility for my use, or misuse, of their basic 'Patapsychologial discoveries, i.e., the First Law ("You can't find a normal person anywhere") and the Second Law ("You can't even find a plumber on week-ends.")

I conclude these murky hints with one more, still murkier quotation from one of my own Immortal Novels, the one which has perplexed as many true-or-false addicts as Mr. Gulliver ever did: a note jotted in a policeman's notebook as he begins to suspect that certain "fantasy fiction" (by Ambrose Bierce, Robert Chambers and H. P. Lovecraft) contains the key to the biggest mystery he ever confronted—

The usual hoax: fiction presented as fact. The hoax presented here opposite of that: fact presented as fiction.

And I add a helpful remark from M. André Gide: "Do not understand me too quickly."

PART ONE

THE MASKS OF REALITY

Like Bertrand Russell and Carl Hempel, fuzzy theorist
Bart Kosko says everything is fuzzy except numbers.
For instance, take *alive*. Viruses can form crystals
and cannot reproduce on their own. Are they alive?
—McNeil and Freiberger, *Fuzzy Logic*

'Pataphysics, will be, above all, the science of
the particular, despite the common opinion that
the only science is that of the general. 'Pataphysics
will examine the laws which govern exceptions.
—Alfred Jarry, *Faustroll*

I have never seen a normal man or woman, or even a
normal dog. I have never experienced an average day
or an ordinary sunset. The *normal*, the *average,* the
ordinary describe that which we never encounter outside
mathematics, i.e., imagination, the human mindscape.
—Timothy F.X. Finnegan, *Nightmare and Awakening*

Qui me amat, amat et canem meum.
—Saint Bernard of Clairvaux

ONE

I GOT RUN OVER ON THE INFORMATION SUPERHIGHWAY

**In Which the Author Learns of His Own Death
and We Begin to Look Behind the
Masks of Art and Magick**

> This is not a normal world.
> —*Batman*

> "Maybe" is a thin reed to hang your
> whole life on, but it's all we've got.
> —*Hannah and Her Sisters*

According to reliable sources, I died on February 22, 1994—George Washington's birthday. I felt nothing special or shocking at the time, and believed that I still sat at my word processor working on a novel called *Bride of Illuminatus*. At lunch-time, however, when I checked my voice mail, I found that Tim Leary and a dozen other friends had already called to ask to speak to me, or—if they still believed in Reliable Sources—to offer support and condolences to my grieving family. I quickly gathered that news of my tragic end had appeared on Internet, one of the most popular computer networks, in the form of an obituary from the *Los Angeles Times*:

> "Noted science-fiction author Robert Anton Wilson was found dead in his home yesterday, apparently the victim of a heart attack. Mr. Wilson, 63, was discovered by his wife, Arlen.
> "Mr Wilson was the author of numerous books... He was noted for his libertarian viewpoints, love of technology and off the wall humor. Mr Wilson is survived by his wife and two children."

This L.A. *Times* obit originally got on the net *via* somebody in Cambridge, Mass. I thought immediately of the pranksters at M.I.T.—the Gremlins of Cyberspace, as somebody called them.

I admired the artistic verisimilitude of the Gremlin who forged that obit. He mis-identified my *ouvre*. (Only 6 of my 28 books could possibly get classified as science-fiction, and perhaps 3 more as science-faction.) He also, more clumsily, stated my age wrong by one year and the number of my surviving children wrong by one child. Little touches of incompetence and ignorance like that helped create the impression of a real, honest-to-Jesus LA *Times* article—just as creaking chairs, background coughs, overlapping dialogue, scrupulously "bad" sound quality etc. make the bogus newsreels in Orson Welles' two greatest movies, *Citizen Kane* and *F For Fake*, seem "just like the real thing."

The forged L.A. *Times* obituary may not rank with Welles' most monumental hoaxes—e.g., his prematurely Deconstructionist "war of the worlds" radio show, where bland music and increasingly ominous newsbreaks thoroughly confused a mass audience about the borderline between "art" and "reality." But the *Times* forgery, if not of Wellesian heft, certainly contained a Wellesian blend of art and magic: in retrospect, it even reminds me, a little, of the 1923 Surrealist art show, in which the audience first encountered a taxi-cab in the garden—a cab which had rain falling *inside* but not *outside*—and then confronted a sign telling them gnomically:

DADA IS NOT DEAD
WATCH YOUR OVERCOAT

I always think that double dip of guerrilla ontology (by Dali and Breton, respectively) carried the baffled audience beyond surrealism into post-modernism, i.e., Total Agnosticism and/or terminal bewilderment. Certainly, art and life, and art and magick, have never gotten clearly disentangled again to the satisfaction of all observers. In this struggle to knock down the Iron Curtain between creativity and "reality," I tend to see the Wellesian men-from-Mars hoax as the second major step after surrealism and, *ahem*, I sometimes immodestly consider my own works a third step.

But the Gremlin who killed me on February 22 carried the "transformation of mind and all that resembles it" (Breton) one quantum jump further than I ever had. He caused real grief and shock, if not Wellesian mass panic.

One friend told me that the first bulletin he saw, on Compuserve, just quoted the alleged LA obit and then added, "This is as bad as learning that Zappa died. I think I'm going to meditate a bit, in his memory."

Another networker, female, keyboarded in a whole chapter of *Ecclesiastes* in my memory—"For everything there is a season, a time for every matter under the sun: a time to be born, a time to die" etc.—and then added "Now get out there and PARTY LIKE HE'D WANT YOU TO!"

Some others had even more exalted lines about the value of my life, but I feel too self-conscious to quote them. I'll just say that they did a lot to cheer me up and remind me that I have admirers.

You see, I've become a bit morbid lately, and have developed a tendency to believe one bad review more than twenty good ones—something that happens to many writers about my age. The two saddest cases among the giants of the generation before me, Hemingway and Faulkner, both got bad-review-itus to such an extent that they submitted to the pain and humiliation of electro-shock therapy in a desperate attempt to break up their depressions. The electro-shock worked for Faulkner, who recovered and wrote one more book before he died, but not for Hemingway, who shot himself as soon as he got away from the helpful doctors and their brain-frying machine. Venomous reviewers have more power than you generally think.

But nobody was writing hostile reviews of me on the computer nets the first weeks after my death. All I read about myself assured me that my works belonged on the same exalted pedestal with Homer, the Rig Veda and Hilda Doolittle, while my soul ranked in the vicinity of Buddha, Noble Drew Ali and Saint Teresa of Avilla.

I felt so overwhelmed by the love and kindness in all the lamentations that I felt a bit guilty about not "deserving" these eulogies by really dying.

My goodwyf Arlen, on the other hand, did not find any of this amusing. She said the guy who started it had "gotten dangerously close to black magic." She tends to regard "Curses," "Maledictions" and "Self-Fulfilling Prophecies" as different names for the same neural sabotage. Sometimes, quoting Mary Baker Eddy, she calls it "mental malpractise."

Shortly, however, other artistic efforts began to appear on computer nets.

One bulletin from "The House of Apostles of Eris, San Francisco" said that "attempts to contact Robert Anton Wilson have been unsuccessful"—hmmm?—but nevertheless reassured all that "RAW is alive and busy with religious works."

I think the author of that bulletin *intended* to sound unconvincing, especially to the initiates of my Classic Novels (Erisian "religious works" consist of mind-fucks or "*shocks*" in the strict Masonic sense). He or she certainly cast contagious suspicion on the other denials being posted on the nets by various friends who had managed to contact me. Certainly, the conspiracy buffs who have followed my career ever since *Illuminatus!* will not believe a report that includes the suspicious admission that nobody could find me ...

Many contributions to the alive-or-dead controversy seemed unsure whether I had died (or hadn't died) in Los Angeles or San Francisco. The funniest one of all claimed I survived, but in Howth (County Dublin, Ireland)—where I lived during most of the 1980s:

"Contacted at his home in Howth Castle, Wilson said 'The reports of my death have been slightly exaggerated. I can still totter about a bit and even crack a weak joke occasionally.'"

To which some wit, recognizing the Joycean jest, replied: "Shouldn't that be Howth Castle and Environs?"

The Howth legend continued to circulate from one net to another, and soon included the news that I had taken over management of the Committee for Surrealist Investigation of Claims of the Normal (CSICON) after the death of its founder, Prof. Timothy F.X. Finnegan, of Trinity College, Dublin, and that CSICON still offers $10,000 to any "normalist" who can produce "a perfectly *normal* person, place or thing—or even an *ordinary* sunset. Or an *average* day."

Of course, Finnegan and CSICON exist in some sense, like Howth Castle, as readers of my works know by now—not quite in the sense in which the Statue of Liberty exists, but not entirely in the metaphoric sense in which the National Debt and the Holy Trinity "exist" either. But the result of all this was beginning to make me wonder if I only exist in some semiotic or metaphoric sense myself, sort of like an elderly male Madonna. I mean, like, man, do I exist the way the Howth Castle in Dublin exists, or the way the Howth Castle and Environs in *Finnegans Wake* exists?

I remembered a Spiritualist treatise I had once read. (I skim all sorts of weird literature, which keeps me from believing totally any of the stuff we get told as Official Truth by the major media). This ghostly tome claimed that we poor spectres often do not know we've died until some medium "contacts" us and explains why people have started treating us so rudely lately— e.g., why even our wives and children ignore us outright unless we knock over the lamps or rap in code on the tables.

I had also read Jonathan Swift's hilarious "pamphlet war" with the astrologer Partridge about whether Partridge had or had not died on the day predicted by a rival astrologer, Isaac Bickerstaff. ("Bickerstaff" sounds a lot like Swift himself, operating behind a Mask as usual, just as Lemuel Gulliver, the scientific world traveler, also sounded curiously like Swift; we shall learn much about Reality and Masks in this enquiry.) Although Partridge insisted vehemently on his continued vitality, Swift's argument, a model of Celtic subtlety, held that just because a man *claims* he hasn't died and may even believe it himself, this does not logically require us to credit his unsupported testimony. This left poor Partridge floundering—(never argue with a Dublin intellectual)—and now I felt myself floundering a bit also.

Obviously, my testimony on the matter would not convince Swift, when he decided to play the Scientific Skeptic, and I wondered if it would convince CSICOP—the group opposing CSICON.

CSICOP (Committee for Scientific Investigation of Claims of the Paranormal) believes that the "normal" actually exists somewhere, and not just in some Platonic spook world. They claim it exists *everywhere*, and that nothing else at all exists anywhere. (If you see any of the 10^{100} not-normal things in this world, they will claim you had a hallucination.)

Anyway, I *thought* I still had a life, but I have often *thought* I had landed in Berlin again and saw Nancy and Andy and Tobias and Tom and all my friends there, when in fact I only had a dream of going to Berlin; and I have even *thought* I had achieved Great Spiritual Revelations when everybody else in the room believed I had merely wigged—gone "over the hills with the wee people" at last, and gotten so stoned I couldn't tell the Great Duck-Footed Whangdoodle from a *Daily Planet* phone booth.

As a famous bard wrote:

> He thought he saw a banker's clerk descending from a bus
> He looked again and saw it was a hippopotamus

I remembered a Phil Dick novel, *Ubik*, about a bunch of dead people who don't know they have died and think the universe has slowly started turning into shit. If that happened to me, I would not and could not know about it—by definition.

Thoughts like that can really unsettle your mental architecture, especially if you wasted a lot of your life on epistemological philosophy, and on cannabis extracts. I, alas, have indulged both those vices on many occasions, and I fear that I have become a horrible example of Aggravated Existentialism. Worse yet: I have also heard Albert Rosenfeld, a distinguished M.D., lecturing on "clinical death," say, "We have come a long way from the day when Marshall Dillon lifts the sheet and says, 'He's dead, all right.' Now it takes a committee to decide."

As noted on the title page of this section, the "committee" of modern science still hasn't decided whether to consider viruses "alive" or not. Some even say that viruses can pass through cycles of life and death, over and over, almost like reincarnating "spirits" in Asian eschatology. Certainly, a virus can act like a dead thing—an inert object—for long, long periods of time before it suddenly starts acting like a living thing again and reproducing faster than bunny rabbits. That little mystery represents just one place among many where I find modern science a lot weirder and more interesting than the speculations of metaphysics.

Can I prove, any better than poor Partridge or the Ebola virus, that I haven't died and come back several times? What committee can decide on a case like mine?

But these ontological doubts got pushed aside when the C.I.A. entered the Trip, playing the Wrathful Demons of this bardo.

Somebody (signing her/him/itself as "Anon.") logged the following into several computer bulletin boards:

"THE C.I.A. KILLED ROBERT ANTON WILSON...

"Wilson did not die of natural causes. He was assassinated. Earlier on that day, Wilson was injected with a time-delay poison based on shellfish toxin, by agents of the CIA's special SUPER SECRET BLACK OPERATIONS SQUAD, using a special microscopic needle made of a plastic which dissolves in the body without a trace. Wilson's body had immediately been taken and cremated and the usual step of an autopsy had been bypassed, BY ORDERS FROM ABOVE.

"It is clear why the power$ that be wanted Wilson dead. Wilson was a dangerous element; the government can only govern if the majority does not question the system (whoever currently "rules" does not matter.) The troublesome minority can be dealt with discreetly, by means of EXECUTIVE ACTION (assassination), which is what happened with Wilson...

"Earlier the same agencies (CIA, NRO, DEA and CFR/TLC/Bilderberger BOLSHEVIK SHADOW GOVERN-MENT) had LSD advocate Timothy Leary neutralized with a neurotoxin which DESTROYS THE MIND and ARTIFI-CIALLY INDUCES A STATE SIMILAR TO SENILITY...

"Dissemination of this information is encouraged. MAKE 30 COPIES."

Cute as a shit-house rat, I thought, when I read this. *Now, whenever Tim tells people I haven't died, that will furnish further evidence of his "senility."*

Of course, I also enjoyed the idea that somebody, somewhere, might consider me important enough to terrorize the C.I.A. and call out their SUPER SECRET BLACK OPERATIONS SQUAD to terminate me. Since CLASSIFIED represents the rating directly below SECRET in government security manuals, I wondered how the CLASSIFIED BLACK OPERATIONS SQUAD spends its time—giving housemaid's knee or genital warts to editorial cartoonists?

A Marshall Yount wrote to deny that Dr. Leary showed any signs of "neutralization" and roundly asserted that Tim "is pretty goddamn sane" and told "Anon" bluntly, "You are probably an Oliver Stone fanatic."

One J. Fleisher wrote on the same net, "I liked that bit about the 'plastic dissolving needle.' Did you make all that James Bond stuff up yourself? Correct me if I'm wrong but aren't most plastics insoluble (in just about anything let alone the human body.)???"

Sci-fi fanzine editor Arthur Hlavaty wrote, "I have contacted Wilson and he tells me he's alive. But I'm pretty gullible."

Others grew more eldritch:

"Maybe the government has installed a VIRTUAL RAW in his place to allay people's fears. Oh, sure, he can respond all he wants, but I know it's not the real RAW." Virtual RAW has also been seen disguised as Christopher S. Hyatt, Ph.D. — so says the publisher of New Falcon. Apparently Falcon receives letters on a weekly basis claiming that Virtual RAW is Christopher S. Hyatt, Ph.D. and secretly owns Falcon. (On the other hand, many people have said that Virtual Hyatt is really Orson Welles.) One thing is funny though: Falcon's checks always clear the bank and neither Virtual Bob or Virtual Hyatt has signed them.

But my favorite contribution of the Wilson Mythos was logged by somebody using the moniker, *The Green One*:

> "There is no toxin. There is no needle. You have not heard of a toxin. You have not heard of a needle. They were not tools of the conspiracy. There is no conspiracy. The toxin and the needle, which do not exist, played no part in the conspiracy, which does not exist. Fnord. Repeat after me. There is no toxin..."

What can I add to that bit of guerrilla ontology, except to say "Fnord indeed?"

TWO

PAINTER JAILED FOR COMMITTING MASTERPIECES

**In Which We Encounter The Mystery Man of Modern Art
and Fall Into Another, Deeper Philosophical Abyss**

> "Logic!" cried the frog.
> "There is no logic in this!"
> —*Mr. Arkadin*

> I can live without God.
> I can't live without painting.
> —*Vincent and Theo*

But perhaps we began at the wrong point. The true nature of our plot might better begin with another, and more elaborate, Deconstruction.

In August 1968 the Spanish government imprisoned a man on the island of Ibiza for creating a long series of sketches and paintings—beautiful, intensely lyrical works that *Art Experts* had universally proclaimed as masterpieces.

The imprisonment of this Maker of Masterpieces did not represent censorship in the ordinary erotic or religious sense.

Nobody even accused the artist of Political Incorrectness. He got jugged for a technical matter—namely, that he had signed the wrong name to his works...or several wrong names, in fact. Names like Picasso and Van Gogh and Modigliani and Matisse, for instance. Not that anybody knew then, or knows now, what name the man *should* have signed. Generally, when the case gets recalled at all, people refer to the prisoner of Ibiza as El Myr or Elmyr de Hory, but neither of those titles have any claim to special eminence among his many aliases. In his long career, the painter had used both of those names, but he had also used Baron Elmyr von Houry, Elmyr Herzog, Louis Cassou, Baron Elmyr Hoffman, Joseph Dory, E. Raynal, Joseph Dory-Boutin and quite a few others—perhaps as many as a hundred pseudonyms, according to Francois Reichenbach, an alleged **Expert** on this case.

One trouble with Reichenbach as an **Expert**: he admits to buying and selling some of "Elmyr's" forged paintings. Another problem: he later collaborated (with Orson Welles, no less) on a film—*F For Fake*—that either exposed "Elmyr" totally or created a whole new set of myths about "Elmyr," depending on which other **Expert***s* you choose to believe.

(Welles himself has said—in the documentary "Orson Welles: A Life in Film," BBC-TV—that "Everything in that movie was a fake." But to post-modernism, all art constitutes fake, or mask, in the Aristotelian sense of an imitation, or counterfeit of something else, and in a new non-Aristotelian sense we will explore as we advance deeper into the murk. We need to think slowly before deciding whether Welles spoke literally or metaphorically in describing *F For Fake* as itself a fake.)

Whatever the facts—if we still dare to speak of "facts" in this age of situationism and deconstructionism—we will, as a matter of typographical convenience, hereafter refer to the prisoner of Ibiza as Elmyr without dubious quotes and without any guessing about his last name—if he had a last name, like ordinary humans, and didn't arrive here by spaceship... "Elmyr" he preferred in his last years, and Elmyr we shall call him. And, for those who don't like to repeatedly see words they can't sound out in their heads, the Hungarian "Myr" rhymes with "deer," and "Elmyr" has the same beat approximately as "cold beer" or "my ear." Just

say "cold beer, my ear, shake spear, Elmyr" and you'll have no
further sounding problems as you read.

Elmyr served only two months in jail and then the Spanish
further expressed displeasure with his chosen profession by
expelling him from their country for one year, because he also
had a reputation as an flamboyant homosexual, or in pop argot,
an aging fairy godmother. But meanwhile, he had told his story
to a young American writer, Cliff, who became his official
biographer. According to *Fake!*, the deliberately outrageous
biography concocted together by Cliff and Elmyr, this man of
variable names, wobbly gender and multiple styles had
committed many more masterpieces than those for which he had
gotten jailed.

In fact, *Fake!* says Elmyr had painted *over a thousand* of the
classics of modern art. Every time you walk through a museum
and see a Picasso or a Matisse that you particularly like, you
should stop and ask, "Now did Picasso or Matisse do that, or did
Elmyr do it?"

Sort of changes your whole view of what critics call "the
canon," doesn't it?

The canon—a term borrowed from the theologians (which
should make us suspicious at once: can we borrow anything of
value from a corporation widely suspected for about 200 years
now of intellectually bankruptcy?)—designates those works of
art and literature which have achieved the rank of Masterpieces.
When does a work achieve this canonicity? When the **Experts**
say it does, of course. But the Elmyr case, far more than
Deconstructionist philosophy, indicates that the **Experts** do not
always know shit from Shinola.

Of course, not everybody believes that Elmyr committed quite
as much great art as he gleefully confesses in the biography.
Many **Experts** claim *Fake!* (a title to ponder, and ponder again)
engaged in shameless bragging and exaggeration, to make Elmyr
seem cleverer than the facts warrant.

Unfortunately, these **Experts** had—many of them—
authenticated some of the fakes that Elmyr undoubtedly did
paint. As Elmyr's co-author, Cliff, says, these **Experts** do not
want their cover blown—they don't want us to know how often,
and how easily, they have gotten duped by Elmyr and other
skilled forgers.

According to Cliff, *all* **Experts** *operate largely on bluff*. Some of the **Experts**, however, have counter-attacked by suggesting that this alleged "co-author," Cliff, may himself have functioned even more as a co-conspirator.

And, in fact, the same co-author, Clifford Irving to give him his full name, subsequently became even more famous, and much more infamous, for persuading a New York publisher to give him a $750,000 advance for an *authorized* biography of Howard Hughes, i.e., a biography in which Hughes himself would talk, for the record, about all the financial, political, conspiratorial [1] and sexual scandals in his Faustian career. $750,000 had a value, in 1969, of about $5 million now, but the publishers shelled out happily. Irving had shown them a contract and various notes *in Hughes' own handwriting...*

You see, even though Cliff Irving had already written *Fake!*, a textbook on forgery, including charming details on forged signatures as well as counterfeit paintings, he had a boyishly sincere manner and a wickedly scintillating personality. Like all good con-men.

He and Hughes had met on a pyramid in Mexico, Irving said with a straight face. [2] In the dead of night, of course... (It would make a wonderful surrealist painting, if Elmyr ever did a Dali: The ambitious young Irving and the rich old lunatic with matted hair and fingernails—*or claws*—like Bigfoot...signing a contract on a pyramid...under, I presume, a full moon...)

Handwriting **Experts** later testified in court, after Irving's own veracity came under suspicion. They said absolutely that Howard Hughes himself, and nobody else, had written the signature and notes produced by Irving. At this point, alas, many people began to share Irving's (and Elmyr's) low opinion of **Experts**, and soon the biography of Hughes got canceled.

---

[1] Hughes believed that the Rockefeller family had "bought" all the legislators and courts east of the Mississippi and himself bought as many politicians as he could, starting from the West, to "protect" himself. He also gave $1,000,000 to Nixon's brother, and Nixon's illegal "plumbers" unit did one break-in for Hughes personally. See Carl Oglesby's *The Yankee and Cowboy War*.

[2] Note that all agents of the IRS, which claims we owe them anywhere from 20 per cent to 80 per cent of all we ever earn (just because we got born here) also manage to keep a straight face.

Hughes himself speaking over a phone (he never did come out of seclusion...) denounced Irving as a fraud; but, of course, some say that the voice emanated from a Virtual Hughes—a double who had impersonated Hughes for years. The Mafia had bumped off the real Hughes, these conspiracy nuts claim, many years earlier. Had Irving faked a meeting with a man already dead and gotten "exposed" by another faker impersonating the dead man? As Swift proved to Partridge, we cannot decide matters of life and death on mere allegation.

But we will deal with that kind of conspiracy later. Right now we only confront the problem of *"the canon" itself as a kind of conspiracy.*

We simply do not know the extent to which Elmyr has entered the canon. Maybe 2 per cent of the masterpieces in modern museums emanated from his wizard's brush, as virtually every-body now admits. Maybe the figure (at least for post-impres-sionism, fauvism and early cubism, Elmyr's specialties) runs as high as 25 per cent, or 50 per cent... An *ouvre* of "more than a thousand" paintings might make up something in that percentage range of canonical 20th Century Classics. These implications appear heavily suggested in Irving's *Fake!* and even more stressed in the Welles-Reichenbach film...

Well, then, we must re-examine the canonicity of art as skeptically as the 18th and 19th Centuries re–examined religion. Religious canonicity survived (in the Occident) only as long as the Pope qualified as the world's leading **Expert**. When other **Experts** arose, with their own cults, religious canonicity became ambiguous and controversial. What happens when the Art **Experts** face a similar challenge?

Some Radical Feminist critics have already begun such a "Protestant heresy", and have dumped such Dead White European Males (DWEMs, in fashionable jargon) as Dante, Beethoven, Shakespeare, Michelangelo, etc. and replaced them with a new canon featuring a lot of long-forgotten ladies whose work, frankly, seems dreadfully inferior to me, and to most art critics.

For instance, Susan McClary has found Beethoven's Ninth Symphony a musical hymn to rape, which will no doubt surprise all those with less androphobic ears, who hear something quite different in it, something of cosmic grandeur... Says McClary,

"The point of recapitulation in the first movement of the Ninth is one of the most horrifying moments in music... which finally explodes in the throttling, murderous rage of a rapist..." Sounds almost as bad as *The Texas Chain Saw Massacre*, doesn't it?

Although I write a lot of satire, I didn't make this up. You can find McClary's analysis in *Minnesota Composers' Forum Newsletter*, January 1987. She also doesn't like Western classic music in general, because of its "phallic violence" and "pelvic pounding." I insist I did not invent McClary or any of her ravings. Honest to God. Some Femigogues just happen to sound like satire when you quote them verbatim.

As for the female masterpieces set against old Ludwig, they only *appear* inferior, the Feminist revisionists say, because all of us have had our perceptions warped by the "patriarchal brain-washing" of our "phallocentric" culture. ("All of us" includes many female art critics, like Camille Paglia, who angrily claims this argument has crossed the line to an idiot caricature of Feminism)

Maybe we all need a long de-programming at a Feminist re-education camp. Then we will realize that Hildegarde of Bingen not only outclassed Beethoven but wrote more first-rate music than Mozart, Bach and Scott Joplin together, and without any rape fantasies creeping in.

Third World revisionists have raised similar objections to the canonical centrality of DWEMs. They ask us, not too gently, do we really believe that *all* the great art of humanity came out of *one sub-continent,* created by *white males* only? Hmmm?

Do we trust these revisionists or do we trust our own sensibilities?

After Elmyr, do we dare trust *anybody?*

As a famous bard wrote,

> He stood in his socks and he wondered, he wondered
> He stood in his socks and he wondered

The post-modernists go beyond even the Feminists and the Multi–Culturalists, by casting relativistic doubts, not only on official Canons but on all alleged "eternal truths"—artistic, religious, philosophical, scientific or whatever. Worse yet, some of the **Experts** have identified me as a postmodernist. For instance, *Post-Modern Fiction: a Bio-Bibliographical Guide* by

Larry McCaffrey includes me as leading post-modern novelist, "in the tradition" of Pynchon, Burroughs and Vonnegut. I have to recognize some truth in this accusation, since Pynchon, Burroughs and Vonnegut certainly lead the list of My Favorite Contemporary Writers, and have therefore undoubtedly influenced me. (James Joyce and Orson Welles, my favorite artists of this whole century, look suspiciously like premature post-modernists.). Sociologist Alfonso Montuori also includes me among the post-modernists in his *Evolutionary Competence*, although he says I have less gloom and pessimism than other post-modern novelists, a distinction that I feel glad somebody has noticed. Despite that, to the extent that post-modern means "post-dogmatic," I do shamefacedly belong with this unsavory crowd; only to the extent that post-modern has come to mean a new dogma do I part company from them.

At the end of Welles' *F For Fake*, after we have suffered prolonged doubt about how many Picassos should get reclassified as Elmyrs, one character cries passionately *"I must believe, at least, that art is real!"*—a noble thought with which I might finish this chapter...

But this voice of Faith and Tradition belongs to another art forger, one who allegedly faked even more of the canonical Renaissance masterpieces than Elmyr had faked of the canonical Moderns. We cannot have faith in this faker's faith...

References:

Fake! by Clifford Irving, McGraw-Hill, New York, 1969—for basic Elmyr material.

F For Fake, directed/produced by Orson Welles and Francois Reichenbach, Sati Tehran Films, 1974—for more on Elmyr, the Howard Hughes biography and some Hughes conspiracy theories.

The Yankee and Cowboy War, by Carl Oglesby, Berkeley Medallion Books, 1968—for Hughes/Mafia/Watergate links.

The Gemstone File, edited by Jim Keith, Illuminet Press, 1992— a chrestomathy of Hughes/Mafia conspiracy theories.

THREE

23 DEAD ROSICRUCIANS

In Which We Encounter An
Occult Order and a More Deadly Mystery

> You likee Chinee New Year?
> —*Shanghai Gesture*

> There's madness in their method.
> —*The Great Escape*

Last night, I got a phone call from a friend in Los Angeles. "Did you hear about the 23 murdered Rosicrucians?" he asked.

I answered with typical wit and brilliance. "Huh?"

He then told me about two groups of Rosicrucians found dead in full ceremonial robes in two locations in Switzerland. I humored him, thinking he had finally wigged and now carried a few gallons shy of a full tank.

This morning I looked in the *Santa Cruz Sentinel* and found on the top of the front page:

CULT MURDER-SUICIDE KILLS 48

The story, from Associated Press, told how Swiss police found 23 people in ceremonial robes dead in a mysterious chapel below a farm-house near the village of Chiery, near Geneva. All wore

black, red and white robes, and ten had plastic bags tied around
their necks with cords. Some had their hands tied and twenty had
bullets in their heads.

(You see? I barely get to the middle of this book[1]—a sequel to
two previous works about, among other things, secret societies,
synchronicity and the number 23—and what happens? The universe provides me a mysterious murder involving 23 members of
a secret society. It makes you wonder, I swear it does.)

Subsequent investigation uncovered two other sets of similarly
robed bodies in two other locations in Switzerland, and
additional dead bodies in another house owned by the same
occult order in Canada. The name of the order, or the "cult" (as
Associated Press calls it), has remained uncertain. The AP story
variously gives it as the Order of the Solar Tradition, the Order
of the Solar Temple and the Order of the Rose and Cross. This
last, of course, translates the Renaissance German *Rosenkruez*,
which we more often see rendered as "Rosicrucian." As readers
of *Cosmic Trigger I: Final Secret of the Illuminati* know, this
order has several mysterious "links" (coincidental or conspiratorial, as you will) with Freemasonry and the Illuminati.

All in all, the Swiss have found 46 bodies and the Canadians,
two. Total: 48. And nobody in the police will speculate about
how many died of suicide and how many of murder, or what
provoked this extreme form of religious behavior.

Maybe the police will obtain more light on this latest
"Rosicrucian" mystery before I finish this book. Maybe.

Or the media may lose interest and return to their usual
preoccupations of this year, namely (1) explaining why we
should view everything President Clinton does with extreme
anxiety, if not outright panic, and (2) explaining again, and
again, and again, that O.J. damn well killed Nicole, by God,
whether the jury eventually rules that way or not.

Well, we know who owns the media and what fears dominate
their lives, do we not?

Meanwhile, this Rose and Cross and Solar Temple mystery
reminds me of why I agree with CSICON, the philosophical
society that claims the "normal" does not occur in sensory-

---

[1] Pages in my works do not appear in the order I wrote them but in the
Significant Form that seems best to me on final re-write.

sensual space-time and exists only as a brain construct, a concept
in theoretical math. (Prof. Finnegan originally got this insight
from one Sean Murphy of Dalkey, a suburb of Dublin on the
southern coast of the Bay. Murphy's actual words, as Finnegan
recorded them in his diary, read "Ah, sure, I never had a normal
day or saw a fookin' average Irishman." This insight hit the
subtle brain of Timothy F.X. Finnegan when he had just finished
his seventh pint of Guiness for the evening, and he immediately
saw their general philosophical import. The next day, he created
the first 2-page outline of 'Patapsychology, in the tradition of
Alfred Jarry's 'Pataphysics.[1] CSICON still offers $10,000 to
anybody who can produce a totally normal person, place or
event.)

And I cannot find any reason to credit CSICOP, the neo-
Platonist cult that believes the "normal" really exists everywhere
and that nothing else at all exists anywhere. Of course, like
CSICON, the noodles in CSICOP also have a $10,000 "reward"
for anybody who can disprove their Dogma that the truly
"normal" exists somewhere even though most of us have never
seen it. But CSICOP has their own judges, so you can't win.

The less fanatic, more sophisticated CSICON will allow 3
judges selected *at random* to decide if any given dog, or cat, or
bobolink, or rat, or vole, or wombat, or man, or woman, or
house, or chair, or Picasso, or Beethoven sonata, or cloud, or
sunset, or *whatever*, fits all the criteria of normalcy. Just
claiming that the Totally Normal must exist somewhere because
we can think of it (Plato's fallacy) does not count as a "proof;" to
collect the CSICON reward you must show, and allow the judges
to examine, a concrete example of the Perfectly Normal.

Nobody has yet produced such a *concrete abstraction* .

I therefore assume that the universe of experience—the
sensory-sensual world, as Marx called it—consists only of non-
normal or eccentric bumps in the space-time continuum. You
never will find a normal person, a normal dog or even a normal
zebra. Nobody can produce an average sonata, an average
Pollock painting or even an average Playmate of the Month. *The*

---

[1]Nothing else about Sean Murphy remains on record except a remark attributed
to one Nora Dolan : "The only hard work that Murphy lad ever did was
climbing back on the bar-stool after he fell off, twice a night."

mathematically normal labels that idea which no actual event exemplifies.

As a famous poet of old Japan wrote,

Mountain pool—
Frog jumping—
Gurgle-gurgle-gurgle!

Reference:

Santa Cruz Sentinel, 7 October 1994.

FOUR

CHIMES AT MIDNIGHT

In Which All the Humor Drains
Out of the Joke About My Death

> What is the purpose of the carbon-based units?
> —*Star Trek: The Motion Picture*

> "Friends" is a mental state.
> —*Miller's Crossing*

Only a week after my alleged passage to the Twilight Zone, or promotion to glory (as the Salvation Army calls it)—my kicking the bucket, in homely American—I woke one morning, planning to call Bob Shea in the hospital.

In a procedure that had grown habitual in the last year, I made my coffee as soon as I got downstairs (grinding my own gourmet beans: a ritual in honor of Epicurus). I carried the steaming cup to the phone alcove. I dialed Bob Shea's hospital number and recited a bawdy limerick to make him laugh. But his voice sounded weaker than ever, and I had that terrible feeling again, the feeling that I just didn't know how to do enough to really help.

We talked about *NYPD Blue,* a new TV show we both liked. We agreed that Sipowicz always gets the best lines—"Once or twice a year I like to keep a promise to a witness, so I remember

35

what it feels like." "This'll rock you in your socks, John, but I gotta tell you: occasionally we don't achieve perfect justice in this building."

"I'm feeling better," Shea finally said in a near-whisper. "A lot better. But I'm tired now."

"Okay," I said. "I'll let you go."

"I love you," he said suddenly.

"I love you, too," I said, hanging up. I sat there thinking that in this society it takes about three decades and a major illness before heterosexual males can say "I love you" to each other... I mulled that over, and thought about Shea's optimism, because I didn't want to think about how weak and tired he sounded.

In retrospect, I don't know if he wanted to sell that optimism to his own suffering body—to rebuild its immunological defenses with the potent neurochemistry of hope—or if he only said it to spare me further worry and pain, to relieve my anxiety for a few hours.

The next time I called the Bob Shea Information Line on Voicemail, the message told me he had gone into coma and no more phone calls should be made to the hospital. Even then, I didn't believe, didn't *want* to believe, the truth. When the Voicemail message finally changed, after about three more days, and said simply that Bob Shea had died, I went into shock. I should have expected the news, but of course I didn't. You never do. I had tried to instill hope into Shea and, by contagion, had instilled so much into myself that I had come to expect a miracle.

I sat at the coffee alcove like Wile E. Coyote when he has just gotten hit with a boulder the size of an elephant but doesn't know it yet and doesn't realize he should logically fall over. I slowly put down the phone, still unable to believe the truth, still in shock. Shea had seemingly beaten the Big Casino (no new tumors in six months); how could he go and die of the side-effects?

The Gremlins of Internet had announced the death of one author of *Illuminatus!* and now the other had died instead.

I looked out the window. The sun had barely appeared—I rise early, with only cinnamon and tangerine streaks coloring the east—but already the breakfast crowd, as I call them, had arrived in my patio. House finches, blackbirds and sparrows hopped and flapped about, pecking at my bird feeder. Two hoodlumish Santa

Cruz scrub jays appeared, scared everybody else off, and dug their beaks into the feeder vigorously. A mourning dove made its usual grieving sound in a tree, as if it didn't believe things would ever become less depressing, and a car drove past, invisible behind the patio wall. I still could not make the concepts "Bob Shea" and "death" fit together in my head. It seemed like "round square" or "giant midget." As Wittgenstein said, some concepts cannot join into a meaningful thought.

I thought of a grave in Sligo, the wild west of Ireland:

> Cast a cold eye
> On life, on death.
> Horseman, pass by.

I thought of Justice Shallow's glorification of the riotous Springtime of his youth ("Jesus, the wild days we have seen") and Falstaff's bittersweet and understated reply: "We have heard the chimes at midnight, Master Shallow." Nobody but Orson Welles ever gave that line the emphasis it deserves... It means "Our revels indeed continued very late" (in an agricultural economy where most people go to sleep at sunset) but it also means "Our day has ended: ahead lies the grave alone."

Another car rumbled in my street, and the mourning dove complained about life's injustice again. I became abnormally conscious of green sexy Nature outside my glass patio door. Then another damned noisy car went by, racing: some guy late for work maybe.

Bob Shea and I had never seen birds and flowers and trees in the first years when we knew each other, but we had heard a hell of a lot of noisy cars. Our friendship grew in Chicago, amid the rattle and scuttle of industry, the blood-and-shit smell of the stockyards: I remember it as Dali's (or Daly's) asphalt purgatory. The friendship became closer when Bob and I inhaled the haze of tear-gas and Mace during the 1968 Democratic Convention, the one they held behind barbed wire because Mayor Richard P. Daly (emphatically not Dali, although his ideas often sounded surrealist) decided he would not allow Americans to meddle in their own government.

The protesters chanted: "One, two, three, four! We don't want your fucking war! Five, six, seven, **EIGHT**: Organize to smash the State!" Another canister of tear gas exploded nearby and, eyes streaming, Shea and I ran down Michigan, cut into a side street, and evaded the clubbing administered to those who couldn't run as fast as we did. If you want to know what happened to those less "wing'd of foot" than us, you don't need to call some archive to dig out the 1968 footage; just look at the Rodney King tape again. Cops enjoy simple animal pleasures, which do not change much over the generations.

I counted back, sipping my coffee, and checked my memory: Shea and I had indeed known each other for just a few months shy of 30 years. A human can grow up in 30 years, from diapers to the first tricycle, to the first orgasm, and even to a Ph.D. A human can learn to work at a regular job or learn how to beg on the streets, or court and marry and become a parent, or join the army and get a leg blown off. Most humans in history, before 1900, did not live longer than 30 years. A friendship that long becomes more than friendship. Shea meant as much as any member of my family.

Way back in '65, when Shea and I both started working for The Playboy Forum/Foundation, we drifted into the habit of lunching together. Soon, we developed the tradition of going to a nearby bar after work every second Friday (read: payday), and drinking a half-dozen Bloody Marys while discussing books, movies and every major issue in civil and criminal law, logic, philosophy, politics, religion and fringe science—insofar as one can distinguish between those last two subjects. We generally couldn't draw any lines between those two topics or any of the others, which explains why each of us found the other's ideas so stimulating, and why, in our years, the Playboy Forum discussed more far–out notions than it has before or since.

I remember our *WHO OWNS ERIK WHITETHORN?* series, in which we publicized a woman, Mrs. Whitethorn, who had sued the government for trying to draft her son, Erik, 18. She claimed she owned Erik until he reached 21, and that the government could not take him from her. Shea and I gave that case all the coverage we could, since we wanted people to really think about whether an 18-year-old belongs to himself, to his mother, or to the Pentagon.

Alas, Erik, like many young people, didn't want to become a tool of his mother's idealism, and finally ended the debate by willingly enlisting in the Army. (Madalyn Murray's son also

rebelled against becoming a battering ram in her assault on
Organized Religion.) We had to drop the debate after Erik
donned his uniform and went off to napalm little brown people. I
like to hope that some *Playboy* readers of those years still occasionally wonder whether humans belong to themselves, to their
parents, or to the that Kafka-esque and labyrinthine Five Sided
Castle on the Potomac. [Due to the continuation of magick in the
collective unconscious, most people (I suspect) still think the
Five-Sided Castle of Yog Sothoth literally "owns" them and their
offspring, just as they think they "owe" money to the I.R.S.]
Mostly, in the *Playboy Forum*, we followed the ACLU's
positions, which Shea and I passionately shared (as does Hefner,
or he wouldn't have started the Forum and the Foundation) but
often, as in the Whitethorn case, we pushed a bit further and
sneaked in some anarcho-pacifist propaganda—never in
Playboy's voice, of course, but as the voice of a reader. Some of
those "readers" later became more renowned as characters in the
three *Illuminatus!* novels we wrote...

Among my sins, I turned Shea on to Weed. I turned a lot of
people on to Weed in those days. I had a Missionary Zeal about
it, but now that I think back, so did a lot of others at *Playboy* in
those days. Maybe I should say that I *helped* turn Bob on to the
Herb.

On one gloriously idiotic occasion we got our hands on some
super pot from Thailand and had the dumbest conversation of
our lives.

"What did you say?" Shea would ask, concentrating intensely,
like somebody enquiring of Socrates about the meaning of
justice...

I'd grapple with that abysmal enigma, but amid millions of
new sensations and a rush of Cosmic Insights, I'd lose the
question before I could find an answer to it. "What...did...
you...say?" I would ask slowly, trying to deal with the problem
reasonably.

"I asked...uh..." He paused to reconsider the gravity of the
problem. "Um what did you ah just ask?"

And so on, for what seemed like Hindu yugas or maybe even
kalpas. That night inspired the "Islands of Micro-Amnesia" in
Illuminatus! Maybe a similar night inspired the Lotus Eaters in
the *Odyssey*?

One payday Friday, when Bob and I sat in our favorite bar consuming our usual Bloody Marys and gobbling our usual honey-roasted peanuts, a priest at a near-by table struck up a conversation. Soon he had joined us and I quickly became convinced that I understood why the conversation persistently veered toward the Platonic ideal of true love between philosophers. I then pulled one of my nastier pranks. I said I had to get home early, and left Bob to navigate for himself. A half-hour after I arrived home and got out of my shoes, the phone rang. Shea had called and asked me, with awe—as if somebody had killed a black goat in the sacristy—"Do you think that priest was a *homo* sexual?"

I admitted the suspicion had crossed my mind. "As Gay as Mardi Gras in New Orleans," I think I said, seeking the *mot juste.*

"My God," Shea said. "You really think it's possible?"

"Well, what made you call me and ask?"

"He kept talking about how only intellectual males can truly love each other."

Shea became much less naive in only a few months after that, since a lot of our Forum/Foundation work involved consultations with the Kinsey Institute. I regard this incident as atypical, and hope it doesn't make Shea seem obtuse, even for a time almost 30 years ago (when the Church brazenly denied all priestly shenanigans and bullied the media into not even reporting the cases that got to court). But this adventure had something strangely typical of Bob Shea also, in showing a kind of innocence that, in some respects, he never lost.

Shea probably, at that time—still young, remember—would not have believed that Roy Cohn, who made a career of driving Gay men out of government, himself led an active Gay life. Shea took a long time to learn how much deception exists in this world, because he himself always acted honestly. He accordingly thought clergymen who preach celibacy will practice celibacy; during the first year of our friendship, 1965, he even believed that politicians who call themselves liberals will think and act liberally.

Anyway, that cruising priest caused enough Deep Thought, for Shea and then for me, that he finally became transformed and immortalized as Padre Pederastia in *Illuminatus!*

Around the time we met the priest, Shea told me that he had remained Catholic until the age of 28 (if I remember correctly after all these years. Maybe he said 27 or 29?) Aside from his shock at the thought of Gay clerics, he did not seem like somebody newly escaped from Papist thought-control and I never did understand how he had stayed in that church so long. (Having quit Rome at 14, like James Joyce, I had assumed all intelligent people got out at around that age...) Shea never did explain why he stayed in so long, but he once told me, in bitter detail, why he finally bailed out.

His first wife, it appears, went totally barking mad shortly after the wedding. After a lot of agony and psychiatric consultation, Bob finally accepted the verdict that he had married an incurable schizophrenic. He found it more than he could handle, and sought an annulment, which led to a meeting with a monsignor.

To Shea's horror, neither psychiatric evidence nor any other evidence nor the church's own canon law itself had anything to do with the monsignor's conversation. The monsignor only wanted to know how much cash money Bob could pay for an annulment. Shea offered what he could afford, as a young man beginning at the bottom of the magazine industry, in a cheesy imitation of *Playboy*. The monsignor told him to go home and think hard about how to raise more coin of the realm. End of interview.

Shea got a civil divorce and never went into a Catholic church again. Still, when I first knew him (only 5 or 6 years after he quit the Church) he considered abortion a criminal act—and didn't know that Gay priests existed. He learned a lot, in those wild last years of the '60s, and he learned it fast. His Kennedy liberalism got gassed to death by Daly's storm troopers and he became another fucking wild anarchist, like me.

I remember one night when we got stoned together (Bob and his second wife, Yvonne, and Arlen and me) and looked at *Frankenstein Meets the Wolf Man* on TV. They still had cigarette commercials in those days and one of them, that night, showed two actors who looked remarkably like Ken and Barbie walking in a woodland and passing a lovely waterfall. As they lit up their ciggies, the slogan said, "You can take Salem out of the country, but you can't take the country out of Salem." I guess they wanted us to get the association "smoking Salems = breathing good fresh country air." As soon as the commercial ended, Lon Chaney Jr. came back on screen and started suffering acutely (remember his expressive eyes?) as he turned into a wolf. "You can take the man out of the jungle," I said with stoned solemnity, "but you can't take the jungle out of the man." Like most of my marijuana whimsies, that went down my Memory Hole and I forgot it immediately.

Imagine my astonishment when that surreal complex of ideas (Darwin/ Wolf Man/ Salems and all), showed up in *Illuminatus!* Shea hadn't forgotten.

And another night comes back to drench me in fond memory and grief: the same four of us—Bob, Yvonne, Arlen and me—all stoned again at Bob's pad; and then Bob silently put a record on his stereo. In my deep cannabis trance, all I heard came to me as pure sound, wonderful sound, Beethoven-rich sound, but I could not for the life of me guess what produced such sound. Finally, I decided it seemed more organic than instrumental.

"The blue whales?" I asked finally. ("Songs of the Blue Whales" had achieved a lot of popularity that year.)

In answer Shea held up the album cover: *The Language and Music of the Wolves.* He had led me into realms of non-human music, indeed.

As a famous bard wrote,

> Poems are made by fools like me
> But only God makes THC

In 1971, after we finished *Illuminatus!,* I quit *Playboy* in the midst of some mid-life hormone re-adjustment. I didn't understand it that way at the time; I just decided that I could not live out the second half of my life as an editor (read: wage slave) who only wrote occasionally; I had to become a full-time free-lance writer, "or bust."

Instead, I became a full-time writer *and* busted. It took five years of off-again on-again haggling with Dell Books to get the Shea-Wilson opus into print (and then they artificially cut it into a trilogy, so I never know whether to say Shea and I wrote one book together or three books together.) Five years of poverty seems just as long as five years in prison: but that's another story. While Arlen and I and our four kids wandered about, looking for the least horrible place to live as paupers, Shea and I started writing to each other almost every week. Dell remained nervous about the monstro-novel: *Illuminatus!* went out of print and came back by popular demand and then went out of print again and then came back bigger than ever and we both became more "commercial" (i.e., publishers paid us bigger advances). We both also became busier, and we wrote fewer letters—two a month or even fewer, sometimes; but for 23 years we wrote about every important idea in the world and filled enough paper for several volumes. I hope some of that will get published some day.

One of our major topics for dispute concerned "reality," which Shea regarded as a word denoting something concrete and external to any observer. I, as my books all make clear, and this book seeks to make even clearer than before, share the view of Husserl, Nietzsche, Korzybski and the Deconstructionists: *"reality," like "illusion," "art," "stoned," "straight," "normal," "abnormal," "fantasy," "mask," "hallucination," "the truth behind the mask," "the mask behind the mask" etc. designates a judgment or evaluation by the observer and has no meaning apart from the observer-observed transaction.* Shea always thought that view leads to solipsism. I always claimed it doesn't. Neither of us ever convinced the other. We both learned a lot, however, by keeping this argument going for more than two decades.

We spent a week in London, when the stage version of *Illuminatus!* played at the National Theatre. I remember going to the Tower of London, because Shea wanted to see it. He lectured me on the lies and propaganda of the Tudor version of history, swallowed whole and turned into *Richard III* by Shakespeare. I admired the poetry in Shakespeare and regarded history as one of those arts, like theology, in which anybody can prove whatever they want to prove, at least to the satisfaction of those who want to believe them. Shea took lots of photos of the rooks, who certainly do fit the historical atmosphere of the Tower: birds that seem to have emerged, not from evolution, but from *Richard III* itself—or H.P. Lovecraft.

Then we went to Westminster Abbey and I paid homage to Ben Jonson, the man who inspired some of my own flights of nomenclature by giving his characters names like Face, Waspe, Epicure Mammon, Fastidious Brisk and (the first parody of an anti-smoking fanatic) Zeal-of-the-Land Busy (who has a great line about the gruesome possibility that before anybody harvests the tobacco plant "the ferocious alligator might have pissed thereon.")

Somewhere, we stumbled onto Buckingham Palace without even intending to visit it. I said something rude about the royal family, under my breath. I found Guiness Stout more memorable, and even more regal, and it played a larger role in my ever-growing love of the British/Irish isles.

When *Playboy* fired him, Shea endured terrible anxiety about keeping his house, and dashed off a few novel outlines while looking for another job, He sold his first novel before finding a job and never stopped writing again. I still treasure his comment on why the Bunny Warren cast him out. "I worked hard and was loyal to the company for ten years," he wrote. "I guess that deserves some punishment." I treasure that as the best comment I ever heard about capitalist ethics.

Whenever I had a lecture gig in or near Chicago, Shea invited me to stay at his house. Yvonne always went to bed early and Shea and I talked and talked and talked for hours, just the way we did in the early years of our friendship. I always felt that Yvonne didn't like Shea's literary friends, but I never took it personally.

And then, suddenly, Yvonne left him for a much younger man, and I don't know (or really want to know) about the details. I worried for a while that Bob would crumble with depression, and I shared in empathy the toxic waste dump he must have felt around him, 60 years old, alone in a big house, and deserted by a wife who ran off with a young stud who might call him "Gramps." Maybe I project too much here. At 62 myself, I perhaps see in Bob's desolation the deepest anxieties of all aging males.

Oh, well, give Yvonne some charity: she just split the scene. She didn't Bobbitize the poor bastard on her way out. After thirty years of Radical Feminism, that perhaps shows some old-fashioned decency.

Then, at a pagan festival where we both had lecture gigs, Shea met Patricia Monaghan. I saw what happened: a kind of magick, real love at first sight. Pat gave Shea's last two years a transfinite boost of TLC and almost youthful joy. The day before he lapsed into coma, he arranged to marry Pat, even though he had not yet divorced Yvonne. I think of the wedding ceremony as the last thing he could do for Pat, and the last thing she could do for him. So Bob Shea died a bigamist, and I respect him for it. He followed the inner light (as the Quakers call it) and acted from a loving heart.

Years and years, in many places—in Ireland, in Germany, in Cornwall, in Switzerland, on the central coast of California—I often found myself wishing Shea could visit me and see the panoramic views that I found so wonderful. I still feel that at times, and find it hard to understand that he will never visit me now. Never.

Shakespeare made the most powerful iambic pentameter line in English out of that one word, repeated five times: "Never, never, never, never, never." I first realized how much pain that line contains when my daughter Luna died. Now I realize it again.

The birds have all flown away and the patio stands empty. Empty? Can an old-time acid-head like me really believe that? I looked again and realized anew that every plant and vine pulsed with passionate life in it, millions of Dionysian cells drunkenly copulating. I started to remember a line from Dylan Thomas but couldn't quite get it: "The force that through the green shoot drives the flower, drives my something something." I grinned, remembering Shea's wit. Once I had written, in one of our disputes, "I find your position amusingly rigid."

"I'm glad you find me amusingly rigid," he wrote back "Many women have paid me the same compliment."

FIVE

LIVING IN ONE'S OWN FICTION

In Which the Author Finds Himself Trapped in his Own Artistic Universe

> Absolute authenticity of detail is essential to
> our Work. Anything less is mere quackery.
> —*The Magic Christian*

> And don't call me Shirley.
> —*Airplane!*

Shea's death set off another bumpy ride for me on the
Information Superhighway.

Computer nets, faxes and phones soon resounded with voices
(or print-outs) declaring that Shea's death, like mine, "was only a
hoax." Some even claimed that Shea and I cooked it all up
ourselves as a publicity stunt. Others insisted that he had died but
I hadn't, or that I had died but he hadn't. Hardly anybody
seemed to believe anything quite as simple and straightforward
as the truth: somebody faked my obituary, but Shea really died.

I saw the irony in this, of course, but I felt too crippled by grief
to enjoy the joke.

Still, I have a weird sympathy for the bloke or blokes in Cambridge who started the original fake, declaring one *Illuminatus!* author dead, and now, like me, having to deal with the other author dying instead. By now, they must feel a little confused, a little guilty and perhaps a bit superstitious. Don't fool around with the masks of reality until you can handle the reality of masks.

Slowly, as March turned to April, the controversy petered out—or I thought it did. The denials of my death, by people who had heard "me" (or the Virtual Me) lecture one place or another in the weeks after my death, or who had talked to "me" on the phone, convinced more and more people; the whimseys and/or paranoias of the more imaginative hackers faded away. I wrote a few obituaries for Shea, for magazines that requested them.

By May, I thought it had all faded away—except my mourning over my best friend, which will never end entirely.

Then around May 22 (3 months after the first forged obituary went on line) I got a phone call from some nice people I know slightly in Nevada City, at the Institute for the Harmonious Development of the Human Being (formerly, the Fake Sufi School, and after that, briefly, the Snake Fufi School.). They had finally heard the rumor of my death and wanted to find out for themselves whether or not I had passed on to the Great Holodeck in the sky.

I broke the news of my continued existence, or my continued delusion of existence. I must say they took it well. I think it even made them happy.

More and more now, I think of Mencken's bath-tub hoax [1], and realize that some fantasies go on forever. New people will hear about my heart attack, or how the CIA poisoned me, every few months now and "I" will have to deny it again and again, as long as "I" live; and whenever "I" do die, many fans will not believe it and will flatly denounce the obituary as a new hoax.

---

[1] H.L. Mencken, literary critic and freethinker, wrote a fictitious "news story" about the violent opposition when the first bath-tub appeared in America. He thought everybody would get the joke, an error I have often made myself with some of my own jests. Instead, millions believed his story, and although Mencken denied it many times, the denials never circulated as fast or as far as the myth. Many people still believe religious conservatives rioted when plumbers installed the first bath-tub in Washington, DC.

Borges finally decided he lived inside a Borges story. Phil Dick definitely spent his last decade inside a Phil Dick story. I think I have gotten stuck now, perhaps forever, in a Robert Anton Wilson story.

As Wilde once noted, Nature imitates Art as much as Art imitates Nature. We never *see* a foggy city the same way after we have encountered a Whistler painting of a foggy city; sea water never looks the same after we've read Lovecraft's stories of Cthulhu, the Deep Ones, the Shoggoths and the other loath-some creatures who dwell at the ocean's floor; friendly strangers never look quite as honest after you've passed through a Thomas Harris novel about serial killers and how they inspire trust and confidence and persuade otherwise sensible people to come with them to lonely places.

SIX

DO ZEBRAS GIVE BIRTH TO IGUANAS?

**In Which We Find a Wonderful New Argument
Against the Possibility of Change or Evolution**

> Tell the General, "Shit happens."
> —*Captain Ron*
>
> Does zoology include humans?
> —*Marnie*

Earth habits die slowly, even down here among the dead men. For instance, I still have my addictions to guerrilla ontology, the Marx brothers and post-modernist literature. In fact, I will now begin my usual post-modernist jig by undermining your confidence that you know what sort of book you have in your hands. Remember the poor folks back in the 1720s reading the latest projector's pamphlet, *A Modest Proposal*, which urged the most humane and economic solution to Ireland's problems: namely, to let the English eat the Irish babies, instead of leaving them to die slowly of starvation. Some readers in the first few decades after publication must have made ten guesses about how to understand this, including the wild notion that maybe that bloody Lemuel Gulliver had done it again.

I will now disprove the theory of evolution.
Nothing up either sleeve. Behold—

1. An animal can belong to only one taxonomic family.

For instance, a critter cannot belong to the set of all kangaroos
and the set of all Irish pub-keepers, can it? Or the set of all
lobsters and also all rhinoceri? Or even to the set of all U.S.
Senators and all ring-tailed baboons—however amusing we may
find that last idea?

*2. The offspring of any two animals also can only belong to the
one taxonomic family, that of its parents.*

When horses mate, little horses get born, never little owls. Rats
bring forth other rats, not hummingbirds. Salmon do not give
birth to wombats. Etc.

Even when cross-species fertilization occurs, e.g., the mating
of a horse and a donkey bringing forth a mule, the mule belongs
to the same *family* (equines) as the parents, even if not to the
same *species* as either.

No biology text will challenge any of these "laws" or
generalizations.

*3. However, if evolution exists, some animals must produce
offspring who do not belong to the same taxonomic family as
themselves.*

Two fish must have brought forth something, some biological
monster, some kind of not-fish...an *amphibian*. Two reptiles
must have produced a *mammal*. And, most crucially for the
evolutionists war with the Bibliophiles, two apes must have
given birth to a *not-ape*...a *human*, or a proto-human.

But we have just seen that this cannot happen, according to
biological and genetic laws. No two animals can produce an
animal not of their own family.

Ergo, evolution cannot occur. Simple as 1-2-3.

(The rev. Jerry Falwell, the rev. Pat Robertson, and similar
certified saints of sanctified Fundamentalism, may use this
argument any time they want, but they must pay me a royalty of
$100,000 each time they use it, or I will sue them for everything
they own, including their bridgework. This warning constitutes
legal notification.)

Of course, if you don't like Creationism, you will want a way out of this bit of seemingly iron logic. Hang on. Maybe I'll give it to you in a little while. Trust me.

Meanwhile, consider that I either belong to the set of all living American writers or all dead American writers. Accordingly, this book belongs either to the set of all works by Robert Anton Wilson or it belongs to the set of all literary forgeries. Assuming some literary Elmyr perpetrated this, do you regard it as a "good" forgery (containing very Wilsonian prose) or a "bad" forgery (a weak imitation of Wilsonian prose)?

SEVEN

HOLY BLOOD,
HOLY MURDER

In Which We Re-Examine P2 and Discover
A Perhaps More Sinister Plot, or Perhaps
A True Sociological Art Work

> Don't you think we all go a little mad sometimes?
> *—Psycho*

> Nobody knows who they were
> or what they were doing, but they left a legacy.
> *—This Is Spinal Tap*

Time to refresh the memories of those who might have snoozed a bit since reading volumes I and II of this trilogy:

We began, in *Cosmic Trigger Volume I: The Final Secret of the Illuminati*, by considering the endlessly labyrinthine legend of the Bavarian Illuminati. For those who snoozed, and those who came in late, we recall that the Illuminati acted as *a secret society within a secret society*. Formed in 1776 by an ex-Jesuit Mystery Man named Adam Weishaupt—a kind of occult Elmyr—the Illuminati recruited only from Third Degree Freemasons (e.g., those who had passed through the terrifying

52

ritual of Hiram, the Widow's Son[1]). In 1786, the Bavarian government, alleging that the Illuminati had engaged in an international plot to overthrow every monarchy in Europe and the Vatican to boot, outlawed the organization.

Every generation since then, a small group of paranoids—or of brave and original researchers, unafraid of the canonical **Experts** in the History Departments—take your choice—has discovered evidence that the Illuminati still exists and continues to plot World Revolution.

Unfortunately, equally sincere Heretics have argued, every generation, the Illuminati no longer plots to take over the world because it has already *succeeded* in taking over and does indeed control this planet, e.g., it owns the International Banks.

Others, you may remember, have alternative theories about the Illuminati, linking them to Satanism, Aleister Crowley, the Rock music industry, Rhodes scholarships, Phi Beta Kappa, Skull and Bones, World Federalism, the World Bank, UFOs, cattle mutilations, crop circles and Hilary Rodham Clinton. We should mention, just out of charity to those who have suffered greatly in perusing these pages and will suffer more, that all the canonical **Experts** endorse the really far-out theory that *the Illuminati doesn't exist at all anymore.*

And remember: all our notes on the uncertainty floating around every Expert Opinion does not contradict the fact that, on occasion, **Experts** know something about their chosen subject.

We also saw, in *Cosmic Trigger I: Final Secret of the Illuminati,* that research on the Illuminati, in several documented cases, most notably my own, activates either (a) acute awareness of every time the number 23 appears in a strange story (as in "23 dead Rosicrucians": a tale that arrived in time to help set the mood for this treatise...) or (b) actual synchronicity in the Jungian sense—a movement of the human collective unconscious flooding the researcher with data involving 23s. But, of course, we admit the latter theory sounds flaky, and we never really endorse it. Not really.

Nor have we endorsed another line of evidence, also in *Cosmic Trigger I,* which *seems* to indicate that, from ancient Egypt

---

[1] Sorry, I cannot explain that in more detail. "Those who know do not speak, and those who speak do not know."

onward, the Illuminati and/or many different occult orders that once called themselves the Illuminati, or at least called themselves something similar, have had a "mystical link" of some sort with the double star system, Sirius, which "rises" behind the sun on July 23, or seems to rise as seen from Earth. My own experiences of *seeming* "telepathic contact" with Sirius I have long since filed as "right brain activity flooding into the left brain," a suitably scientific-sounding hunk of jargon which leaves me agnostically uncommitted to my own early theory that real interstellar communication has gone on since ancient Egypt.

In *Cosmic Trigger II: Down To Earth*, we traced the history, insofar as it has leaked so far, of a real, documented conspiracy that acts a great deal like the legendary Illuminati allegedly acts—*Propaganda Due* or (its usual abbreviation in English) P2. You will find it a strange story, since it involves spies, dope dealers, Freemasons, the Council of Cardinals and hundreds of banks that existed only in Virtual Reality... As our national bard wrote,

And much of Madness, and more of Sin
And Horror the soul of the plot

P2, like the Illuminati, grew within Freemasonry, and within the same brand of Freemasonry as the Illuminati did—namely the Grand Orient Lodge of Egyptian Freemasonry, formed c. 1780 by the duc de Orleans and that mysterious "charlatan," Count Cagliostro. Sometime in the 1960s—details remain even more obscure than in the 200-year-old original Illuminati conspiracy—P2 began recruiting among Third Degree Initiates of Grand Orient lodges in Italy. By around 1982, when the whole plot began to unravel, P2 had more than 900 members in high places in the Italian government, including General Musumeci, chief of the Secret Police, i.e., the man responsible for seeing that no illegal or terrorist conspiracies infiltrated the boot-shaped peninsula. Alas, Musumeci died (apparently of natural causes) while under indictment for conspiring in terrorist acts carried out by the P2 crew and blamed at the time on "left-wing elements."

We also saw a great deal of evidence linking P2 with both the Mafia and the Vatican; and some evidence that P2 heavily influenced 1970s/1980s C.I.A. involvement in Mafia/Vatican drug-money laundering. (Those who came in late and want details should rush out and buy *Cosmic Trigger II: Down to Earth* at once. Suffice it to say that at least 200 non-existent banks seemed to exist long enough to make a very strange loop between the Vatican Bank, the Cisalpine Bank and Franklin National Bank, and much cocaine and heroin money got laundered in that labyrinthine puzzle box.)

We noted the odd fact that the three best-known leaders[1] of the P2 cabal all held the rank of Knight of Malta in the Sovereign Military Order of Malta (SMOM), the Vatican's own secret police. This fact seems very, very odd because the Vatican has always maintained a firm, almost fanatic opposition to Freemasonry, and the Freemasons have always abhorred the Vatican and have a special commitment to fighting the Knights of Malta. (This commitment, and a pledge to fight to death in defense of the separation of Church and State, remain essential parts of the 32 degree initiation. I reveal no secret here. Any book on secrets of Masonry will tell you *this* much...)

Such dual membership creates the archetypical conspiratorial puzzle: Did P2 serve the Vatican and betray the Masons, or serve the Masons and betray the Vatican? (Personally, I suspect they betrayed both sides, and profited vastly by so doing. Licio Gelli, grandmaster of P2, received pay from both the C.I.A. and K.G.B., and evidently profited thereby.)

Turn we now to the year 1973, a most interesting time for this planet. In Washington, the "Watergate" scandals slowly revealed conspiracies as underhanded and Machiavellian as anything in the history or lore of the Illuminati or P2 (and Howard Hughes remained the one Mystery Man whose involvement Congress never fully explored). In Northern California, I had the "weird" experiences of 23s and Sirius links recorded in Vol. 1.

And in Switzerland that year, journalist Matthiew Paoli published *Les Dessous* (in English, *Undercurrents*), a book about a monarchist conspiracy, the Priory of Sion, which he had uncovered in his own country and in France. This "conspiracy" (or this "affinity group," if we wish to avoid loaded language) originally

---

1Licio Gelli, founder of P2 and, according to Italian magistrates, a double agent for both the CIA and KGB; Roberto Calvi, P2 member, President of the Banco Ambrosiano and manager of numerous "ghost banks" where drug money got laundered; Michele Sindona, P2 member, President of Franklin National Bank and Mafia lawyer.

came to Paoli's attention when, in the late 1960s, he found some copies of their internal newsletter, *Circuit,* in a chapter of the Grand Loge Alpina, the largest Masonic order in Switzerland.

Two thoughts "leap to mind" (at least to my mind) at once.

1. European conspiracy buffs have long believed the Grand Loge Alpina controls the finances of the Western world through the banks they own in Zurich and Basel and Geneva. Former English Prime Minister Harold Wilson referred to them as "the Gnomes of Zurich" and said they had more power than all the governments in Europe together.

2. In David Yallop's anti-Vatican blockbuster *In God's Name,* he alleges several suspicious links between the P2 conspiracy in Italy and the Grand Loge Alpina. He even claims some members of the Council of Cardinals belonged to either the Grand Loge Alpina or to P2 or to both...

Let me state clearly: I do not take all of David Yallop's charges with total seriousness. Unlike other **Experts** on the P2 frauds and murders, Mr. Yallop does not rely on court records and similar public documentation alone; he also cites alleged "sources" within the Vatican whose names he has pledged to keep secret. These sources reveal astounding crimes, worse than anything yet proven in court, *if we believe them:*

Alas, anonymous sources do not count for a hell of a lot of mass or weight, in my view—but I do not discount them entirely, of course, since sometimes they do ultimately appear in court, or elsewhere, with a front name, a hind name, and an address. Until that happens, however, I regard Yallop's sources through the lens of n-valued logic, floating in some indefinite maybe-world between a yes (100) and a no (0)...

Anyway, after these irrelevant but irresistible reactions to the very name of the Grand Loge Alpina have passed, we still think Mr. Paoli has written a most curious and provocative book. The journal he found in a GLA temple, *Circuit*, seemed concerned only with vine cultivation, genealogy and astrology—an odd trio, wouldn't you say?—but had many odd kinks and hermetic references, evidently intelligible only to Initiates. Paoli found it listed its publisher as the Committee to Protect the Rights and Privileges of Low-Cost Housing—although it seldom discussed housing, low-cost or otherwise—but when he went to the address given, he found no such Committee there.

With helpful hints from a few uncharacteristically communicative GLA members, Paoli finally found the true address of the Priory of Sion, the actual publishers of *Circuit*. The address turned out to lie within the de Gaulle government in Paris, at the Committee for Public Safety (once the engine of terrorism during the French Revolution, under the leadership of Robespierre, but now quite respectable.) The managers of the Committee appeared men of high culture and proven patriotism—André Malraux, Nobel Laureate in literature, influential art critic[1] and Resistance fighter during the Nazi occupation; and Pierre Plantard de Saint Clair, scholar, occultist and another former Resistance fighter (who had survived capture and torture by the Gestapo.)

Both men had a long record of loyalty to de Gaulle. Nonetheless, Paoli felt that much of the mystical politics of *Circuit* either intended to restore the remnants of the Royal Family to the throne in France, or else it didn't mean anything at all—a shaggy dog story, or "mere" hoax (as distinguished from a purposeful or profitable hoax.)

Most of Paoli's book tries to show, from a few issues of *Circuit* that he managed to get his hands on, that the group behind this magazine, the Priory of Sion, wrote in a kind of code (wine-making = a very specialized eugenics, because wine = human "blood," i.e., human genes in modern language) and that they seemed concerned with the special "blood" (genes) of the French royal family and of some related noble families in Spain, England and elsewhere.

Alas, a great deal of Paoli's evidence does not quite lend itself to this theory or to any other rational explanation. For instance, the cover of the first issue of *Circuit* he saw—the one that originally aroused his curiosity—shows a map of France with the Star of David superimposed upon it, and something that looks much like a Flying Saucer hovering above...

Now, the Star of David means something positive to Jews everywhere, but it also means a great deal not-positive to anti-

---

[1] He invented the term and concept of the "museum without walls," which sees modern art as developing, not from previous Western traditions alone, but from African, Hindu, Chinese and various other Third World traditions also. I consider him the godfather of multi-culturalism.

Semites. Superimposing a Star of David on a nation, in anti-Semitic literature, generally implies that the nation has come under control of the alleged "International Jewish Conspiracy." Could a group named after Sion (an alternative title for Israel) also preach anti-Semitism? Evidently not, in this case. *Circuit* strongly implies that the "wine"(genes) of the French aristocracy relates directly to the "wine" (genes) of the Kings of Judea in Old Testament times, especially David and Solomon.

Paoli never saw it clearly, but in the light of later "revelations"—or later hoaxes—his evidence indicates that the Priory of Sion wants us to believe the French royal family (and several related European noble clans) descend directly from King David.

Just like the carpenter who 2000 years of Europeans have called the King of Kings...

But what does this have to do with that flying saucer on the cover of *Circuit?*

Oddly, after the publication of *Les Dessous*, Paoli took a journalistic assignment in Israel. The government there soon arrested him on suspicion of spying, found him guilty, and shot him. Funny coincidence, wouldn't you say?

Returning to 1973: the same year, in Paris, Gerard de Sede published an odd tome called *La Race fabuleuse.* I regret to say that I can find no hard evidence of conspiracy or complicity between Paoli and de Sede. I feel really sorry about that, because what follows would make more sense if we knew for sure the two rascals hatched this monkey business in collaboration...

La Race deals with a dozen or more mysteries in French history, and only at the end do you realize that the author has explained, or pretended to explain, very few of them. In other words, much of the book deals with oddities that the author leaves dangling, for the reader to puzzle over...or perhaps to incite the reader to do some original research...?

The book begins, for instance, with the odd coat of arms of Stenay, a city near Paris. This coat of arms shows the head of Satan. (Neo-pagans might say "the head of a horned god," but it really looks much more like a conventional Christian image of the Devil than like any other horned god.) De Sede asks, reasonably, why the deuce would a Christian city in a Christian country want the Devil on their coat of arms? This leads to other oddities about Stenay, and about the Merovingian kings who had their capital there c. 400-700 A.D...and only at the end do we realize that de Sede never did get back to that bizarre coat of arms and explain it.

Similarly, we learn that a familiar Fortean phenomenon—the fall of frogs from the sky, without any evidence of whirlwind to provide a rational explanation—occurs more often in the records of Stenay that in any other European city. This, also, never does get explained. It merely leads to a theory that the frog on the royal Merovingian coat of arms refers to these mysterious frogs that kept falling out of the sky onto the heads of the royal Merovingians.

I don't know about you, but if mysterious frogs kept falling out of the sky all around me, I wouldn't want to brood too much about the subject, which might make me nervous. I certainly would not put the aeronautical amphibians on my Coat of Arms.

We also read a great deal about Adruina, the early European bear-goddess, and about her etymological/mythological link with the Greek Artemis, also a bear goddess originally, and about the Ardennes forest, named after Adruina, but all this leads up to some shadowy speculations about why somebody murdered the last Merovingian king, Dagobert II, in the Ardennes forest on December 23, 679 A.D.

Damn. That accursed 23 again.

De Sede also mentions, almost casually, that the principle church in Stenay faces South, so that on summer mornings you can stand at the altar, look out the front door, and see Sirius rising behind the Sun.

So 23 and Sirius both have links to this mystery. I might almost suspect somebody wanted to lure me toward this subject, except that de Sede's book appeared in 1973 and I did not write about my 23/Sirius experiences until *Cosmic Trigger I* in 1976. Three years later.

One of my favorite parts of *La Race* deals with Nostradamus, who de Sede interprets in a novel fashion. After informing us that Nostradamus, a pen-name, means one devoted to Our Lady (*nostra Dame,* in a blend of French and Italian), de Sede suggests that this strange physician's Jabberwockian poems have not remained in print continually because they "reveal the future"—a thesis that only makes sense to those who can believe in one century that "Gobble Gobble Turkey Farm/Many camels come to harm" must refer to the birds slaughtered for the First Thanksgiving and then believe a few hundred years later that it refers to Mustafa Kemel because it mentions Turkey and massacres.

No: de Sede does not propose such absurdity. He says the quatrains stay in print because a secret society keeps them in print, and they do this because the verses *reveal the past.* (How's that for reaching?) The quatrains tells what *really* happened in past history, as distinguished from the lies of a certain sinister group that controls Europe.

The sinister group remains unnamed even at the end, but I think few will examine the text without agreeing with my feeling that de Sede has arranged the evidence to point a strong finger of suspicion at the Vatican. The secret society opposing the Vatican also remains unnamed but sounds a lot like the Priory of Sion in Paoli's book.

A certain Marquis de B. (de Sede's abbreviation) reveals some of the hidden history. The Vatican murdered poor Dagobert II on December 23 in the Ardennes forest for mystical reasons having to do with astrology and numerology. The Priory of Sion, or some similar but nameless group, serves to protect those who have carried the genes ("wine") of Dagobert down to the present. These genes have special value because—hold on now—the Merovingians descended from intermarriages between a few distinguished ancient Israelites and superhuman extraterrestrials from the Sirius system.

Well, at least we know why the church in Stenay faces Sirius on July 23, even if we remain in the dark about that bear-goddess...

Alas, shortly after this interstellar revelation, the Marquis de B. himself got murdered, in the Ardennes forest, on December 23, 1972. The book ends with de B.'s son fleeing Europe to hide in Asia, and de Sede left with only some of his questions answered.

A delightful novel, I would say, but also one that, like my own works of guerrilla science-fiction, blends in enough facts to keep the reader uncertain about how much to believe.

We will use Fuzzy Logic in estimating *how much* of all this we choose to take seriously. Wait. Meanwhile, try not to jump to too many conclusions about the fact that everything about the Priory suggests a Rosicrucian and/or Illuminati order. Those 48 dead bodies probably have no link to any of this, at all, at all.

Principle Sources:

La Race fabuleuse, Gerard de Sede, J'ai Lu, Paris, 1973.
Les Dessous, Matthieu Paoli, Lyons, 1973.

EIGHT

PRIDE AND PREJUDICE

In Which We Contemplate Gay Pride,
Straight Pride and IQ Tests
for Dogs and Other People

> Gort, Klaatu barada nikto.
> —*The Day The Earth Stood Still*

> I 'm the bad guy?
> —*Falling Down*

Yesterday a Gay Rights demonstration occurred in Washington. Naturally, the **Expert** police estimate of the crowd (300,000) falls far short of the estimates given by the **Expert** organizers (1,000,000 or more.) Even in counting heads, people "see" in accordance with pre-established programs.

Back in the Vietnam War days, I attended dozens of anti-war demonstrations and the police's crowd-count never agreed with the organizers' count. My own observations never gave me clear reason to believe anybody's estimate. I don't know how people judge the size of large crowds, or how they can use techniques they sincerely believe have "objectivity." Even in looking at spilled marbles, I think people estimate very subjectively.

Gay Pride puzzles me even more than counting the dots in a blur. In my own naive way, I don't understand why some people feel they have to announce, in public, that they feel proud of their sexuality. In my simple mind, sex seems a hell of a lot of fun, and often includes deep emotion, even "religious" emotion, but has never provoked the kind of pride that one has for straight A's on a report card, or a Nobel prize, say. Sexual "pride" makes me think of young boys bragging to each other in a locker room—and usually lying their heads off about their "conquests."

But militant "Gay Pride" has become so established in this part of the country that I often feel tempted to start a Straight Pride movement, in order to "create a dialogue" as the current jargon has it. Maybe if we all bragged about our sexuality, just like those adolescents I just mentioned, eventually we'd get bored with the topic. Or—maybe most of us have nothing else left to brag about?

Of course, I don't really think a Straight Pride movement has much chance in this part of California, though. Out here, under the new tyranny called Political Correctness, Straight People remain "in the closet." We "enjoy" (or don't enjoy...) a certain tolerance, but only of the sort given to minor household pests. (To quote Mr. Dooley, "All the liberties I enjoy, I don't enjoy.")

If we dared to proclaim Straight Pride, we would immediately get accused of homophobia—although the Gay Pride people, most curiously, never, never get accused of heterophobia.

Counting heads: last night on the radio, several talk shows debated whether Gays constitute 1% of the population or 10% of the population. Sociology and sexology seem like a worse mess than I ever imagined. At least physicists can count accurately— outside the quantum realm. And even in the quantum realm, they can calculate probabilities.

My final conclusion on Straight Pride: we couldn't organize such a parade because most straight people just don't really feel proud of their sexual dalliances. They really do it just for fun.

Meanwhile, I find myself bemused by two recent IQ studies that have made headlines. They concerned dogs and people, two of my favorite species.

The first study appeared about six or seven months ago, and I didn't save any news stories about it, mostly because it didn't arouse any controversy among the **Experts.** This survey rated 150 breeds of dogs for comparative IQ. The border collie scored highest (number one) and the Afghan hound the lowest (number

150.) The Australian Shepherd, a favorite of mine, scored ninth. I don't remember much of the other details.

As I said, this report aroused no controversy. Defenders of the Afghan did not rush into print charging the authors of the study with afghanophobia, breedism, political incorrectness, sloppy research technique or inadequate methodology. Supporters of the gallant but embattled dachshund did not dispute its relatively low position in the canine hierarchy. The whole incident passed without fire or fury.

More recently, a book called *The Bell Curve* has appeared. It ranks Americans of European, Oriental and African gene-pools in terms of comparative IQ, just like the dog study did with breeds of dogs, and establishes, or alleges, a hierarchy. Naturally, all hell has broken loose. The authors have had every imaginable charge placed against them, and every single article I have seen says their results do not stand up to scientific criticism. What I find fascinating about all this lies in the singular fact that, although I have seen that line—"does not stand up to scientific criticism"—at least a hundred times (well, maybe only ninety-seven), not one writer who has repeated it has ever cited a single scientific paper refuting the methodology of *The Bell Curve.*

Frankly, I think no such studies ever get quoted because no such studies exist.

Scientific work refuting *The Bell Curve* does not exist for the simple reason that the book has only appeared in print within the last 3 or 4 months, and *nobody can do an adequate scientific examination of its claims in that short a time*.

For example, the latest polemic to come my way—in the January/February 1995 issue of *Extra!*—devotes itself from beginning to end to the one tactic of guilt-by-association, which we all supposedly learned to despise when Joe McCarthy used it in the 1950s. The authors of *The Bell Curve,* according to *Extra!,* have links with the Eugenics movement, and one of their principle sources of statistics also has a link with that movement, and ergo the book "is" racist. This does not amount to scientific rebuttal; it sounds more like table-pounding.

In the first place, if somebody proved Einstein guilty of child molestation or Darwin guilty of multiple ax-murders, the theories of relativity and evolution by natural selection would still stand or fall on the scientific evidence, not on such moral failures of their creators. In the second place, I don't necessarily believe 100% that these "links" to Eugenics exist just because *Extra!* asserts them; I would like some confirmation of these links. *Extra!* emanates from a group called Fairness and Accuracy in Reporting, and I don't trust them much, partially for the same reason I count the silverware after a visit by a chap who calls himself Honest John, and partially because "fairness" and "accuracy," in their minds, always coincidentally confirms the dogmas of a bloke who wrote over 100 years ago, named Karl Marx.

I now offer for your examination a few characterizations of this inflammatory little chapter. Check each sentence "yes" or "no."

1. Wilson dislikes Gay people.
2. Wilson believes in *The Bell Curve.*
3. Wilson believes IQ tests exist which accurately and adequately measure the one and only type of intelligence possessed by dogs and/or humans.

If you checked any of these sentences "yes," go back and try to find the sentences that justify that reading of my words. When you find them, or think you find them, make a logical chain from such sentences to the conclusions you checked "yes," and *count the number* of inferences contained in each such chain.

Then ask what if anything justifies any of those inferences.

In cold fact, all three statements [1, 2 and 3] contradict my actual ideas. I just wanted to remind you how easily humans can go from statement S_1 to conclusion S_5 without noticing that the inferences in between—S_2, S_3 and S_4—have no basis in logic, and result only from mechanical reflex. I already quoted André Gide about that. Now I quote the father of linguistic analysis, Josiah Warren: "It is dangerous to understand new things too quickly."

NINE

FAKE DOCUMENTARIES AND "REAL" MONEY

**In Which We Consider Mask as Art
and Examine Picasso's Claim that
He Could Fake Picassos as Well as Anyone**

Games? Must we?
—*North by Northwest*

Stronger? You see!—You see!—Your
stupid minds! Stupid! Stupid!
—*Plan 9 From Outer Space*

If we consider Clifford Irving's *Fake!* a fake itself—a fake biography of a fake painter, revealing only what the faker, or fakers, care to reveal, and dumping a great deal of disinformation on us in the process—then we must regard Orson Welles' *F For Fake* as a fake movie about a fake biography of a fake painter. But perhaps we would more accurately dub it a fake documentary about the impossibility of ever making a "true" documentary.

In this interpretation, *F For Fake* does not represent something new or different in the Wellesian *ouvre*. Even before the "war of the worlds" hoax, way back in his 'teens, actually, Orson wrote a play called *Can You Hear Their Voices?* about John Brown, the anti-slavery fanatic who killed quite a few people because he loved humanity so much. In this play, John Brown never appears; other people talk about him and try to judge the morality of what he did; the audience never sees or hears Brown, because that would come dangerously close to "revealing the truth," and Welles, heavily influenced by Nietzsche from the age of 14, did not believe that humans could know or reveal "the" "truth." Orson belonged to the post-modernists before "post-modernism" itself had a name or definition.

Thus, in Beatrice Leaming's biography, *Orson Welles*, she tells how, after she persuaded him to cooperate in her book, he cajoled her into writing it in a narrative style similar to his John Brown play and many other of his works, especially *Mr. Arkadin* and *Citizen Kane*—not as "the truth about Orson Welles" but as the story of her *attempts to find the truth* about Orson Welles. To think she had *found* the truth, he told her emphatically, implied that she had become God.

(Post-modernism, in art and theory, evolved out of the linguistic analysis of recent semantic/semiotic philosophers, who have discovered that [1] any system of words or concepts covers *part, but not all*, of human experience, and that [2] social factors play a role in which systems dominate at a given time. The opposition consists mostly of Christian theologians like Jacques Maritain and C.S. Lewis, who claim the total truth remains accessible to us through Faith in the Christian mythos. More recently two blokes named Gross and Levitt, in a curious book called *Higher Superstition*, repeat most of the Maritainish and Lewisoid arguments for Faith in Authority and rejection of relativistic skepticism—except that Gross and Levitt believe that current mainstream science, not mainstream Christianity, contains the repository of Total Truth which skepticism should never question. More about those extremely odd birds later.)

Of course, long before *Kane* or the invaders-from-Mars broadcast or the John Brown play, before Orson was out of diapers, James Joyce wrote *Ulysses—the* classic of our century's literature, all the **Experts** say (and I, for once, agree)—in which the surface "realism" conceals a thousand spooky jokes, and critics have, in 70 years, learned that every narrative voice that originally seemed to speak "objective truth" has an element of quantum uncertainty about it. In fact, some of the things that definitely seemed undeniably true for the first 40-to-50 years of not-very-stupid readers—e.g., Molly Bloom's rampant promiscuity—no longer appear true at all.

It now appears the consensus that Molly had, at most, one lover before marriage, and one after. Well, some say, *maybe* two after. All the rest of her sexual "history" appears only as Mr. Bloom's masochistic fantasy and Dublin's malicious gossip. Early readers believed this mountain of fable and hearsay—even after Conan Doyle had shown how easily a writer can *fake out* his audience—because nobody then thought a "serious" writer would play Holmes-and-Watson Games with them.

Similarly, nearly 60 years of readers wondered *why* Bloom asked Molly to make his breakfast in bed the following morning—a reversal of their usual ritual—but nobody wondered *if* Bloom had indeed asked that. Finally, in *Joyce's Voices,* Hugh Kenner offered the very plausible theory that Bloom never asked for breakfast at all. Bloom, dozing off, started to dream about Sinbad and the Auk's egg (end of chapter 17) and talked in his sleep; Molly heard *something like* "bed" and "eggs" and decided he wanted eggs in bed next morning. This makes more sense to me than theories that Bloom did ask for eggs served in bed and the Scientific Narrators of that chapter "forget" to include this odd fact.

Joyce's status as the canonical post-modernist, or prime Irish bull in our signer shoppe, stands out most notably in his sphinx-like silence all during the years when commentators and scholars tried to interpret the Breakfast Request that Bloom never made. He happily left that joke, and God knows how many others, for the "500 years of Ph.D. candidates" he expected to pour over his text.

But the games Joyce played—and the games played by Welles, and M.C. Escher, and Borges, and Pynchon, and a lot of our current post-modernists—while just as cute as Doyle's games, have a serious side, just like cutting-edge science and philosophy, which have also encountered Uncertainty. A Final Answer seems impossible, to post-modern artists as to current philosophers and most scientists (except Gross and Levitt.). *Ergo*, the postmodern artist now offers us, not the Problem Solved, but the Problem as Puzzle, for each of us to work at solving, as long as it continues to amuse (or annoy) us.

Do you know the true character, the moral failure, of Charles Foster Kane? Look again at the short, intense scene in which he surrenders his corporation to Stanford, the banker, and listen to what he confesses about his true ambitions in words and what he further confesses in body language; you will not feel so sure about Kane after that.

Did the Martians *really* land in 1938, and have they falsified records about Orson Welles and everything else since then, to maintain the myth that the "landing" never really happened and consisted only of Orson cleverly counterfeiting news bulletins? This thesis appears in the gonzo thriller, *Buckeroo Banzai*, a joking attempt to make us believe one of Orson's best jokes.

What Final Analysis does Welles' *Touch of Evil* offer us on Hank Quinlan, a tragic monster almost as grotesque, as frightening and as pitiful as any horror film "Creature," and yet a human like us? Tanya the whorehouse madam, clearly a woman who knows people well, states it: "He was some kind of a man. What does it matter what you say about *people?* "

This Verdict, or this post-modern Suspended Sentence, concludes the only truly frightening "thriller" Welles ever made, which also comes closest of all his works to a loutish slapstick farce (midway between Shakespeare's vulgar Clowns and the Three Stooges, actually), a balancing act keeping classic horror and classic burlesque in simultaneous orbit, a feat that Orson performs with easy aplomb, the way he always performed the rabbit out the hat routine he had learned at age twelve.

According to a story I got from *F For Fake* —and which probably therefore never happened (or did it?)—an art dealer once went to Picasso and asked him to look over some *alleged* Picassos he'd been offered, and pick out the fakes. Picasso obligingly stacked the paintings into two piles, "real" and "fake." Then, as he threw one canvass into the fake pile, the art dealer cried, "But no, Pablo. That's not a fake. I was visiting here the week-end you painted it."

"No matter," said Pablo with the dignity of a great magician. "I can fake a Picasso as well as any thief in Europe."

While digesting that, consider also this true parable, from Prof. Hugh Kenner, a man not known for hoaxing his readers: Andy Warhol always kept a stack of Campbell Soup cans in his pantry.

Then, if he liked a visitor, he'd autograph one of the cans and present the guest with a "genuine Warhol."

As Kenner points out, the next logical step in this progression from art to magick would occur if Warhol had sued Campbell Soup for making cheap imitation Warhols.

And, to repeat one of my own speculations from a novel, if Warhol found a dollar, put a frame around it, and a gallery exhibited it as "found art" would the value relate at all to the origin of the "dollar"—i.e., whether the wizards in the Federal Reserve Bank had passed a magick wand over it making it "real" money (paper blessed by the Fed's magick wand), or the Mafia printed it in a cellar making it "counterfeit" money (paper lacking the magick wand)? Of would the value *in the gallery* depend entirely on Warhol's current market price? (In any case, it would certainly have a value far higher than the declared $1 face value... Ever wonder about that?)

In this connection, we take note of a slight disagreement between Elmyr and Zsa Zsa Gabor. When *Look* magazine scooped the art world by exposing Elmyr as the "onlie begetter" of numerous forgeries previously attributed to some sinister Committee of criminal geniuses, Zsa Zsa, never shy about seeking publicity, announced that she had once purchased two alleged Dufys from Elmyr. He immediately denied it: "That's absurd. Can you imagine her buying even *one* Dufy?"

According to Elmyr, he and Zsa Zsa had only one commercial relationship: she had posed for him, as a nude model, before she became rich and famous. Zsa Zsa immediately denied Elmyr's insulting yarn. "All Hungarians are liars" she said flatly, refurbishing the famous logical paradox of the Liar Who Asserts He Lies since she and Elmyr both came from Hungary originally... And in *F For Fake*, Welles does not forget to include the classic Hungarian joke: "How do you make Hungarian chicken soup? First you steal a chicken..."

Meanwhile, the Lilienfield Gallery in New York offers us, in its January 1948 catalog, a relic of the Great Imposter's early days, when he still tried to sell paintings under what some consider his own name, Elmyr de Hory. One of the nudes has the title *A Portrait of Zsa Zsa.* It sure looks a lot like Ms. Gabor.

At this stage, I feel inclined to suspect that Eva posed for it.

References:

Orson Welles, by Beatrice Leaming, Viking, New York, 1985.
The Counterfeiters, by Hugh Kenner, John Hopkins University
    Press, 1985.

TEN

FLYING SAUCERS, PHONY PHOTOS AND FUZZY LOGIC

In Which Another Fake Gives Birth to An Even Weirder Mystery

The only time to make up your mind about people is never.
—*Philadelphia Story*

Is that foolish enough for you?
—*The Lady From Shanghai*

In 1966, while on sunny Ibiza the evil wizard Elmyr happily painted more in his seemingly endless series of "masterpieces by Picasso and Matisse" almost every day—with no forewarning of the legal Ax soon to fall on him—somebody in mainland Spain *evidently* cooked up an even more audacious fraud. The scrupulous italics will justify themselves. *Many extremely intelligent and well-informed people will assure you that no element of fraud or hoax enters the story I will now recount.* These people, some of them **Experts** in one field or another, believe that the events in Madrid that year began a still-continuing "conversation" between humans and more highly evolved aliens from another star system.

The first "contact," or the first "hoax"—as you will—occurred on Feb. 6, 1966, when a whitish disk descended from the clouds and landed near an airfield outside Madrid. The disk, described as thirty feet in diameter, changed from white to yellow to orange as it landed, according to several soldiers who saw it, or *think* they saw it.

A civilian named Jordan Pena, driving nearby, also saw it, or imagined that he saw it. He also says he saw it take off again abruptly soon after landing. And he saw on its bottom a strange symbol:

)+(

This symbol later became known as the sign of UMMO. But let's not rush into these very deep waters. Let us proceed as slowly and cautiously as possible.

The first incident ends there—except that investigators later found three deep, rectangular marks in the soil where the alleged disk had allegedly landed.

These marks represent one of the 4000-odd cases where, according to physicist/UFOlogist Stanton Freedman, we find "hard evidence" at an alleged UFO sighting. The reason that UFO deniers insist "no hard evidence" ever appears seems on all fours with the reason that Radical Feminists fail to see any artistic or scientific merit in DWEMs like Beethoven, Shakespeare, Newton and the other good old boys. As Korzybski and de Bono (among others) have demonstrated, *Opinions result from perceptions, and perceptions reinforce Opinions, which then further control perceptions, in a repeating loop that logic can never penetrate*. (Only a shocking new perception, too strong to get edited out by Opinion, can break this self-hypnotic loop.)

Of course, the "hard evidence" found at UFO sites never quite proves what the True Believers want it to prove. Like the marks in the soil in the above landing, the evidence proves that more than hallucination occurred. It proves no more. In this case, for instance, we can only say that *somebody* or *something* made marks in the soil. Who or what remain open questions.

Curtain on act one.

When the curtain rises again, a year and a half has passed. On June 1, 1967, in another suburb of Madrid, several dozen witnesses saw another disk, this time estimated at 120 feet in diameter, rising from an unknown spot and shooting across the sky. It also changed colors—yellow to orange to red. Then it sped off—but not before several witnesses noticed on the bottom of the craft the same mysterious symbol:

)+(

Two photographers, who never identified themselves, sent a total of seven photos of the "disk" to the newspaper, *Informaciones*. Spanish UFOlogists quickly obtained these and sought scientific analysis of them.

The major scientific findings, from the French aero-space researcher, Dr. Claude Poher, indicated that:

(1) the disk in the photos must measure no more than 8 to 9 inches in diameter in order for the sharpness of its details to match those of the landscape;

(2) the disk must have floated no more than 10 feet from the camera; and,

(3) under magnification, a string holding the disk in front of the camera became visible.

As Sherlock Holmes would say, from these facts, certain inferences appear undeniable. Somebody made a disk 8-to-9 inches wide, hung it from a string and took the photos with a camera 10 feet away. This does not suggest a "technology far superior to the human." It suggests a technology pitifully inferior to George Lucas' Industrial Light and Magic. It suggests Ed Wood and *Plan 9 From Outer Space*.

But if the photo results from clumsy fakery, at which a sophisticated professional faker like Elmyr would sneer, what sort of fakery produced the original disks in the sky (seen by dozens of witnesses)? Industrial Light and Magic did not exist then, nor could its technicians—then or now—operate in public far from their computers. Not with today's technology, yet...

Then, this: In the neighborhood of the June 1967 disk, people began finding more "hard evidence"—cylinders bearing the symbol)+(. (More hard evidence edited out by those who wish to banish the subject by intoning the mantra, "We have seen no hard evidence. We have seen no hard evidence.") When pried open, the cylinders contained inscribed strips of a plastic called Tedlar, developed by NASA. These "messages" looked like some exotic inhuman language, or like meaningless doodles—as you will—but they only represented the curtain raiser.

So far the "hard evidence" doesn't seem to prove much... But to avoid any suggestion of the weird, you have to hold a really dogmatic faith that (a) the "normal" really exists, and (b) you know *all* of its contents...

But ever since these Madrid masques, many people in Europe, and elsewhere—including some very learned and respectable people—have received neatly typed letters from "UMMO," the Highly Advanced Space People who allegedly flew those disks and dropped those cylinders. (Retarded, or even Dull Normal, Space People never seem to come here...) The author or authors always signs off with both the name UMMO and the symbol)+(, evidently the spelling of UMMO in their language...

None of this *per se* differentiates UMMO from a few dozen similar cults. For instance, millions around the world believe fervently in messages allegedly received by a Swiss farmer, Eduard Meier, from "the Pleiades," and Meier only ranks as the most successful of numerous similar dealers in alleged Cosmic Wisdom. (Of course, aliens who say they come from the Pleiades might as well say they come from "the galaxy." The Pleiades covers less area than the Milky Way, but only to the extent that saying you found a book in Boston conveys a bit more information than saying you found it in the Eastern U.S.)

UMMO differs from Meier and the other cults in one very significant way. All of the other outer space messages peddled by "contactees" have low-to-zero information content.[1] They say nothing new. They have all the philosophic, scientific and literary value of Hallmark cards.

The UMMO messages do not have this platitudinous dullness about them. They have high information content—real intel-

---

[1] In modern mathematics, information content has a precise numerical value, based on the reverse of the probability that you can predict it in advance. Thus, an astrology column has virtually no information, a great poem has high information, and the ravings of an acute schizophrenic have such enormous information that nobody can predict them or make use of them.

lectual "bite"—and have intrigued many scientists and philosophers. They really do say things that sound *innovative*—a unique trait in the UFO field.

Wait a minute now. Let's not jump to conclusions. Dr Jacques Vallee, a very open-minded and well-trained scientific investigator of UFOs estimates the scientific level of the UMMO messages in his book *Revelations: Alien Contact and Human Deception* as about the level of a few dozen bright 1970s Ph.D. candidates. Not bad for 1966...but not necessarily extra-terrestrial, you must admit.

For instance, consider one typical UMMO transmission:

> WE DENY THE EARTH PRINCIPLE OF THE THIRD EXCLUDED TERM (THE EXCLUDED MIDDLE, ENUNCIATED BY ARISTOTLE) ACCORDING TO WHICH PROPOSITIONS CAN ONLY BE TRUE OR FALSE. THE WHOLE ONTOLOGY OF TERRESTRIAL THINKERS IS SATURATED WITH EXPRESSIONS LIKE "TO BE," "I AM NOT," 'I EXIST," WITHOUT ANY OPTION FOR OTHER FORMS OF DIFFERENT CONTENT.
>
> UNLESS YOU YOURSELVES CLARIFY YOUR FORMS OF INFORMATIVE COMMUNICATION, THE PROCESS OF SEEKING THE TRUTH WILL BE VERY LABORIOUS AND SLOW.

)+(UMMO

If you regard this as a revolutionary contribution to philosophy, I quite agree. However, although still resisted by the majority of Academia in the Western world, non-Aristotelian logics, *including* the previously excluded middle, have appeared from quite terrestrial sources since the 1920s. In that decade, while quantum uncertainty first hit home in physics, two different mathematicians, Brouwer and Lukasiewicz, both proposed multi-valued logics, not limited to Aristotle's either/or.

Other notable contributions, to non-Aristotelianism came from mathematician John von Neumann, who proposed in 1933 that we could best discuss the new paradoxes of quantum mechanics in a three-valued logic of true, false and maybe (the excluded middle); and semanticist Alfred Korzybski who, the same year, proposed that most human conflict, including war, results from the either/or, and that we could communicate with less hostility in a n-valued logic *bounded by* **yes** **and** **no** *but including a middle with as many degrees of probability as each situation demands.* E.g.:

1 = no
2 = 20 per cent probable
2.5 = 25 per cent probable
...etc...
9.0 = 90 per cent probable
10 = yes.

Back in the 1950s, mathematician Anatole Rapoport offered a four-valued logic which I often find useful, classifying statements as *true, false, indeterminate* (at this date) and *meaningless* (forever indeterminate, because no experience can either prove them or refute them.)

And in 1964, mathematician Lofti Zadeh invented a fuzzy logic, much like Korzybski's but more mathematically precise, which, although still "controversial" in the Occident has already gotten incorporated successfully into some of most exciting computers and other electronic innovations coming out of Japan in 1994.

In Zadeh's fuzzy logic, we can not only estimate degrees of probability *a la* Korzybski but also degrees of presence or remaining presence. In other words, where Aristotle only lets us say "The U.S. Senate consists of imbeciles" or "The U.S. Senate does not consist of imbeciles," and von Neumann and Korzybski allow us to estimate the probability that the Senate consists of imbeciles, Zadeh's math allows us, if we know the facts, to state precisely how many imbeciles we will find present among the 100 persons in the Senate... 1, 10, 25, 53, 90 or whatever...

To use an example less amusing but perhaps clearer: in Aristotelian logic, we must classify a Coca Cola can as either *present* in the refrigerator or *not present* in the refrigerator. In Koryzbskian n-valued logic, we can estimate the probability that the coke remains in the refrigerator, from 0 per cent, through ten percent...up to 100 per cent, depending on how much we know. In Zadeh's fuzzy logic, we can estimate *how much* Coca Cola remains present in the can, e.g., full can, three-quarter full, half can...etc.

Similarly an animal does not have to belong to one taxonomic family or else simply not belong to it. (The Creationists, so happy a few chapters ago, get shafted!)

In Zadeh's math, we can say "This animal belongs 90 % to the fish family and 10% to the amphibian family." "This animal belongs 60% to the ape family and 40% to the hominid family." See? Just like the Coke can contains 60 % coke and 40 % air. I told you I wouldn't leave us wandering in the dark with the Fundamentalists...

(For the remainder of this book, I will—solely for convenience—use "fuzzy logic" as a generic label for Zadeh's fuzzy logic and also for the other non-Aristotelian logics of von Neumann, Korzybski, Lukasiewicz, Brouwer, Rapoport etc.— i.e., for all three-valued or multi-valued logics that do not limit themselves to Aristotle's either/or.)

So: as revolutionary as multi-valued logics seem, they do not prove an extraterrestrial mind has communicated with us. (In addition to the Western scientists mentioned above, most Oriental philosophy has a multiple logic, transcending two-valued either/ors.) UMMO could communicate such "radical" ideas and still arise from some clever committee right here on Earth, or even from some super-genius who plays the role in philosophy that Elmyr played in painting.

(Everybody who has examined the UMMO documents without accepting them as extraterrestrial seems to think some *committee* devised them. Curiously, when the first Elmyr fakes came to light, most art **Experts** assumed a *committee* had done *them*...)

A problem arises here, one that can baffle us, amuse and entertain us or enrage us—whichever we choose—as much as the Elmyr mystery in art.

Let us say that the UMMO messages do emanate from a clever hoaxter right here on Earth. He—or they, if we want to think of the Puppet Master as an intelligence agency (say, the C.I.A.)— rounded up a herd of smart, hungry young science majors, and a few philosophy majors, and brewed up the whole UMMO hoax in 1967. Then they all continued it until the present (it hasn't stopped yet...)

Can you really believe in such a conspiracy? Many people can, but I assume most of my readers find the concept preposterous.

Can you seriously credit that in nearly 30 years none of the participants has had pangs of conscience, or gotten worried about his/her future reputation—or just couldn't stand the heat inside a truly Machiavellian conspiracy—and blown the whistle on the others? Or do you think such overly scrupulous types get "eliminated" before they can tell all to the media? If you can swallow this, you may next try believing that all the evidence for the Nazi Holocaust results from faked photos and perjured testimony devised by a Vast International Conspiracy of Zionists...

(By the way, why don't the Holocaust Deniers try something really daring and question all the evidence *that World War II happened?* A brave soul named Donald Holmes has done that in a philosophical novel called *The Illuminati Conspiracy: The Sapiens System* (New Falcon Publications, 1988). Kerry Thornley argues the same thesis in his remarkable privately printed poem, *Illuminati Lady*, adding the notion that the Virtual Reality of the war resulted from collaboration between incarnate Illuminati led by Gandhi and discarnate Illuminati led by Madame Blavatsky.)

On the other hand, if we can't believe in a terrestrial UMMO conspiracy, anymore than we can believe in conspiracies that faked the Holocaust or the whole of World War II, where in hell, heaven or outer space do the UMMO messages come from?

As Mason said to Dixon, "We've got to draw the line *somewhere*."

Or does that desire to *draw a line* underlie our notion that, for evolution to work, two fish must have given birth to an amphibian?

Can we begin to consider that sharp demarcations emerge from human analysis only and do not exist in sensory-sensual experience?

Can we begin to ask "*how much* truth does this book contain?" or "*how much* fiction does this book contain?" instead of the Aristotelian "Is it true or false?"

Reference:

Revelations: Alien Contact and Human Deception, by Jacques Vallee, Ballantine, New York, 1991.

Fuzzy Logic, by Daniel McNeil and Paul Freiberger, Simon and Schuster, New York, 1993.

ELEVEN

HANGED BY THE NECK

In Which We Encounter the Priory of Sion Again and a Possible Link to Three Hanged Men

> Isn't it silly?
> —*The Lady From Shanghai*
>
> *Mein Führer!* I can valk!
> —*Dr. Strangelove*

In the years following Paoli's *Dessous* and de Sede's *La Race*, various persons seem to have privately published various books and pamphlets about the Priory of Sion, evidently for limited circulation, and deposited them in the Bibliotheque Nationale in Paris. With virtually no exceptions, this "literature" bears no authors' names or obviously fraudulent, joking pen-names. All of it also shows an interesting blend of information and disinformation, as if the proprietors of this show wanted us to get curious but also to remain skeptical. Few hoaxes work that way, I think.

As in Illuminati literature, we find in this Priory material a variety of contradictory "explanations" of what the Priory means and intends. Some sources would have us consider the Priory a right-wing Catholic plot, masterminded by Archbishop Lefebvre, but other tracts try to persuade us that the Priory represents a Romantic chivalric order, sort of like our U.S. group, the Society for Creative Anachronism, which likes to play-act as if the Renaissance had never happened and the Dark Ages still survive. Support for de Sede's model of the Priory as an anti-Papist "resistance movement" also appears occasionally.

The Lefebvre "evidence" seems like a rather obvious joke at the expense of a somewhat paranoid old man. Archbishop Lefebvre had a falling out with the Vatican during the reign of Pope John XXIII (that number again...) and led a faction of right-wing Catholics who regard the Post-Vatican II curia as puppets of a "Satanic and Freemasonic" conspiracy, or sometimes as the classic Illuminati conspiracy itself. No solid evidence at all, at all, links this old crank with the actual Priory and its decidedly Masonic allies in Switzerland.

The chivalric theory rests on alleged revelations by insiders and the seemingly "documented fact" that Jean Cocteau served as Grand Master of the Priory of Sion, the 23rd Grandmaster amusingly enough.

This "fact" rests on a charter of the Priory signed by Jean Cocteau. If you can forget about Elmyr and the Howard Hughes contract, you will find encouragement in the "authentication" of the Cocteau signature by two **Experts** hired by later researchers (Baigent, Lincoln, Leigh).

When Arlen encountered Cocteau's possible involvement in this dark carnival, she immediately formed her own theory. The Priory of Sion, she says, came into existence in a Paris basement c. 1930 when Cocteau, Breton, Dali and other first-generation surrealists decided, while smoking opium, to start their very own International Conspiracy—the first surrealist conspiracy and therefore the first one to deliberately appear batshit crazy.

(I recall a BBC film about Cocteau in which he says, as well as I recollect, "The poet must always be a suspicious character. Only if he is under police surveillance can he be sure his work is important." I saw it in Ireland about ten years ago, so I paraphrase his words from memory...)

Other material sounds more like de Sede's hermeticism, leaving a distinct impression that the Priory somehow serves the alleged Masonic goal of total abolition of the Roman Catholic Church and appointment of a Rosicrucian Emperor to govern all Europe.

An especially provocative work, also privately printed and deposited in the Bibliotheque, has the title, *Le Serpent Rouge*, and deals with the Merovingians, the murder of Dagobert II, a hidden race of kings, Rosicrucian symbolism, astrology and Mary Magdelene. The authors' names appear on the title page as Louis Saint-Maxent, Gaston de Koker, and Pierre Feugere.

In the two days after this hermetic little book appeared, the Paris police investigated three cases of men found hanged in conditions where suicide and murder both seemed possible. (Like our current Solar Temple deaths in Switzerland...or the deaths of Calvi and Sindona in the P2 conspiracy...) The victims, of course, had the names Louis Saint-Maxent, Gaston de Koker and Pierre Feugere.

Sort of takes you back, doesn't it? Could the Priory of Sion have a serious side, after all?

"Le Serpent rouge," of course, means the Red Serpent. This symbolizes male sexual energy in many occult traditions and relates to the Hindu kundalini theory of induced brain change by sexual/yogic stress. The book seems to hint at some sort of astro-logical sexual mysticism, but it also insists, again and again, that only Mary Magdelene fully received the Divine Transmission that came through Jesus... The Fatimid Moslems, similarly, hold that only the tradition coming through Fatima, the Prophet's daughter, contains the true teaching of Islam. I don't know if that helps matters or just plunges us deeper into the murk...

Reference:

Holy Blood, Holy Grail, by Baigent, Lincoln and Leigh. Delacorte, New York, 1982.

TWELVE

CROP CIRCLES NOT INCLUDED

**In Which We Explore Something in Uganda
That May Qualify as a New Art Form
or a New Mental Illness**

> There's something I'd like to show you…
> —*Out of Africa*

> What business are we in, Dad?
> —*The Magic Christian*

In the August-September 1994 issue of the *Fortean Times,* I read about an alleged "madman" in Uganda, who certainly belongs in this book. I do not know if the *Fortean Times* editors themselves want to label this creative and imaginative chap "mad" or just picked up the term while condensing and paraphrasing a story about his exploits which they cite from the *Coventry Evening Telegraph*, 24 February 1994. Anyway, "mad," "eccentric" or just a unique case of artistic enthusiasm combined with insensitivity, this Ugandan has a truly original hobby.

He goes about in the jungle, you see, with a tranquilizer gun. When he spots a gorilla, he fires—pow! (Have you ever gotten hit with one of those things? Imagine what it feels like…) The gorillas sink to the jungle floor, "out like a light"—just like you or me after too many Irish whiskeys—and the culprit then inflicts his own divine[1] imagination upon the helpless creatures. He dresses them in clown suits before they can wake up and object to this undignified proceeding. Then he blithely skips off through the under-brush to lie low for a while before seeking further "subjects" (or victims) for his strange art.

So far the game wardens haven't caught him. I know some Animal Rights activists in California who would gladly tar and feather him and then hang him by the neck. His "art," if we must call it that, offends New Age sensibilities even more than wearing animal hides or skins as clothing.

I wonder a lot about this bizarre Ugandan. Once having found his *metier*, will he repeat himself endlessly (the usual fate of the inferior artist)—more and more gorillas in clown suits—or will he begin experimenting more broadly? Can we look forward to reports of wildebeests in polka-dot pajamas, chimpanzees in tuxedos, zonked zebras waking in the garb of a Gay Leather Bar?

I wonder about the gorillas, too. I bet they hate it — feel acute terror and rage—when they wake up covered in *something constraining* which they cannot possibly understand. Do the game wardens mercifully knock them out again with another tranquilizer dart, and gently remove the disgraceful circus costumes? Or do the gorillas themselves tear the damned weird *stuff* off the bodies just as soon as they wake? Or do some of them simply wander off, not quite able to cope, like you or me after a bad drunk? In that case, how many tragic gorillas in clown suits might wander the Ugandan jungle this very day?

It makes me think of Pagliacci and the sad clowns of the first Picasso masterpieces (only a *very few* of which we owe to Elmyr... I hope...)

And I contemplate with wonder the 'patphysical hypothesis that the UMMO messages really do come from an extraterrestrial source that wishes to educate and improve humanity. If the UMMO chaps flew over Uganda and looked down upon scores of gorillas in clowns suits, how would this alter their perception

---

[1] I use the word in the sense in which the surrealists dubbed de Sade "the divine Marquis."

of the human mind, the human imagination and of what sort of retraining we need?

And, of course, I also wonder if all this primate clownery has really occurred in Uganda or does the *Coventry Evening Tele-graph* just have a drunken and unreliable part-timer covering animal news from Africa...[1]

---

[1] On 16 February 1995 I heard on KPIG (107.5) that this ritual or artwork continues. The gorillas cannot remove the clown suits unaided, and the wardens do re-tranquilize and unclown them. "We are dealing with a very sick mind," the chief warden told reporters.

THIRTEEN

AN INFORMATION-RICH ENVIRONMENT

In Which We Consider the Influence of
Magic and Marijuana on Orson's *Touch of Evil*

Your methodology sucks!
—*Cannibal Women of the Avocado Jungle of Death*

It's okay—we're on the side of freedom and justice.
—*Steelyard Blues*

Critics have endlessly analyzed and re-analyzed the celebrated opening shot of Orson Welles' *Touch of Evil* (1958) and yet, as in all dangerous art, one can still discover new shocks in it. For one thing, it contains a magic trick which no commentator has yet noticed. The shot also functions to disorient our conditioned expectations—as "a reorganization of the data of perception in order to betray the spectator" (as Terry Comito wrote in his introduction to the published script). More precisely, Welles actually sets the spectator in a *stoned out* space. In a film about dope and border-crossings Welles uses the first shot to immediately drag the audience across the border into a psychedelic world.

To exemplify:

87

1) The shot lasts 2 minutes and 15 seconds, and drenches the audience in so many bewildering information bytes that an ordinary director would use about 20 shots, edited in montage, to convey all this.

But montage, as Jean Collet has written, always functions "propagandistically" and "brutally"—it insistently directs the audience's perceptions into a pre-created reality-tunnel. Any Wellesian tracking shot, with the actors moving in various different directions and the camera wandering nervously among them, works against this totalitarian bias and does not propagandize you: it incites you to decide which elements to notice and how to relate them into a coherent "meaning."

2) At no place in the 135 seconds does Welles allow the camera to settle into what the French New Wave directors called *le plan Americain*—the typical Hollywood frame, in which the camera lens stands at the eye-level of an "objective" spectator a few feet from the action.

Le plan Americain delimits ordinary "space" and ordinary "reality" as formula Hollywood directors have trained us to see them and think of them. Welles sets you firmly in a contingent space that continually redefines itself (in the manner of the best works of Picasso or Elmyr or whoever did those great "1920s" cubist mindmaulers.)

3) Specifically, Orson mounted the camera on a 22-foot crane to accomplish the cramming of the information of 20 montage shots into one fluidly moving, anxiously restless single shot. The camera never goes where we expect it to go, but always precisely where we do not expect it to go.

Like marijuana, a Wellesian long shot creates an information overload and provokes you to enlarge your reality-tunnel to accommodate it. Montage and *le plan Americain* put you in a trance; Welles' maneuvers shake you violently and uneasily awake. Lurching wildly, and uncomfortably, back and forth between comedy, melodrama and tragedy, *Touch of Evil* looks at narcs (and other cops) with trippy eyes, and although made two years before the '60s began, now seems like the archetypal '60s film.

4) Welles, of course, uses his favorite 18.5 mm lens, which gives an unusually wide angle and a deep focus. This creates that

"blend of realism and surrealism" (as a BBC commentator once called it) that we consider Wellesian cinema.

Realistically, the 18.5 brings the background into sharper focus and approximates more closely to what the eye sees in the ordinary non-filmic world; it allows Welles, a would-be painter in his adolescence, to frame every shot in his gloriously composed, "painterly" style.

Surrealistically, the 18.5 sets us in what I have called "stoned space." Mathematically, with the normal Hollywood lenses, if an actor walks forward three paces, he appears on screen walking forward *three* paces. With the 18.5, he moves relativistically in filmic space *nine* paces closer to the audience and seems to loom ominously—or ridiculously. This blend of sharper-than-normal focus and non-Euclidean relativistic space seems the best cinematic translation (thus far) of psychedelic perception.

The prejudices which hold what the "normal" tight-angle lens sees "reality" clearer than the 18.5, or that human eyes sees "reality" but dog's eyes don't, represent the kind of cultural chauvinism that post-modern art attempts to subvert, so that we may see with multiple vision. As the Bard of Lambs and Tygers said, we need to perceive beyond "Single Vision and Newton's Sleep."

(Yes: we know in fact that Welles used the Devil Weed at least some times. Jazz singer Billie Holliday mentions that she and Orson smoked a lot of it during the shooting of *Citizen Kane;* see her autobiography, *Lady Sings the Blues.*)

To look in more depth at the stoned-out space of the opening 135 seconds of *Touch of Evil:*

Ominous music (Rock'n'Roll with a heavy mechanical tick-tock beat) begins before we *see* anything. The camera fades in on a tight middle shot of a time-bomb in a man's hands; we see the suit and shirt of the bomber, but not his face. A woman's drunken (or demented?) laughter "causes" the camera to dart nervously to the left and we see an intoxicated man and woman coming across a parking lot toward us. The camera jerks around with more anxiety, peering here and there, placing us in the murderer's perspective, then moves decisively forward as he attaches the bomb to the bottom of a car. From now until the end of the shot, a tick-tock beat under the music will remind us of the bomb.

The camera meanwhile has moved back and the murderer runs quickly in front of it, fleeing, but the camera has accelerated and every commentator seems to miss what Welles, the magician, has just done. (We will return to that.) The "retreating" camera, as if trying to get away from the bomb, rises as it leaves the parking lot; we barely catch a glimpse of the man and woman getting into the car and starting it. The camera "loses" them as it zooms over a row of buildings, picks them up again briefly in the distance as it descends to another street, and continues to lose them and find them until the end of the shot. The tick-tock music never lets us forget the bomb.

Meanwhile, we find ourselves amid the "whirling labyrinth" (Terry Comito's phrase) of Los Robles, a border town bridging the U.S. and Mexico. Miguel Vargas, a Mexican narcotics cop (Charlton Heston) and his new wife, Susan (Janet Leigh) loom as shadowy figures, then appear in clear light, then get lost again. The camera slows down to allow the car to approach us and the Vargases, then speeds up to leave them behind. Two American MPs appear, static elements; a dozen Mexican and American pedestrians, moving elements, also appear; and then we "find" the car again. Other cars cross in front of the camera, an old Mexican pushes a vegetable cart, garbage blows in the streets, we see honky-tonk strip-joints, bars and the inevitable JESUS SAVES of a storefront mission. Never does anybody move directly toward or away from the camera, except very briefly; somewhere between 50 and 70 extras keep moving in different directions, at oblique angles, until we suddenly land in a comparatively "normal" cinematic space—just as the Vargases and the car both arrive simultaneously (synchronistically?) at the border.

The ticking beneath the music rises several decibels: we have recognized the "hero" and "heroine" and now they stand a few feet from a bomb, in deadly peril, unaware of their danger.

The moment after we *cross the border* the camera teasingly loses the car again as we follow the Vargases and begin to learn something about them. Susan, a "nice girl" from Philadelphia, has had the courage to marry a Mexican, but she inadvertently reveals genteel latent racism still lurking within her; Miguel appears over-protective—a trait which will continue throughout (ironically—since he gets distracted by his job and totally fails to protect her when she really needs him.) When they pause to kiss each other, the 135-second shot finally ends as the bomb violently explodes—off-screen. (We only see its reflected light, not the explosion itself.)

The story that follows (insofar as we can reduce this "whirling labyrinth" into a story in any conventional sense) soon becomes a deadly contest between Vargas (Heston), a "good" narcotics cop who goes by the book and Captain Hank Quinlan (Welles), a racist homicide dick and dried-out alcoholic who follows a mystic "intuition."

In the pivotal scene—another tracking shot, lasting 200 seconds (three minutes, 20 seconds)—Welles performs his second magic track. (We will return to the first.) Cramming over a dozen actors into a small apartment, Welles keeps them moving between living room, bedroom and bathroom. They quarrel, bicker, talk over each other's lines (in typical Wellesian fashion) and harass the dweller in the apartment, Manolo Sanchez (Victor Milan), principle suspect in the bombing.

Quinlan's racism and Vargas' resentment keep flaring up, Sanchez protests his innocence with passion and fervor, and as the actors wander back and forth between the three rooms, the camera excitedly follows first one actor or group and then nervously darts back to "check out" another actor or group. Somehow in this confusion, important things happen off-screen (we hear Quinlan punching Sanchez, but we don't see it). The most important event remains not only unseen by the inquisitive camera but lost to the microphones as well. While Sanchez distracts us with oaths of innocence, swearing on his mother's grave, *somebody* unobtrusively plants two sticks of dynamite in the bathroom, allowing another cop to find them and justifying Sanchez's arrest.

The rest of the film tracks Vargas' attempts to prove that Quinlan has planted the dynamite and framed the Mexican suspect, and Quinlan's attempt to discredit Vargas by framing him and Susan on a marijuana-and-heroin rap. Vargas, smart and tough despite his Liberalism, fights back effectively. In a mere 24 hours, Quinlan's whole world collapses on him. Re-examined evidence calls into question not some or most but *all* the convictions he has obtained in 30 years as a detective; as the trap closes, he starts drinking again, after 12 years of sobriety; and he ends up—blind drunk, frantic, pitiful—killing his partner, a cop who virtually adored him and believed his "intuition" had a supernatural element.

Liberalism, as in a "normal" Hollywood film, has triumphed over fascism, and we can all feel warm and fuzzy.

Then Welles pulls the rug from under our feet. Sanchez confesses that he did plant the bomb. Quinlan did have reliable intuition, after all—at least *part* of the time; meanwhile, we uneasily note in retrospect the liberal Vargas has, in fighting his way out from under the narcotics frame, increasingly used Quinlan-like tactics, further undermining our faith in the moral conventions assumed by good guy/bad guy thrillers.

We never find out how many of the people "framed" by Quinlan actually committed the crimes for which he framed them—just as we never find out the definite position of a quantum particle, or how many Picassos we should really call Elmyrs. *Post-modernism does not result from whim, but from growing evidence that we simply do not live in an Aristotelian true/false universe. As UMMO says, we live with a middle (or muddle) excluded by Aristotle.*

Amusingly, some commentators, especially in France, have refused to believe in Sanchez's confession; they want a simple Moral Tale, evidently. Such critics missed the magic trick in the first 135 seconds. If you re-run the film on video, using rewind over and over, you can eventually convince yourselves, as I did, that Sanchez did indeed plant the bomb. We see only his suit and shirt and a very brief side-angle on part of his face, but we can identify him. Welles, with the assurance of a man who practiced stage magic from childhood on, even allows Sanchez (Victor Milan) to wear the same suit and shirt when we see him again in his apartment. The magician knows that in an information-overload situation, spectators only see what they came prepared to see.

Welles' ambivalent concept of human "character" derives from Shakespeare, his favorite writer from the age of nine onward; his politics emerged from the anti-fascist movement of the 1930s. This tension between Shakespearean shades-of-grey ambiguity and idealistic black-or-white morality underlies all the ironies and anxieties that give Welles' plays and films their off-kilter and pessimistic humanism. After Quinlan dies, a madam speaks his only epitaph—already quoted but worth looking at again, since it does not soften our judgment but merely exacerbates our uncertainties—"He was some kind of a man. What does it matter what you *say* about people?"

In a deeper sense, the *whole* of *Touch of Evil* has aspects of a magic trick. Commentators all agree that Quinlan wins our sympathy at the end, when doomed and dying. It remains a curiosity that Welles, who knew all the "tricks" to make a villain sympathetic—and played the most charming sociopath ever seen on film in *The Third Man*—systematically avoided any ordinary devices to "humanize" Quinlan. Acting as his own make-up artist, he made Quinlan as ugly as a circus freak; he padded his already obese body to create an obscene flabbiness; he sternly controlled his irrepressible humor in one area only, not letting Quinlan have any of the witty lines he gave other villains; in total, Quinlan embodies everything the Sixties would later mean by the concept "Pig."

And yet when Quinlan drunkenly tries to wash his partner's blood off his hands—incongruously, in dirty, muddy water—we confront a mad, surrealist sense of Shakespearean tragedy, which elevates this racist "pig" to a flawed Tragic Hero. When Quinlan himself falls dead—in the same dirty water—he seems the center of the film, and Vargas, the conventional "hero" has shrunken to a *deus ex machina,* the engine that destroyed Captain Hank Quinlan. (Charlton Heston, in an interview on BBC's documentary "Orson Welles: A Life In Film" described Vargas as "a witness" to the Quinlan tragedy.)

Since Welles as a liberal has always said he despises Quinlan—even though he also said "Every villain has his reasons" on the BBC documentary just cited—we cannot explain how this monster became a Tragic Hero in the last third of the film. James Naremore, in *The Magic World of Orson Welles* found several "human" traits in Quinlan, but I don't think he convinced anybody but himself. (Of course, everybody knows, as soon as Quinlan comes on screen, that this fat, limping wreck plagued with food-and-alcohol addictions has some terrible inner

vulnerability. We may, if we wish, assume the addictions indicate a terrible self-doubt that he never verbally acknowledges. [1])

*Quinlan looms up there alongside Macbeth and Othello and
Lear only because Orson Welles put him there*. And Welles did it
entirely with the "magic trick" of artistic *rhythm.* The structure
of *Touch of Evil*—the clockwork of the parts clicking together
into an esthetic whole—creates a tragic crescendo just as
formally classic as Welles' Shakespearean films (*Macbeth,* 1948,
Othello, 1952, *Chimes at Midnight,* 1966). Quinlan serves as a
figure of high tragedy because tragic structure—abstract artistic
form—raises him out of his piggish world into the world of film
poetry.

One of the first lessons of marijuana: the world contains too
many information bytes to fit into any one model. The second
lesson: any model you create changes *perceived* information
bytes until they fit it. Viewed through the eyes of paranoia, your
best friend appears part of a conspiracy against you. Viewed
through the eyes of a Shakespearean humanist like Orson
Welles, a Hank Quinlan becomes, not just a redneck racist pig,
but an enlarged and tormented image of the flaws in all of us.

And this uniquely *noir* case of *film noir* also reminds us that
fake evidence may support a true thesis: a paradox to ponder...

---

[1]Even at the end, Quinlan insists on the guilt of all the people he convicted with
planted "evidence"—"Guilty! Guilty! Every last one of 'em—guilty." He
knows. His intuition tells him.

FOURTEEN

JESUS AND MARY CHRIST

In Which We Learn More, and
Understand Less, About the Priory of Sion

> It's *good* to be king!
> —*The History of the World, Part One*

> Stand back—we're on a mission from God!
> —*The Blues Brothers*

The next "revelation" in the Priory of Sion mystery—or the next "hoax," if you will—came in 1982 with the publication of *Holy Blood, Holy Grail* by Baigent, Lincoln and Leigh, the only book on this subject to reach best-seller status.

HBHG re-explores some of the same data as de Sede, Paoli and the pseudonymous authors in the Bibliotheque Nationale: the murder of Dagobert II, evidently by agents of the Vatican; the bear-goddess who appears again and again in these works, and never does get explained; astrological and hermetic mysticism... the usual stuff...but then come Shocking Discoveries.

Or shameless leg-pulling.

For one thing, the authors interviewed Gerard de Sede, who more or less admitted, or certainly hinted strongly, that he did not write as an outsider studying the Priory but as an initiated member engaged in a process of gradual revelation which the Priory has orchestrated for several decades.

For one with a mind as Byzantine as mine, this raises the question: should I also consider Paoli, the Swiss journalist, an insider play-acting the objective outside investigator? How about the anonymous and pseudonymous authors of the Bibliotheque booklets? And, of course, the instrumental question: can we rely on the lens we now look through?—i.e., how about Baigent, Lincoln and Leigh themselves? Shall we consider them outside the masque, or inside? The *real fun* of conspiracy hunting comes when you realize you can't trust anyone, as all the paranoids know.

For the paranoids, this increases their paranoia, which they seem to enjoy. For a guerrilla ontologist like me, it increases my agnosticism, which I prefer to paranoia, because I find it more amusing and less depressing.

Whatever or whomever we suspect, according to *HBHG,* when Baigent, Lincoln, Leigh met M. de Sede they discussed mostly another of his books, *L'or de Rennes-le-Chatteau* (The Treasure of Rennes-le-Chatteau) which deals with further Merovingian mysteries and with a strange church in the town of Rennes-le-Chatteau, built in the 1890s by an even stranger priest named Bergener Sauniere. This church, called the Cathedral of Mary Magdelene, has an inscription over the door saying *THIS PLACE IS ACCURSED* and has some oddities inside as well: the Stations of the Cross, for instance, show a Scotsman in kilts witnessing the crucifixion. Father Sauniere allegedly financed this theological Fun House out of the "treasure" of Rennes-le-Chatteau which, in turn, he discovered by deciphering an old document. The decoded message itself, alas, requires explanation, rambling along incoherently about "the horse of God" and "noon blue apples" before it mentions "Sion" and "treasure" at all.

We've all heard of "the house of God," but what do we make of a "horse of God?" According to some archeological evidence, the first Gauls and Gaels worshipped a horse-god, but like the bear goddess, this primordial divinity doesn't quite relate to the other Priory mysteries...(or does it?) Or should we recall the mysterious *Travels in Remote Parts*, delivered from a closed coach (by an unknown dwarf, allegedly Mr. Alex Pope, allegedly for the author, Lem Gulliver of Nottinghamshire)—a book in which a horse of superhuman intelligence teaches Gulliver the Enlighted (i.e., equine) view of our own accursed human species? Did Swift only serve as another mask for the Horse of God?

As for "noon blue apples"—I admit this stumps me, although a friend in Arizona, Eric Wagner, has started a poetry magazine with that name.

Arlen, incidentally, conceived her theory that the surrealists invented the Priory of Sion after she read about that code and that church. Alas, the church dates to c. 1895 and surrealism to 1923. Maybe some mysterious 'Pataphysicians, in league with Jarry, invented both the Priory of Sion, first, and surrealism, later? (And why does "the Priory of Sion" as a name deliberately invoke a famous forgery about the Elders of Zion?)

As the French themselves say, it gives one furiously to think, and to wave one's arms about...

Another station of the cross inside the cathedral of Mary Magdelene shows conspirators smuggling Jesus's body out of the grave during the night, recalling the famous heresy that Jesus never died: somebody slipped him a narcotic that simulated death and, after hiding out a while, he either faked a resurrection, and/or went off to preach in India, and/or ultimately died in Japan. (Several versions of this yarn have circulated at various times, including the enigmatic verse in the *Koran*, where Jesus says, "They thought they crucified me, but I laughed at them." An even more remarkable passage in *some*, not all, early manuscripts of Tacitus says Jesus led riots in Rome 40 years after his alleged death.)

Other details about the Mary Magdelene temple provoke further curiosity. As noted above, a priest named Father Sauniere built it in the 1890s, after allegedly finding a "treasure" in Rennes-le-Chatteau. Various versions of the identity of the "treasure" have appeared in the hundred years since Sauniere, and some claim that it consisted of neither gold nor silver but pure information. Sauniere, this theory says, found documents that allowed him to blackmail Important Persons. In fact, a royal von Hapsburg allegedly deposited a lot of money in the priest's bank account. Since I have no access to 100-year-old French bank accounts, I can only report this claim, not verify or refute it. (Time for more fuzzy logic, folks…)

Baigent, Lincoln and Leigh eventually tracked down the Grand Master of the Priory of Sion—the same Pierre Plantard de Saint Clair whom we encountered earlier, publishing *Circuit* out of the office of the Committee for Public Safety which he shared with André Malraux. Plantard spoke at length but mostly in riddles, as befits the Grand Master of a secret society. As to the treasure of Rennes-le-Chatteau, Plantard described it as "spiritual" rather than "material," said it belonged to Israel and promised it "would be returned to Israel at the proper time."

HBHG also links the Priory—sometimes convincingly, sometimes weakly—with some interesting folks. Such as:

(a) the Knights Templar, the chivalric order which had 123 members burned by the Inquisition in 1307 (Templar teachings got passed on to all later anti-Papist secret societies, according to many theorists).

(b) the rituals of Freemasonry and especially the archetype of the Widow's Son (all taken from the Knights Templar, according to Masonic historians).

(c) the Rosicrucians and Illuminati.

(d) such worthies as Isaac Newton and Claude Debussé, who allegedly served as Grandmasters of the Priory before Cocteau or Plantard de Saint Claire.

The authors do succeed, I think, in documenting that Father Sauniere belonged to one or more occult orders in Paris, although they do not mention what any student of modern occultism recognizes at once: all of these Parisian hermetic groups influenced Aleister Crowley and, through Crowley (or through P.B. Randolph) further influenced all modern magick orders that have both a Masonic style of ritual and symbolism and a hidden Tantric ("sex magick") teaching.

Ultimately, Baigent, Lincoln and Leigh present their own theory of what the Priory intends to reveal in slow stages. This theory holds that (a) Jesus married Mary Magdelene[1] (b) they

---

[1] A strong possibility, I think. Various people address Jesus as "Rabbi" in even the censored, edited and rewritten canonical gospels given to us by the Vatican Experts (and, oddly, accepted even by Protestant Experts.) No man could hold

had a child, the really important Widow's Son of tradition and (c) this child escaped to France after the crucifixion and became the progenitor of the Merovingian kings.

In short, Baigent, Lincoln and Leigh want to sell us the oldest of all millennial legends: the True King will return soon, very soon, and cast out the usurpers. They even claim that this archetypal myth occurs in all European countries *because the Priory planted it,* to prepare us for the day when the seed of Jesus sits in judgment on all nations.

Since this archetypal *agon* occurs as early as the climax of the *Odyssey*, I doubt that the Priory seeded it in Bronze Age Greece, although they may hope to capitalize on it. And the idea that the Priory persuaded Shakespeare to put the same myth into *Hamlet* seems on all fours with the Baconian phantasy. No: the myth of the True King who casts out one or more usurpers exists independently of the Priory.

Among the descendants of Jesus and Mary Magdelene you can find in the genealogies the authors give us, I find three especially interesting.

1. Pierre Plantard de Saint Clair himself. An enormously learned occultist, a very rich man, a proven Hero of the Resistance, an associate of de Gaulle with some of de Gaulle's aura clinging to him, Plantard de Saint Clair just might, with a good PR campaign, sell himself as the Seed of Jesus and reestablish "divine" monarchy, abolishing the democratic chaos and disorder of recent centuries and leading us back to the Dark Ages. (But what "treasure" will he then return to Israel?)

2. Prince Bernhard of the Netherlands. He not only descended from Jesus, according to the *HBHG* genealogies, he also appears in several popular conspiracy theories. He founded the Bilderbergers, the ultra-secretive group of rich white males who meet once a year and (according to those not personally rich enough, white enough or male enough to get into the club) plot how to exploit the rest of us. The Prince also belonged to David Rockefeller's Trilateral Commission, another international club for rich

---

the rank of Rabbi in orthodox Judea, especially in those days, without having a wife. Bachelorhood appears almost as unGodly as suicide to Jewish tradition. God told the sons of Adam to enjoy the earth, keep the faith, and *multiply.*

white (and nonwhite) males, also suspected of plotting against the rest of us.

All of these suspicions about the Bilderbergers and Trilateralists come from people who usually don't qualify as rich or male or even white themselves, not at all. I think this has the same explanation as the oddity noted by philosopher George Carlin: You never see a "SHIT HAPPENS" bumper sticker on a Rolls Royce. (For the record, neither the Bilderbergers nor the Trilateralists have ever gotten convicted in any court, of any crime whatsoever. However, I must admit that, without getting sinister about it, I share the general suspicion that when a parliament of rich men meet in secret, they do not usually exercise their brains to accomplish anything of benefit to folks like you and me.)

3. Dr. Otto von Hapsburg. He bears the family title, King of Jerusalem, dating back to the Crusades, and serves as the president of the Society for the United States of Europe, the group which has tirelessly worked over many decades for the European unification now occurring. But he also belongs to the Knights of Malta, a Roman Catholic secret society, which many Protestants and a few humanists suspect of plotting to overthrow democracy and Protestantism, re-establishing Papal domination over all Europe.

This Knight of Malta connection intrigues me. Several of the key members of the P2 conspiracy in Italy also belonged to the Knights of Malta. For instance: Roberto Calvi, whose Banco Ambrosiano served as laundromat for both Mafia and C.I.A. drug money; Liccio Gelli, Grandmaster of P2, master of political blackmail, and, in the 1970s and early 1980s, a man on the payrolls of both the C.I.A. and the K.G.B.; Michele Sindona, whose Franklin National Bank underwent the most drastic bankruptcy in recent history: Sindona himself, a former Mafia lawyer, stands convicted of 65 counts of stock and currency fraud in New York and of murdering a bank examiner in Rome. He died mysteriously of poison while awaiting trial on charges of plotting a fascist *coup* in Italy with Gelli, Calvi and others.

Some accounts claim Sindona committed suicide. Others say he shouted "They poisoned me!" before he keeled over. The death of Calvi in London, by hanging, also appears as either murder or suicide, depending on which Expert you trust...

The only conclusion that makes sense of this data, it seems to me, would hold that many powerful and/or "conspiratorial" groups that have different or even inimical goals can on occasion cooperate when they feel frightened enough of each other to think cooperation more profitable than gang war. Coppola's film *Godfather III* presents this thesis rather well, I think, and refers openly to P2 while only hinting of another group, elsewhere in Europe, even stronger and more sinister than P2... (Larry Gurwin of the *Financial Times* of London has reported that Italian investigators share this view, thinking P2 acted under supervision of an even more secretive group in Monte Carlo. See his book *The Calvi Affair* for details.)

Incidentally, the von Hapsburgs not only served as Emperors for a long time and still hold the title of Kings of Jerusalem, but one of them legalized freemasonry in Austria and abolished the all-Catholic school system, replacing it with the kind of secular public schools we have in non-Catholic countries today. I refer to the Emperor Joseph, son of Marie Theresa, and hero of Beethoven's first major work, *The Emperor Joseph Cantata*. Per Maynard Solomon's *Beethoven* (Schirmer, New York, 1978), Beethoven received his commission to write this hymn to the pro-Masonic anti-Catholic Emperor Joseph from—guess who?— the Illuminati of Bavaria.

Solomon seems unaware that conspiracy buffs still worry about the Illuminati. He mentions Beethoven's links with them several times, just as examples of the composer's deep involvement with the "Enlightenment" and the "democratic ideas" of his time.

Reference:

Holy Blood, Holy Grail, *op. cit.*
The Calvi Affair, Larry Gurwin, Pan Books, London, 1984.
In God's Name, David Yallop, Jonathan Cape, London, 1984.

FIFTEEN

HOW TO LIVE ELEVEN DAYS IN 24 HOURS

In Which We Take a New View
of Locality in Space-Time

> You gotta save Christianity, Richard! You gotta!
> —*The Crusades*

> Every day is Christmas in heaven.
> —*The Meaning of Life*

For about a year now, I have dated all my letters with my own no-bias multi-cultural calendar. Of course, I know a multi-cultural chronology seems very Politically Correct, but don't let that shock you. I happen to agree with the P.C. cult about many things.

(In fact, I only differ with them in not liking their intolerance, their fascist tactics, their introduction of Maoist brainwashing to our groves of Academe, their utter lack of humor, their continuous violations of ordinary common sense, their evident desire to destroy our Constitution and their lack of simple human decency. Aside from those minor issues, I almost approve the P.C. agenda.)

Actually, I started using a single non-Western calendar back in 1969-71 when working on *Illuminatus!* with Bob Shea. I had realized that the Gregorian calendar (the standard Occidental system) dates everything from the alleged birth of a god or demi-god I regarded as fictitious (he supposedly had a virgin for mother, a pigeon for father, and cured the blind by throwing dirt in their eyes...you can see why I had doubts, even before I encountered the claim that his genes got passed on to some of the European royal families notable for their idiots, imbeciles and lunatics.)

But dating everything *a la* Pope Gregory not only subliminally conditions to us to the mythology of the Vatican, but also divides written history artificially in the middle, creating a certain off-kilter view of how things actually transpired since Neolithic times.

For instance, in the Gregorian calendar, the first Egyptian dynasty began c. 3400 "B.C.", the founding of Rome 509 "B.C." and the nomination of the boar hog Pigasus for President of the U.S. in 1968 "A.D." To try to escape the Papist trap here by writing "B.C.E." (Before the Common Era) and "C.E.") "the Common Era", doesn't really help much. We still remain stuck in the Romish reality-tunnel.

Even worse side–effects of the Gregorian calendar arise when you try to sense the time-span covered in the dates just mentioned. It requires hard thinking, a historical imagination and even, for those as close to senility as myself, possible paper and pencil work. In the Illuminati calendar, however, these events fall into place in a single time line: Egypt's first dynasty begins around 600 A.L., the founding of Rome 3491 A.L. and the apotheosis of Pigasus 5968 A.L. (A.L., as in Masonry, means Anno Lumina—year of light.) Fill in a few more dates—Alleged date of creation in orthodox Judaism 240 A.L.; Battle of Marathon 3510 A.L.; Paper invented in China, 4105 A.L.; Brian Boru unites Ireland and drives out the Danes 5014 A.L.; Hassan i Sabbah illuminated 5092 A.L.; Native Americans discover Columbus 5492 A.L.; U.S. Declaration of Independence 5776 A.L.; Noble Drew Ali born 5886 A.L.; the 92nd and last naturally occurring chemical element discovered in 5932 A.L.— and history begins to make sense as a single orderly sequence, not bent in the middle.

The Illuminati chronology (in which year one A.L. = 4000 BCE Gregorian) begins with the birth of Hung Mung, the ancient Chaoist (pre-Taoist) Chinese philosopher who answered all questions by shouting loudly "I don't know! I don't know!" Thus, this system begins with a date around the first dawnings of civilization and writing; it thereby allows us to see all history as a single sequence, not interrupted by an artificial minus-to-plus changeover to commemorate the god of a single weird cult.

As I say, I worked all this out, including the five seasons of the Illuminati year, back in 5969/5971 A.L.—just as "the sixties" died under the clubs and tear-gas of the Nixon counter–revolution. Only c. 5992 A.L. after discovering Noble Drew Ali and the Moorish Science Temple, did I realize that any *one* calendar, even my own lovely Illuminati chronolog, imposes a *single* order on a *complex* system and thereby has reductionist and almost totalitarian implications, at least subliminally. I therefore have switched to a multi-cultural system which, I dare to think, adequately represents what historian Crane Brinton called the growing *multanimity* (as distinguished from *unanimity)* of Spaceship Earth today.

For instance, in my multi-cultural chronology the date on which I began writing this chapter looks as shown below:

Poundian—19 Artemis, 72 p.s. U.
Thelemic—19 September, Anno XC
'Pataphysical—12 Absolu, 122 E.P.
French Revolutionary—Le Travail, 202
Islamic—12 Rabi-2, 1373 A.H.
Gregorian—19 September 1994 C.E.
Erisian—43 Bureaucracy, 3178 y.C.
Chinese—15th day of the 8th month, Year of the Dog 4692
Mayan—6 Reed, 5106
Hebrew—14 Tishri, 5755 A.M.
Illuminati—43 Beamtenherrschaft, 5994 A.L.

A few quick, and valuable lessons, leap out of this chronolog immediately.

First of all, the much-touted "Millennium" only appears close in some calendars, and remains e.g., 245 years off in the Hebrew, 798 years away in the 'Pataphysical, etc. *All Millennialist hopes and anxieties, however "New Age" in flavor, unconsciously*

*assume that the Papist calendar represents the only correct form
of dating.* Most of these Millennialists—whether apocalyptical or
Utopian—don't follow the Pope in any other doctrine, so why
should they accept a Papal calendar?

Second, when I called this system *mine* I did not intend to
brag, but to indicate personal limitations and emic realities:
many alternatives can exist, at the preference of the user. You
can drop the Chinese and Mayan, if you want, and add the
Tibetan and Aztec, etc. Personally, I would love to include
Wiccan and Druidic dating systems, if somebody would find
them or create them.

A few additional words of explanation:

The Poundian calendar, designed by Ezra Pound (a poet feller),
attempts to define the post-Christian era and dates everything
from midnight 30 October 1921 (Gregorian)—the date Joyce
wrote the last words of *Ulysses*.[1] (The "p.s.U." means *post
scriptum Ulysses*, "after the writing of *Ulysses*.") 31 October
1921 accordingly becomes 1 Hephaistos in the year 1 p.s.U. The
year has six male months for the solar-phallic male gods (Hephaistos, Zeus, Saturn, Hermes, Mars, Phoebus, corresponding in
Gregorian to November [with one extra day], December, January, February, March and April) and 6 female months for the
lunar-female goddesses (Kupris, Juno, Athene, Hestia, Artemis,
Demeter i.e., in Gregorian May, June, July, August, September,
October.)

In this system, we have progressed 72 years into the post-
Christian epoch and will soon enter the 73rd.

For those who have other ideas about when the post-Christian
era began, the Thelemic calendar dates everything from 1904
Gregorian, when Aleister Crowley received—(or)—conceived
The Book of the Law. That makes this the year 90, which like all
years gets written Latin style by Thelemites—Anno XC. For
some reason, Crowley did not rename the months, so I keep the
Gregorian month names here.

As a multi-culturalist, I play no favorites. In one sense we have
evolved 72 years beyond the Christ cult, and in another sense we

---

[1]Pound had his 36th birthday on that date also. You can't expect an egomaniac,
even one as generous as Ez, to leave himself entirely out of the dating of the
New Age.

have evolved 90 years. As Sri Syadasti said, "All systems are true in some sense, false in some sense, meaningless in some sense, true and false in some sense, true and meaningless in some sense, false and meaningless in some sense, and true and false and meaningless in some sense." (A secret Illuminati teaching holds that if you repeat that 666 times you will achieve Total Illumination, in some sense.)

For those who, like Prof. Finnegan, CSICON and myself, feel that we have entered the 'Pataphysical Era, I include the 'Pataphysical calendar, starting from Alfred Jarry's birth on 8 September 1873. (He shares the 8 September birthday with the Blessed Virgin Mary in the Catholic mythos and Molly Bloom in the Joycean mythos. 'Pataphysically that "coincidence" must mean *something*.) Thus every 'Pataphysical year begins on Jarry's birthday, renamed 1 Absolu, and proceeds through 13 months of 29 days each (Absolu, Haha, As, Sable, Decervelage, Gueles, Pedale, Clinamen, Palotin, Merdre, Gidouille, Tatane and Phalle.) Since each week has seven days and each month four weeks, and 7 x 4 = 28, we have one extra day each month. We call these days "imaginary" by analogy with imaginary numbers. Every month starts on a Sunday, which simplifies the system and ensures that the 13th will always fall on a Friday.

As UFO sightings, UFO abductions, poltergeists, spontaneous human combustions, Bigfoot encounters, falls of fish and frogs, political triumphs of sci-fi creatures like Newt Gingrich etc. get reported more and more often, many may find the 'Pataphysical calendar the most plausible of all. As Jarry said, all other sciences deal with dull generalizations but 'Pataphysics deals only with the astounding and exceptional. (Every day when frogs fall out of the sky somewhere, or Newt announces a new figure for the number of card-carrying pot-smokers in the Democratic party, becomes a 'pataphysical Jubilee Day.)

The French Revolutionary calendar dates everything from 1792 Gregorian, and as I write this amid the five Sansculotides or feast days (Les Vertus, Le Genie, Le Travail, L'Opinion and Les Recompenses, i.e., Virtues, Genius, Labor, Blather and Wages) no month name gets used. In three days (22 September) the month of Vendemiaire in the year 203 begins, followed by Brumaire, Frimaire, Nivose, Pluvose, Ventose, Germinal, Floreal, Prairial, Messidor, Thermidor and Fructidor. (i.e.,

Vintage, Fog, Sleet, Snow, Rain, Wind, Sprouts, Flowers, Pasture, Harvest, Heat, Fruit—a good description of a year in Paris).

The Islamic calendar begins with the flight of the prophet (*hejira*) in the year 4621 A.L. (621 Gregorian.) A.H. means after the Hejira, the usual abbreviation used by Muslims writing in English; this year thus becomes 1373 A.H. You can look up the months in any encyclopedia. I don't intend to do all the work for you, and if I did this chapter would run longer than the rest of the book.

You already know the Gregorian calendar. It gets drummed into our heads in our allegedly "secular" "public" schools and everybody in our society who holds Power (banks, corporations, even governments) uses it. My system intends to break the conditioning/hypnosis created by this artificial uniformity.

The Erisian calendar, which we owe to the sublime genius of Malaclypse the Younger, dates events from 2816 A.L. (1184 BCE, Gregorian), the year of the Original Snub. (If you don't know about the Original Snub, go thou and read Mal's *Principia Discordia,* from Loompanics Unlimited in Port Townsend, WA, wherein you will find the Snub, together with the Golden Apple, the Trojan War, and everything else in the universe, explained once and for all.) Each year has five seasons, representing the five degrees of SNAFU imposed upon us by the Original Snub— Chaos, Discord, Confusion, Bureaucracy and International Relations. That gives us 73 days to each season, which equals one Chokmah day in Cabala. Herein the Wise and Subtle will find a profound secret hidden, if they can Know, and Dare, and Will, and Keep Silence.

Every fourth year, of course, we run into that damned extra day that also perplexes the Gregorians. We Erisians call it St. Tibb's Day, since everybody now agrees that St. Tibb never existed.

The Chinese calendar makes more sense than any of the others, but I find it too complex to explain in full. You look it up, eh? Meanwhile, rest satisfied that we now live in the year 4692, and you don't have to worry about any damned Millennium for another 308 years.

I find the Mayan calendar even more perplexing, but keep it on my letters because I like the names of the days—Crocodile,

Night, Snake, Deer, Jade, Monkey, Reed, Eagle, Thought, Storm, Wind, Net, Death, Rabbit, Dog, Tooth, Jaguar, Wax, Knife, Hunter. Sort of sounds like my last acid trip, four years ago. This year counts as 5106 of this cycle, but numerous cycles roll on and on and do *not* necessarily end in 2012 Gregorian, whatever you may have heard; that may just mark the opening of another mega-cycle.

You can look up the Hebrew dating system for yourself, too. Really, do you think you can learn anything important without personal effort?

The Illuminati years you already know. The five seasons have the names Verwirrung, Zweitracht, Unordnung, Beamtennherr-schaft, and Realpolitik, each 73 days long. Like the Gregorians and Erisians, we thus have an extra day dangling loose every four years. We call it
Heiligefliegendekindersheissetag,
and it has rituals that beat all hell out of Saint Tibb's Day.

The beauty of this multi-cultural system, to me, resides in its total lack of allegiance to any one emic reality and its condi-tioning the users to think in comparative realities. Thus, to most Americans December 25 1994 means Christ-mass and even the atheists feel dragged into the Reality Grid of the Romish cult. But on my multiple calendar system, the same date appears in many guises—

It appears in Poundian as 25 Zeus, 73 p.s.U. (celebrated with rites of Zeus and gratitude to Joyce for writing *Ulysses*);

or as 25 December Anno XC (with rituals to Horus and toasts to Crowley and the Inner Head);

or as 25 Sable 122 E.P. (with toasts to Jarry and rituals of Ubu Roi);

or as 5 Nivose, 203 (with toasts to Voltaire and Tom Paine);

or as 22 Rajab, 1373 A.H. (with holy herbs for Mohammed, Hassan i Sabbah and Noble Drew Ali);

or as 67 International Relations, 3178 y.C., (with toasts to Malaclypse the Elder and *orgia* for Eris);

or as the 22nd day of the 11th month, 4692, (with a polite bow to Kung fu Tse and a wink to Lao Tse);

or as 11 Dog, 5106, (with rituals to the Centipede God);

or as 23 Teves 5755 A.M., (with monotonous chants of YHVH ELOHIM YHVH ACHAD);

or as 67 Realpolitik, 5994 A.L. (with toasts to Adam Weishaupt, Theobold Wolfe Tone, Mr. G. and Helena P. Blavatsky.)

You have a wide choice of what to celebrate. Why not celebrate all of them? (But don't go driving afterwards.)

I want to thank Hakim Bey, James Koehnline, Malaclypse the Younger and John ver der Does for help with parts of this multi-calendar. If anybody finds any mistakes, please notify me at once.

Of course, my basic motive in trying to popularize this system lies in the hope that some people will use it and get cured of asking "But which *is* the real date?" Then they might start to see the fallacy of all questions in that form and we will achieve a large part of the goals of General Semantics, Erisianism, Deconstructionism and Buddhism. Some may even understand why no form of "is" or "be" appears anywhere in this book (except when I quote somebody else.)

Once you have given up asking "what day *is* it?" you will soon find it easy to give up asking what anything really *"is."* Then, in Melville's fine phrase, you can *strike through the mask*—pierce the veil of cultural conditioning (emic tunnel-reality) and see and hear with your own eyes and ears.

In the words of a great poet,

> Don't believe the human eye
> In sunlight or in shade:
> The shadow-show of sight and sense
> Is the Devil's masquerade.

SIXTEEN

LOOKING BELOW THE SURFACE

In Which We Peer Inside the Hollow Earth

> New York is full of creatures.
> —*Jacob's Ladder*

> We're sending Bibles to El Salvador.
> —*Repo Man*

In *Cosmic Trigger II: Down to Earth,* you may remember, we touched briefly on the career of John Cleeves Symmes, soldier, hero, philosopher—the man who convinced a lot of people, in the early 19th Century, that the Earth has the shape of a balloon, i.e., a skin with nothing inside. President John Quincy Adams even, somewhat grudgingly, joined Congress in helping to fund an expedition to the South Pole to find the hole that Symmes claimed must exist there, according to his calculations.

The expedition never got to the Pole—skepticism ran high and funding ran low—and, as geology advanced, the hollow Earth theory suffered. Educated people knew too many facts that just did not fit any model but the rock-solid Earth that we all learn in school. The **Experts** all say so.

The hollow Earth theory never died, however. In 1871, a chap named Lyon, who claimed a professorship, and an associate named Sherman, who claimed an M.D. (both credentials seem dubious) brought forth *The Hollow Globe* , which not only argued the hollowness of our planet again but bluntly challenged the 2000-year-old Occidental habit of thinking of the only possible theological alternatives as Monotheism (One God) and Atheism (No God.) Lyon and Sherman proclaimed that many gods or spirits have collaboratively created the Cosmos.

Every primitive entity, every sub-atomic particle, in this philosophy, represents a simple spirit with an inner drive to expand in space and transcend all its limitations. The more advanced forms become "life as we know it"—all living creatures evolving toward perfection in a kind of blend of Darwinian and Lamarckian biology. Really advanced forms become hollow planets and, later on, virtual divinities. The onward movement of consciousness-and-power has no end and aspires ever to infinity. (Without the cranky pseudo-scientific details, something of this model survives in the much more sophisticated philosophies of both Henri Bergson and Aleister Crowley. H.L. Mencken also said the cosmos seemed to him more like the work of a committee than of a single mind, but he appears to have intended that only as a sour comment on the general disorganized cussedness of existence.)

This spiritualized "matter" evolving toward perfection in infinity has its greatest representation on Earth among "the American or Anglo-Saxon race," Lyon and Sherman tell us, cheerfully unaware of how terribly, terribly Politically Incorrect that would sound in our own time. But most white Americans thought that way in *their* time. We can only feel deep gratitude that we have transcended all such ignorance and now have a philosophy proven 100% Politically Correct, and the future will therefore never laugh or sneer at *our* opinions.

Several similar "hollow Earth" books have appeared over the last hundred years, but I won't bore you with all of them. Most exhibit great ingenuity, some even achieve near plausibility, and all show total lack of proper "respect for Authority"—i.e., the **Experts** . I think the last fact explains why most people have never heard of them.

Some of this literature deserves at least a brief note. Madame Helena P. Blavatsky believed in a hollow Earth, and so did Lewis Spence. She formed the Theosophical Society and he, the AMORC Rosicrucians in San Jose, California (as distinguished from all the other Rosicrucians.) These two groups have so heavily influenced modern occultism that no amount of scientific evidence, now, can ever dislodge the hollow Earth from the Belief System (B.S.) of millions of Seekers of Higher Wisdom.

As Krishnamurti said to Rajneesh, "You want a Rolls Royce? Go to America. Over there, there's a Seeker born every minute." Rajneesh found so many seekers that he eventually owned 93 Rolls Royces.

Cyrus Teed, one of my favorite dingbats, a real rival to Emperor Norton, actually turned the hollow Earth theory inside-out and created a whole new cosmology worthy of Rube Goldberg and Salvador Dali working together. Let me tell you. Teed's inside-out Earth represents only part of his astounding originality. (His cousin, Joseph Smith, also founded an oddball science-fiction-style religion: the Mormons. They had some bodaceous imagination/creativity genes in that family, I'd say.)

In youth Teed studied medieval hermeticism and eventually built an "electro-alchemical laboratory." I have never found an adequate description of how this place worked, but it certainly did trigger a total transformation in Teed. One night in October 1869 toiling over his electro-alchemical devices, he achieved an erotic and mystical experience, similar to the orgasmic ecstasies of Saint Theresa. (You know: all that "pelvic pounding" that Ms. McClary finds so distasteful in the music that the Politically Incorrect still consider "classical.") In this blissful trance, Teed contacted Goddess, who told him She alone had created the Earth, the male God of Christianity having no role in that enterprise. She also said he, Teed, would resolve the "war between science and religion" by producing the first *true* model of the universe, under Her Divine Inspiration.

Cyrus Teed changed his name to Koresh[1] (Hebrew for Cyrus) and went forth to preach to all nations. His universe consists of

---

[1]I have found no connection between Teed a.k.a. Koresh and the more recent "David Koresh" whose cult had a tragic shoot-out with the FBI in Waco recently ending in a fire that each side blamed on the other.

solid rock from here to infinity, with one hollow spot "in the middle of infinity" where we live. The sun, moon, stars, etc. represent lights reflecting from various sources in our cave. If this seems unclear, just imagine a balloon again, and this time, instead of thinking of us *outside* the skin, visualize solid rock surrounding the balloon and us living on the *inner surface* of the skin. We would see all sorts of lights from other parts of the inner skin, reflecting in various patterns.

Koresh actually acquired several thousand followers, and they all believed that Koreshanity, as they called their faith, would quickly replace Christianity. Soon they had their own city (in Florida) and their own national newspaper; a few survivors, today, still live in the city and print the paper, which they send to leading libraries.

Koresh scored one real hit, you'll notice—the Goddess, indeed, has staged a dramatic comeback. Look in the neo-pagan or Feminist section of any large bookstore. You'll also find a lot of fervent debate about Her in the archeology and psychology shelves. (See my book, *Ishtar Rising: Why The Goddess Went to Hell and What to Expect Now That She's Returning,* New Falcon Publications, 1989.)

Personally, I don't *trust* mystic experiences, including my own—although I seek them and enjoy them. I think Altered Consciousness offers new ways of perceiving/conceiving and should *start* philosophical investigation, not *stop* it. Koresh, for instance, had a lovely mystic union with Goddess, I would judge, but he took it too literally. In addition to his unbelievable cosmology, his Goddess sold him a strange blend of political liberalism and racism: he wanted to end segregation, treat black and white Americans exactly alike—very progressive ideas for his time. But he also wanted to keep all Orientals out of the country forever. In fact, his cult had a slight revival in the 1940s, because the Japanese attack on Pearl Harbor made it seem to some that Koresh's most paranoid warnings about the Yellow Peril had come true.

In my boyhood, I used to read *Amazing Stories*, edited by the incredible Ray Palmer—the Ed Wood of science-fiction editors. Palmer printed science, science-fiction, pseudo-science and sheer lunacy in about equal amounts, and loved it all, but his greatest hits came from a writer named Richard Shaver, who allegedly knew more about the hollow Earth than anybody before him, because he had visited the interior.

Shaver claimed two "races" of humanoid robots lived down there, left over from Atlantis. The good robots, named Teros, seem dull and uninteresting and I can't remember much about them; neither can most other writers about Shaver. The bad robots, called Deros, nobody can ever forget. Due to some design flaw, these mechanical bastards had no passion except using advanced Atlantean technology to perform cruel assaults on us surface people. These totally sadistic monsters and their "invisible ray machines" caused all the paranormal or anomalistic events you ever heard of—poltergeists, spontaneous combustion, teleportations—just to torture and frighten us.

Lavishly porno-sadistic illustrations in Shaver's stories always depicted the awful Deros doing nasty things to lovely young women who wore flimsy nightgowns and had big hooters.

According to *Fantasy Commentator*, a sci-fi fan magazine, believers in the Shaver revelations numbered over a million at the height of its success in the 1950s. (Senator Joe McCarthy did well in those years, too.)

Reference:

Subterranean Worlds, by Walter Kafton-Minkel, Loompanics Unlimited, Port Townsend, 1989.

SEVENTEEN

HIGHER WISDOM,
NEW PHYSICS AND
HEADS IN JARS

In Which We Learn More About
Those Helpful Blokes From IUMMA

> We have Thamthon the Thadduthee thtrangler…and Thyrus the
> Athyrian aththathin…and uh…
> —*Life of Brian*

> Ike made the deal with the aliens in 1957. "Give us your
> technology and you can have all the cow's lips you want."
> —*Sneakers*

The UMMO letters began immediately after the second, 1967
UMMO "sighting" (and those blatantly fake photos.) Originally,
only UFO researchers in Spain received these communiqués, but
later many scientists in many nations, in diverse areas of
research, received some.

UMMO informs us that it speaks for a civilization in the
system of the star IUMMA, 14.6 light-years from our sun. They
even tell us where in the night sky IUMMA exists, but that
doesn't allow verification, because between IUMMA and us lies

an area of "absorbing matter." If you can figure out what "absorbing matter" means, I wish you'd tell me.

Each letter runs 6 to 10 pages, sometimes including equations and diagrams. At first they all bore Spanish postmarks, but later they came from addresses all over the world. The science they use usually makes sense, aside from that "absorbing matter" which still bothers me. They use a duodecimal (12-base) number system, which oddly enough a lot of human cultures used before inventing the decimal system. (Coinage remained duodecimal through most of history, continued 12-based until a few decades ago in the British Isles, and our juries and eggs still come in dozens.) The UMMO use of Earth languages alone sounds stilted and a bit like the usual balderdash in UFO cases or "channeling." For instance, one letter sent to many Spanish and French scientist begins, "We are aware of the transcendence of what we are about to tell you."

Dr. Jacques Vallee got his first UMMO letter in May 1981. It had a Flushing, New York, postmark and had ten times the required amount of stamps, showing that it had either come from real extraterrestrials or from somebody who thought it added verisimilitude to assume non-Earthians, however bright, would not understand our postal stamps. It also began, "We are aware of the transcendence of what we are about to tell you."

Many learned persons have felt genuinely impressed by the ideas in UMMO letters.

Col. Wendelle Stevens (USAF, ret.) published a volume of UMMO epistles in 1985 and seems to think they contain information crucial to human survival. A Spanish edition of UMMO letters has gone through several hard–cover and paperback editions.

One French physicist, Dr. Teyssandier examined all available UMMO communications and found not one mathematical error. The duodecimal math seems fluently used, as if by somebody or some group who found it as natural as we currently find the decimal system.

Another French physicist, Dr. Jean Pierre Petit, acknowledges openly that several recent papers by him, about mirror-image universes, derive directly from ideas in the UMMO letters.

For whatever you make of it, the humans most highly praised by UMMO make an interesting lot: agnostic mathematician

Bertrand Russell, Hindu mystic Mohandas Gandhi, Catholic liberal Pope John XXIII, Protestant radical Martin Luther King Jr., and, of course, Albert Schweitzer. I seem to sense a pattern: these men had vastly different philosophies, on the surface, but all had a passionate underlying commitment to peace and non-violence. If Madison Avenue wanted to "sell" pacifism, they might make a similar selection of ikons, all of whom appeal to different sub-cultures and all of whom urged us to ban the bomb and beat our swords into ploughshares.

In 1969 in a letter to a Spanish priest, UMMO told of animal experiments they had conducted in Albecete. After a year of letting that circulate, and stir speculation among UFO buffs, UMMO provided further details, in 1970, in an open letter sent to several researchers—and to the C.I.A. This time they gave names and addresses. The experiments had occurred at the home of the Marquise of Villasante, Baroness of Alcatrali.

The estate of this noble lady had stood empty since her death in 1954. Subsequent investigations, however, revealed that a large cemetery there had many dogs with organs surgically removed and some dogs actually mummified.

Investigators also found various animal heads kept in jars in one room of the main house. That sounds more like obsessive-compulsive behavior than science, I'd say. But a worse, or weirder, discovery followed.

The Marquise herself had suffered a similar fate after death. Between her death and her funeral some unseen "vandal" had removed both her eyes, her tongue and one hand.

Just as if Hannibal Lecter had dropped by.

The "benevolent" UMMO suddenly seems akin to those creepy cattle mutilators. Maybe we have not understood what game we have stumbled upon; we certainly do not feel sure of the names or purposes of the game-masters.

Reference:

Revelations, Vallee, *op. cit.*

EIGHTEEN

HORSEMAN, PASS BY

In Which We Once Again Confront
the Universal Ash

> Life stinks! Life stinks! Life stinks!
> —*Life Stinks*

> No, you can't win.
> Give my regards to the sunset.
> —*The Lady From Shanghai*

Last October, Arlen and I and our daughter Alex went to Don's last birthday party. I didn't know that it would prove his last, although I should have suspected it. As you can see from the chapter about Bob Shea, I resist knowing that friends will soon die. I want to think they will all recover, or at least—in Don's case—live on without too much pain for a few more good years at least.

Don had AIDS, in its cruelest form—AIDS dementia. In that horrible variant of the disease, which strikes only five per cent of the victims, the symptoms include a rapid decline in brain function, much like an accelerated Alzheimer's.

I had met Don back in the mid-70s, while living up in the Berkeley hills with Arlen and Alex and my son Graham and a Gay computer whizz named John and Alex's husband (at that time), Mike. Between the lot of us we had enough to pay the rent on a virtual palace that made us all look far richer than our actual bank accounts would confirm. Don had read one of my books and wanted to interview me for a Gay magazine, *Advocate*, on which he had some editorial position.

When we first met, Don struck me as young-looking for his age (he admitted to thirty-something and looked a boyish twenty.) I mentally jotted this down in my brain's Observations On Gay Men file, another case of a phenomenon I had already often observed. Gay men, I think, tend to look younger than straight men of the same age. They also look thinner than dieting alone can explain, and often look shorter than average. This inclines me to suspect that genes do play a crucial role in the "choice" of Gay or straight sexuality.

I don't think, contrary to fashionable opinion, that genes play the *only* role, and I feel acute boredom whenever I hear another round of the current debate between Gay Pride advocates and Fundamentalists about whether homosexuality (or heterosexuality, if you think about it) results from genes (alone) or "choice" (alone.) That particular either/or seems even dumber to me than most Aristotelian dualisms.

Science does not limit human behavior to either genetics or "free will." Although they may use other terminology, most current psychologists would agree in general, I think, with Dr. Tim Leary's notion that all behavior (Gay or straight, "mental" or "emotional," "crazy" or "sane") results from a synergy of (1) genes, (2) early imprinting, (3) conditioning, (4) school-and-other learning, and (5) blind circumstance.

Imprinting occurs only at moments of "imprint vulnerability" and Gay genes without a Gay imprint, I suspect, explains the men who seem "a little Gay" but never get attracted to other men and lead ordinary heterosexual lives.

Conditioning probably does not create Gayness, without genes and imprints, but almost certainly reinforces it.

Learning, contrary to the Fundamentalists, seems to have little to do with Gay or Straight orientations, although it influences most of our Belief Systems (B.S.)

Blind circumstance includes e.g., imprisonment or Army service. A surprising number of straight men become Gay for a while, when thrown into that kind of all-male bondage. For instance, John Dillinger, whose appetite for women seemed inexhaustible on the outside, got caught in homosexual acts twice during his ten year prison term.

Considering that these five factors—genes, imprinting, conditioning, learning and circumstance—all play a role in human (and animal) life, and that *sixth, seventh and other factors may yet emerge* in future research, all Simple Simon either/or debate about "genes or choice" seems reductionist and medieval. This point of view, if you haven't guessed, I tend to apply to most personality traits, and not just to sexual orientation. But back to the story:

Besides looking young and thin, facts I mention only to show that I do occasionally notice things about people besides their minds, Don had a nice, engaging personality. Even on first meeting me—an older man with a visible wife and children—he seemed less defensive about his Gayness, and less suspicious of possible latent homophobia, than just about any Gay man I ever knew. But, of course, what most interested me did not involve Gayness, youthfulness, or lack of defensiveness. His mind struck me as absolutely first rate. After the interview, I asked him to drop by again, just for conversation, whenever he could.

We became close friends over a period of about five or six years—until 1982 when Arlen and I moved to Ireland. Up until '81, Don and Arlen and I all attended Paideia University, an alternative educational institution that only California could spawn. Sometimes, all three of us thought Paideia had become so far out that even the California Board of Education would eventually withdraw its approved rating; but it never did, and recently I learned that, instead, Paideia has split into two even wilder and more creative new universities, one state authorized and one totally anarchistic. After Arlen and I went to Ireland, our friendship with Don continued by mail, although he did not write as often as Bob Shea. When Arlen and I returned to the States in 1988, I saw Don a couple of times a year, because he still lived in San Francisco and I had settled for a while in Los Angeles.

Don helped turn me on to the rapidity of the computer revolution and the fact that even I could afford a home computer to write my books. He introduced me to networking. He also called to my attention several important writers, including William Gibson, and I rekindled his interest in James Joyce.

From others in San Fran (I lived there once myself and know a lot of people there) I heard constantly about Don's activism in promoting computers, Gay Lib and (hot damn) my own books, which he admired extravagantly. I suppose Don inspired whoever put up all the graffiti, so widespread in the Castro District that it got mentioned in the San Fran *Chronicle*, *STAMP OUT SIZEISM.*

I had created that slogan, in my *Schroedinger's Cat* novels, for a disgruntled midget named Markoff Chaney, who had as much hostility to the concept of "the normal" as Prof. Finnegan of CSICON does. Chaney, like Finnegan, insists that the whole concept of normalcy confuses neurological levels of abstraction, substituting abstract mathematics for existential experience, and that it further dehumanizes and degrades everything that does not approximate to a dull average in all respects. (I can think of at least *two* reasons why a lot of Castro Gays, who probably read that book due to Don's missionary work, might cotton to Chaney and to the slogan *STAMP OUT SIZEISM.*)

The last time I saw Don, before the final birthday, I had flown up from L.A. to participate in a psychedelic conference at Stanford University. He drove down from the Castro and we had lunch together. He seemed witty, brilliant, boyish as ever (he must have passed 40 by then), and in excellent health. We talked about bloody everything, as usual, but mostly we talked about George Bush, who scared hell out of both of us. We both thought Bush might prove the worst president in American history and the all-around worst man of the 20th Century, even considering such competition as Hitler, Stalin and Mao. I remember how riotously I celebrated when Clinton beat Bush in '92; I presume Don celebrated also.

I don't remember the date, but early in '93 I got a phone call from Stan, once Don's lover long ago and still a very close friend. He broke the news to me, and explained what AIDS dementia involved.

Over the following months I called Don several times on the phone, conversations he seemed to enjoy (I think) but which I found a hellish duty. Nothing quite has the pathos of talking to a good mind which does not quite have its moorings anymore. You never know how much a man in that state understands, but you know he still has some of his intelligence and does understand something; but then you find he doesn't remember his illness or your first name or what you just said. Then he remembers again.

Over several months I experienced the grief and terror of watching a first-rate mind crumble, come back a little, crumble again.

I sent Don several letters. Stan told me that Don could read them, and did read them, and even quoted from them a few times. But he had more and more dementia—blank out periods. Once, on the phone, he said to me, "I don't want to get like some of the cases I saw in the hospital...drooling imbeciles..."

Nonetheless, AIDS dementia, like ordinary Alzheimer's, remains unpredictable. One doctor told Stan that Don might live on for several years with "relatively good" brain functions.

Sometimes, when I called Stan for details I couldn't ask of Don, I heard that some improvement had occurred. Then on the next call I would hear that the illness had advanced further once again. And all through this Bob Shea's cancer advanced, and retreated, and advanced, and retreated.

Naturally, with two friends dying, I became a bit of a hypochondriac myself: every minor symptom I experienced seemed like a fatal illness for an hour or so. Most of them went away before I got concerned enough to see a doctor. (So far, I have nothing serious, although I have had to learn to watch my diet more than I did as a young man. Twenty-three years after first moving here, I finally eat more or less what all Californians allegedly eat—or at least I eat that way *most* of the time...)

When we arrived at the last birthday party, which I did not know would mark the end, I found several friends and several strangers already there. Some seemed to know Don through the Gay community, and some through the computer industry. (He co-founded a network called CommuniTree.) At one point, I wondered idly which of the guests belonged to the straight world and which to the Gay.

Like many idle and stupid questions, this proved worth thinking about, for I realized with *thunderous* emphasis how little Gayness or straightness mattered in human terms: what *did* matter, in the moral dimension, jumped out at me like a chord in Beethoven—everybody at the party manifested love, care, kindness and support to an almost superhuman degree.

These people all loved Don and they exemplified the compassion that, when it appears, makes humans noble and admirable creatures.

Don himself spoke little and could hardly hold his head erect; it kept tilting over. I talked a lot to him, about intellectual matters, or telling him the latest jokes, or praising movies I liked. He seemed vaguely happy to see me, but not quite happy enough to raise his obviously depressed spirits.

When we left, I had that feeling that you get after such occasions: I should have said something wiser, or done something I hadn't done, or reared back and performed a miracle...

Two weeks later, Stan called and told us Don had died.

I can't remember what I said.

Don represents my second close brush with AIDS death. Back in the early '80s, another friend, Mike Symonds, a psychologist, had died of AIDS. I loved Mike. After my daughter Luna's death in 1976 he used to drop by at least once a week, saying he "found himself in the neighborhood" and would chat with me; I realized that he wanted to offer grief counseling if and when I needed it. A few discussions did help me process my pain, but he helped even more by his persistence in coming by to offer aid if I needed aid. Kindness remains, to me, the most wonderful miracle in this incomprehensible universe.

Two others guys I knew only slightly, but liked a lot, have also died of AIDS, which Our Lady of the Flowers, a Catholic medium who channels the Blessed Virgin Mary, says Jesus Himself created to punish homosexual acts. In this scenario, Jesus seems either as dumb as Forest Gump or batshit crazy (to me.) He's also killing a lot of non-Gay people who got blood transfusions at the wrong time. I don't know why any god, even the Christian god, would hate Gays, but I find it even harder to understand a god so underprivileged in the brain department that he kills more or less at random, like a madman with an automatic weapon.

However, I do find grim humor in the picture invoked by Our Lady of the Flowers: Jesus, wearing the *adorable* pink dress he usually has in pop Catholic art, holding a couple of test-tubes and cackling like a mad scientist in an Ed Wood movie, "This'll kill a few million of those goddam fags! Hee hee hee.!" I still can feel astonishment that many people worship a god like that. They wouldn't trust a cop so totally malign and so blunderingly incompetent, would they?

Death, death—how well I have come to know you...

At 36—on my birthday actually—my brother called from Florida to tell me my father had just died. I remember sitting there looking at my birthday cake and thinking this scene could never appear in a novel: it had too much irony to seem real... Since then, my brother has died, my mother has died, my brother's wife has died, you know that one of my daughters has died, and several friends have died of conditions less horrible than AIDS or cancer but just as final. At 62, I feel well acquainted with grief and loss, and expect to see a lot more of them in the next few decades.

I still agree with a speech Orson Welles makes toward the end of *F For Fake*, in which he reflects that all art, by Picasso or by Elmyr, by the anonymous masons of Chartres Cathedral or by Homer, will eventually get lost in chaos and perish in "the universal ash."

But Orson intones the eternal rebuttal in that marvelous baritone he used for his more oratorical moments: 'What of it?', cry the dead artists from their tombs, 'Go on singing!'

Or, if that seems too obscure, let me quote Sean O'Casey: "Life contains tragedy, but life itself is not a tragedy." I intend to enjoy every moment I still have left, and expend my energy in joyous creativity, even while part of me mourns those I have lost.

NINETEEN

HONO INTELLIGENCE SERVICE 1901

In Which We Perhaps Encounter the
Elmyr of the UMMO Mystery

People will say we're in love.
—*State Fair*

People will say we're in love.
—*The Silence of the Lambs*

The last time we turned back to the UMMO mystery, we found some nasty business involving tortured animals and a mutilated corpse. Of course, all these "experiments"—or mutilations—occurred before 1954, i.e., 15-to-16 years before UMMO took the credit, or blame, for them. The committee, or the "criminal genius," behind UMMO could merely have read about this mysterious Spanish atrocity and decided to hook its own myth to these facts, and form a suggestive link, also, to our own cattle mutilations.

I like that theory and find it comforting. I don't want to think UMMO, or any other alleged extraterrestrials, actually engage in "experiments" on lower life forms like dogs or cats—or you or me... And yet...

Further suggestions of UMMO "research" on this planet surfaced next in Argentina in 1973. A humanoid, allegedly totally human, using the name Carlos Jerez, opened a cancer center in Canuelas, called the International Medical Research Facility. Next to the main building, Jerez had a model "flying saucer" twenty feet in diameter and twenty feet high. I've seen a photo. It looks just like the ones in cheap 1950s films, although not as bad as the ones in Ed Wood's *Plan 9 From Outer Space.*

The main building, where Jerez treated cancer patients, bore a plaque with the inscription

HONO INTELLIGENCE SERVICE 1901
)+(

Aha! The sign of UMMO once again! Definite proof that we have stumbled upon superhuman intelligence, or an expensive hoax, or a conspiracy, or an art work of some sort we haven't begun to fathom...

By 1979, Jerez had attained a certain fame. He claimed to have cured over 200 patients, alleged that he represented UMMO and came from Outer Space himself, and had achieved official approval for medical work from the Argentine government in 1966. 1979, however, led to further governmental investigation and they withdrew approval after Jerez failed several medical competence tests, including a failure to detect an advanced tumor in one patient.

Jerez disappeared after this defeat, and has never surfaced again. We have left for our bemusement a building with a lot of real scientific equipment (none of it known to help cancer patients at all), a model 1950s Hollywood UFO in the front yard, and one more annoying and inconclusive UMMO riddle.

Several UFO investigators have tried to prove that all the UMMO letters emanated from Jerez. They have not succeeded, and most have abandoned that idea. We still don't know who or *what* has staged the UMMO game for all these decades or what purpose they have...

In the words of a great statesman and poet:

> When I dined with the Duchess of Dee
> It was just as I feared it would be:

Her rumblings abdominal
Were simply phenomenal
And everyone thought it was me!

References:

Revelations, Vallee, op. cit.

PART TWO

THE REALITY OF MASKS

Permit me to introduce myself:
I'm a man of wealth and taste...
　　—Sympathy for the Devil

　　　　The Prince of Darkness is a gentleman.
　　　　Modo he's called, and Mahu.
　　　　　　　　— King Lear

It used to be that being crazy meant something.
Now everybody is crazy.
　　—Charlie Manson, *San Jose Mercury News,* 20 Nov 1994

　　　　Judge not, lest ye bore the audience.
　　　　　—Orson Welles in *This Is Orson Welles*,
　　　　　　　　Welles and Bogdonovitch

　　　　　Is this a pubic hair in my coke?
　　　　　—Justice Clarence Thomas (attributed)

TWENTY

DANGEROUS EXPERIMENTS

In Which We Encounter Some People
Who Actually Test Their Theories

> I was misinformed.
> —*Casablanca*

> I want to show you something...
> —*Indecent Proposal*

For nine months in 1838 a Mr. Samuel Rowbotham conducted extensive experiments at a canal called the Old Bedford Level in Cambridgeshire, England. This canal contains an uninterrupted length of six miles between the Welney and the Old Bedford Bridges. Like every other experimenter, Mr. Rowbotham had a theory in mind, and wanted to test it—and, of course, to vindicate it. (But you know that, if you've read volumes one and two of this encyclopedia of blasphemy. The "disinterested observer," the Lemuel Gulliver "objectivist," exists only in fiction. In the real world, experimenters always want to prove some darling theory they have made an Idol, so that all may join them in bowing down to worship it.)

Mr. Rowbotham's pet theory derived from Holy Scripture and held that, as Moses wrote, our planet consists of a *flat* circle (like

131

a coin)[1]; it does not have a spherical or globular shape at all. He calculated, correctly I think, that over the six miles between the two bridges, the curvature of Earth should make objects on one bridge seem several feet lower than on the other—a difference that should appear quite visible to a telescope, if modern notions had validity. And, of course, no height difference would appear between objects on the two bridges, if Moses got the straight scoop from Papa Tetragrammaton Himself.

Well, for nine months Rowbotham measured and measured, standing on Welney Bridge and looking through a telescope at various markers on Old Bedford Bridge. Like most other experimenters he found only and always what he looked for. Not once did he see any displacement caused by curvature.

After the traditional nine month gestation, Rowbotham brought forth the child of his labors: his experiments, he announced, demonstrated conclusively that no curvature existed. He reiterated this, many times, traveling about England and lecturing everywhere on the triumph of the Bible over heathen geologists.

He even repeated the experiments, with audiences of various sizes. They all thought they saw what Rowbotham thought he saw.

He further popularized his experiments and theories in a book called *Zetetic Astronomy*. and formed a Zetetic Society.[2]

By 1870, the Zetetics had made enough converts that one of them, Mr. John Hampden, offered a reward of 500 pounds—a large sum, then—to any defender of geology who could duplicate Rowbotham's experiments and demonstrate curvature. Alfred Russell Wallace, co-creator with Darwin of the natural selection model of evolution, accepted the challenge and the tests occurred on 28 September 1870, to the everlasting bedevilment of all parties involved.

Briefly, the globalists led by Wallace measured curvature and the zetetics led by a flat-Earther named William Carpenter

---

[1]The "flat Earth" theory does not demand literal Euclidean flatness. Flat-Earthers admit some thickness, as in the coin example.

[2]In ancient Greece the term "zetetic" meant much the same as the modern "agnostic." How Rowbotham purloined and misapplied it remains unclear. The ancient Greek meaning—skepticism about all ideas, including one's own ideas and those of other skeptics—has re-emerged in the writings of sociologist Marcello Truzzi, and I also have used it that way.

measured flatness. The referee, an editor named Walsh, ruled that the globalists had won and awarded the prize to Mr. Wallace. The Rowbothamites cried "Foul!" and insisted that Wallace had cheated. They sued and the matter went to court.

The three judges who heard the suit refused to pass judgment on the scientific evidence, which they held to lie outside the domain of statute law. They ruled only that wagers do not have the legal force of contracts and that, since Mr. Carpenter and Mr. Hampden did not accept Mr. Wallace's measurements, they could have Hampden's money back.

This did not soothe Carpenter's wrath. Still convinced that Wallace had rigged his experiments, Carpenter grew more embittered as time passed and developed a paranoid suspiciousness about all **Experts**, especially alleged **Experts** in geology. He embarked on a "campaign for justice" (as he saw it) which took the form of sixteen years of ruthless persecution of Wallace, including vile letters to Wallace's wife and children and slanderous accusations of Wallace's total perfidy delivered *ad lib* to anyone who would listen to him.

Wallace finally sued for relief and Carpenter spent a year in prison. As soon as he got out, his campaign of harassment and vilification resumed. We haven't seen anything like this missionary zeal until James Randi's hellfire-and-brimstone Crusade against Uri Geller.

I don't suppose it helped Wallace's peace of mind much that, although he and Darwin each invented evolution-by-natural-selection at the same time, Darwin got all the credit in most text books and Wallace, at best, got acknowledged in footnotes... If they had ever crowned the poor man king, I think he'd have the title Alfred the Unlucky in history books.

Anyway, Wallace, almost bankrupted by legal expenses and driven to nervous exhaustion, became a spiritualist. Carpenter eventually migrated to America where he continued to preach Moses, Special Creation and a flat-as-a-pancake Earth.

In 1901 an orthodox scientist named Oldham repeated the Old Bedford Canal experiments. He reported his results in a paper for the British Association for the Advancement of Science. He, of course, had measured curvature, as an orthodox scientist should.

In 1905, Lady Elizabeth Blount, then the head of the Zetetic Society, financed further experiments at the Old Bedford Canal,

involving a photographer named Clifton, who recorded the
results for posterity. They measured no curvature, i.e., straight-
line flatness. You didn't *really* think they would measure
curvature, did you?

In the midst of all this Old Bedford malice-in-wonderland, our
old friend Koresh—the one whose Goddess told him we lived
inside the hollow Earth, and that Whites and Blacks in America
sound stand shoulder to shoulder, as equal brothers, to keep out
the heathen Chinese—*that* Koresh, not the Waco wacko,
conducted his own experiments in Florida.

A disciple named Morrow had invented a device, called the
Rectilineator, which allegedly would measure curvature, or
departure from flatness, more accurately than the telescopes and
cameras at the Bedford bridges. Morrow and Koresh used a 2
mile section of the Florida coast and performed over a month of
measurements testing for flatness (Bible theory), convexity
(globular theory) or concavity (Koreshanity theory.)

You guessed it. They measured concavity. The Earth curved
upward a little more than ten feet over the two miles measured,
just as it should if we live inside a 8000-mile diameter bubble
within solid rock.

None of these results astound me too much. I once measured
the acceleration of a falling body (a marble, actually) at 68 feet
per second per second, even though every physics book insists
that all falling bodies fall at 32 feet per second per second. I may
have witnessed a genuine fluctuation in Earth's gravity field. Or
I may have needed a new pair of glasses and not realized it yet.
Or, even more likely, the apparatus that released the marble may
have malfunctioned. I don't know, but I incline toward the
theories that the apparatus malfunctioned or my eyes read the
clock wrong.; I doubt I had the good luck to witness a sudden
anti-gravity wave.

But in considering the above experiments, I feel we need to
accept some sort of post-modernism, or at least some of the
"neurological relativism" I preach in all my books. The
instrument that measures all other instruments—the human
nervous system—has its own laws, and one of them involves
always seeing the results one wants to see until and unless
something really *startles* the brain enough to reframe its
experiences.

References:

Subterranean Worlds, op cit.

Eccentric Lives and Peculiar Notions, by John Michell, Citadel Press, Secaucus NJ, 1984—for details of the Bedford and Rectilineator experiments.

TWENTY-ONE

CREATIVITY, CRIME AND TESTOSTERONE

In Which We Re-Examine the Fast Westward/Fast Forward Trajectory Discussed in Earlier Volumes

> I ate his liver, with some fava beans
> and a nice Chianti.
> —*The Silence of the Lambs*

> I'm still hungry.
> —*Citizen Kane*

In *Cosmic Trigger II,* and a few other works, I have discussed the evidence that information-rich locales have steadily moved westward during the past 5000 years. I would like to re-examine that phenomenon, looking at it this time from the point of view of neuro-chemistry.

Specifically I will attempt the death-defying feat of looking at the chemical differences between men and women, and will not limit myself to the parameters defined by Feminist dogma. In short, I will expect denunciations from the Politically Correct. This predictable (because mechanical) reaction does not bother me, especially at my age. I have grown accustomed to hostile criticism. Besides, I cannot imagine a first-rate artist or scientist who could possibly qualify as Politically Correct, since P.C., like all dogma, creates an information-impoverished environment and art and science always seek information enrichment.

Information, mathematician Norbert Weiner once said, consists of signals that you do *not* expect. Remember?

For thirty years some Feminists have insisted that *all* the differences between men and women are created by social training. In the same thirty years, however, other Feminists (the so-called Feminazis) have insisted that men carry some form of Original Sin or biological stigma that renders them less than fully human. A third group of Feminists manage to believe both contradictory theories at the same time, in the manner of Orwell's "doublethink." ("All people are created equal, but female people are more equal than others.")

In this chapter, which I regard as suggestive rather than definitive, I offer a theory of male "difference" based on a series of recent discoveries in biochemistry.

First, however, an important *caveat:* All chemical "triggers" for human (or animal) behavior act statistically, not absolutely. In other words, every generalization in neuro-genetics has a fuzzy value, not an absolute true/false value. *The best generalizations refer to most cases, but none apply to all cases.* As I have argued elsewhere, we should use the word "sombunall" (some-but–not-all) habitually, to counteract the strong tendency toward dogmatism built into our culture by Christianity and Aristotelian logic.

Hitler met, perhaps, 0.0000000001 per cent of all the Jews in the world. His anti-Semitic generalizations, ergo, had an insufficient data base. Similarly, Gloria Steinem has met maybe 0.00000000000000001 per cent of all the males in the world, and her androphobic generalizations also have an insufficient data base.

The word "sombunall" might have saved both of these fanatics, and their starry-eyed disciples, from their worst excesses.

In gender differentiation, *most* men have more visual orientation in general, and show more interest in visual erotica than most women, and this probably relates, as we shall see, to the amount of testosterone in the male body-brain system, and of estrogen in the female. That's why a hell of a lot more men than women buy *Playboy*. Nonetheless, *some* women read and enjoy

Playboy and some even enjoy hard-core porn. *You cannot predict an individual, male or female, in all their quirky unique-ness, from gender generalizations, anymore than you can do it from race generalizations.* As Prof. Timothy F.X. Finnegan of CSICON says, nobody has ever found a normal man or woman, or even a normal mathematician—or an ordinary rose, or an average symphony.

All of us, men and women and those who don't feel sure, have some testosterone (the principle "male" hormone) and some estrogen (the principle "female" hormone) from conception onward, but before we even get out of the womb our chemistry starts to change. Males have more testosterone, females have more estrogen, from birth onward—and after puberty, the amount of testosterone in men and estrogen in women increases steeply, strongly influences most of our adult behavior for the next 30 or 40 years, and only decreases again in old age.

For instance, men "see" more sexuality than women do. Psychologist Frank Sal, showing a film of a man and woman talking, found male students perceived more sexual flirtation in the film, while women saw only friendliness. *We "see" what the chemicals in our brain program us to "see" and this governs all perception, not just sight.* (Ask any acid-head.) Brain chemicals and imprinted/conditioned/genetic neural networks determine what we perceive, and how we conceive what we perceive, at the Bedford canal, in a political debate, or looking at a statistically unusual Light in the Sky.

Some tests also indicate a circular-causal or "feedback" loop in testosterone level. Testosterone makes us guys act "male," but acting that way also increases the production of testosterone. Thus, one study of male tennis players found higher testosterone levels among the winners than among the losers, one hour after competition. Wrestlers at Harvard also showed higher testos-terone among the winners than the losers, and on a more intellectual level of competition, medical students showed higher testosterone one day after graduation.

Conversely, the humiliating and terrifying experience of arriving at Army boot camp lowers testosterone.

The testosterone/estrogen ratio also relates directly to the fact that most men (*sombunall* of them) exhibit more hostile/domi-nant behavior than most women. Researcher June Reinisch of

Rutgers University found that both boys and girls given precursors of testosterone—chemicals that increase testosterone production in the body—immediately become more aggressive. In fact, Reinisch's subjects, both boys and girls became *twice* as aggressive as a control group not given the hormones. The aggressivity indexes were:

Boys given the hormone: 9.75; other boys 4.88.

Girls given the hormone: 4.0; other girls 2.6.

Note that testosterone boosters approximately doubled aggression in both sexes, and that boys already have so much more testosterone than girls that, even without boosters, they still act nearly twice as aggressive. This result appeared so totally contrary to Behaviorist doctrine that Reinish was unwilling to publish her findings at first. As she later said, "The results were so shocking that I actually sat on them for a year. I was afraid to publish them."

Behaviorist dogma, like Creationism, refuses to recognize that the hormones and neurotransmitters found in both humans and other animals serve approximately the same functions in "higher" and "lower" species. In humans, the Behaviorists and Creationists would have us believe, the hormones and neurotransmitters serve merely as artistic decoration and do not trigger the same behaviors, physical or psychological, as in other primates. (Similarly, bones older than 6000 years merely indicate, according to some Creationists, that God, after creating the universe in six days, included artistic details to make it look much older. Others say He did it "to test our faith." I suspect that the Feminists will eventually invoke one or both of these arguments to explain human hormones and neurotransmitters— except, of course, they will say She instead of He.[1])

Onward: in a joint study by the Clarke Institute of Psychiatry and Mount Sinai Hospital, both in Toronto, the hormone levels of 20 rapists were compared with those of 20 non-rapists. The rapists consistently had higher precursors of testosterone.

---

[1] Although, in a serious pursuit of nonsexist language, they should say "It"—as I suggested in "The Semantics of God" (*The Realist*, May 1959), my first published article. You can find this reprinted in my book, *Right Where You Are Sitting Now*, Ronin Press, 1982.

In another study males with a history of low sex drive showed an increase in sexual fantasy and desire when given testosterone. Physiologist Julian Davidson, who did this research, says that "testosterone is the biological substrate of desire, at least in men."

Looking at infant boys and girls, it is often hard to tell them apart visually when they have their diapers on. Behaviorally, however, the boys can be recognized by their higher energy and higher violence; and Annelise Korner has actually shown that at birth boys have greater muscle strength than girls. Psychologists Eleanor Maccoby and Carol Jacklin, in *The Psychology of Sex Differences*: demonstrated that, even in cross-cultural studies of many societies, boys are more likely to engage in hitting, kicking, and verbal aggression (insult).

At puberty, when the boys suddenly have their brains and glands flooded with testosterone and its side-products, and girls get a similarly high dose of estrogen, their bodies change totally, and not even Unisex fashions quite conceal the gross morpho-logical differences. Thus, the males develop facial hair, bigger bones and more muscles; they also begin to produce high levels of sperm, which always gets discharged one way or another (in the rare case of nonmasturbating "celibates," it drains off in "wet dreams.") The females meanwhile begin to menstruate, grow conic breasts and develop wider hips (to make childbirth possible.)

Young males, bursting with sperm, want sex persistently. The females usually require persuasion. The males who do not succeed in persuading any females tend to turn nasty or cranky, as psychologists since Freud have all noticed. In the nicely chosen words of psychologist John DeLamater, "Men initiate sexual behavior and women control it." Thus, *evolution resulted from female choices,* since virtually all the males (except for a few eunuchs and teratological cases) compete desperately to find sex partners, and the females, less driven by testosterone, can always pragmatically choose which males to accept. It may seem an odd thought, but humans have become the sort of people we see today—"we" meaning the whole human species, on all continents—because *females have chosen, since we became human and even before, which genes to accept and which to reject.*

Testosterone as an anabolic steroid promotes growth; thus, most men (not all) measure taller than most women. Estrogen as a catabolic steroid, promotes storage of fat in the body; thus, women can survive without food longer than men (and carry a fetus for nine months and breastfeed it after.) As Bob Goy of the Regional Primate Research Center at University of Wisconsin says, "The female (is)...given large fat deposits as a protection against lean times, so that she and any future breast-feeding offspring will survive when there's no food...(the male) invests much more heavily in growth and muscular strength...(to serve) male-male competition and hunting."

Evidence of the extent testosterone programs sombunall male behavior and perception continues to accumulate. More males masturbate even before puberty than females do; University of Wisconsin psychologist John DeLamater concludes from four studies of behavior in different societies that, whatever society teaches, averages remain consistently different for the two sexes—around 66% of the males masturbate before adolescence and only 33% of the females do.

Neuroscientist Candace Pert explains it this way: "Of course men and women have entirely different attitudes toward sex, and these attitudes are hard-wired in the brain, not learned... The brain doesn't know the Pill was invented." I think Dr. Pert means the "old brain"—the thalamus and cerebellum. The neo-cortex or "new brain" can learn about the Pill, of course, and about changing social mores in general; but the old brain, driven by chemicals, still has the reflexes of our past evolution. Thus, almost all educated people all have a sense of being "at war with themselves" at least part of the time.

Research on testosterone in females sheds further light on its role in the male brain. Like men, women have less sexual desire if their testosterone decreases; and if they are given testosterone pills, both sexual desire and sexual activity increase. Harold Lief, emeritus professor of psychiatry at U-Penn, found female testosterone levels highest just before and during ovulation, when sex desire also has its monthly peak.

In several studies, female rats given high doses of testosterone became more aggressive, fought more often and, in some cases, turned homosexual, mounting other females in typical male fashion. I have seen films of these rats and the sexual behavior after mounting—the rapid thrusting—looks as if the females "think" they have actually grown penises.

Testosterone also seems to have a direct *inverse* link to male homosexuality. Psychologist Brian Gladue of the State University of New York at Stony Brook gave estrogen to 29 heterosexual males, 14 homosexual males and 12 heterosexual women. The heterosexual males showed a purely temporary increase in LH (lutenizing hormone) but the homosexual men showed a pattern similar to the females—a longer-lasting rise in LH to a level 38 percent higher than the baseline. In 1964, Gunter Dorner of the Institute of Experimental Endocrinology found a similar pattern in heterosexual and homosexual rats: the Gay rats had a response (increase in LH) similar to females.

Ingebord Ward of Villanova U found that when pregnant female rats are subject to stress, their male offspring showed unusually low testosterone and showed homosexual or bisexual behavior as adults. Ward went on to study homosexual humans and found "about a third" showed a maternal history of stress, such as bereavement, rape or severe anxiety. Ward concluded that fetal events influence not only sexuality but a wide variety of behaviors, including lifelong mood and energy.

Similarly, Anna Ehrhardt of Columbia College of Physicians and Surgeons spent years studying females with adrenogenital syndrome (high testosterone while still in the womb) These females exhibit "tomboyish" behavior, prefer boys rather than girls as playmates, and have more athletic success than most females.

More: L. Kreuz and R. Rose found that testosterone level of convicts correlated with age of first arrest. Other studies of juvenile offenders found aggressive behavior correlates with testosterone level, and that male juveniles given testosterone become even more aggressive. Candace Pert concludes, "There is now a proven connection between violent behavior and testosterone level." This inspired Carl Sagan's typically reckless generalizations about "testosterone poisoning" in males and the whole "Original Sin" school of Feminism.

(The Christian doctrine of Original Sin holds that all humans have an inborn "perversion of will and defect of reason"—as St. Augustine stated it. The Feminist revision of Original Sin holds that only 49 per cent of humans have these incurable inborn defects: the males. The Nazi version attributes Original Sin to about 12 per cent: Jews and Slavs. I don't like any of these notions, but the Christian version at least has the "democratic" spirit in spreading the heritage of guilt equally among all of us.)

A different perspective emerges, however, from another line of research.

An unexpected result of high testosterone, discovered by Norman Geshwind of Harvard, shows slower growth of the verbal left brain hemisphere among us allegedly "testosterone poisoned" men and corresponding increased growth of the more visual right hemisphere. This might explain why little girls develop high verbal skills before little boys, and remain more verbal most of their lives. (Guess the first artistic fields in which women became successful, back in the 19th Century. Poetry and the novel, of course. One still sees more women than men in editorial jobs.)

Males, with bigger right hemispheres, have more left-handers ("southpaws") than females, a most interesting fact. Left-handedness and high right-hemisphere development both correlate with creativity and, to a lesser degree, with immune deficiency. Some well-known left-handers who therefore had highly developed right brains include such creative titans as Leonardo, Michelangelo, Beethoven, Nietzsche, Einstein and Picasso—and such pathological cases as Billy the Kid and Jack the Ripper (as shown by the direction of his knife slashes.) Geshwind has also collected evidence that right hemisphere dominance produces high ability in music, art and mathematics.

In this connection, Camilla Benbow and Julian Stanley discovered that 20 per cent of mathematicians have left-handedness (twice that of non-mathematicians) and 60 percent had immune system disorders (five times that of the non-mathematicians.) Both of these male tendencies, Geshwind's work implies, result from the effect of high testosterone on right-hemisphere brain growth.

Interestingly, Neurologist David Hier tested men with small testes (idiopathic hypogonadotropic hypogonadism) and, thus, low testosterone. These men scored the same as normal men in verbal skills, but 30 per cent below normals in visual-spatial ability. (Those with lowest testosterone scored lowest in visual-spatial ability.) Similarly, Anke Erhard of Columbia found that spatial abilities appear statistically more often in men than in women and strongest in those of both sexes who matured late. Many geniuses (Einstein, for instance) matured so late that parents had serious concern that the child "was retarded. "

Thus, most visual erotica and porn tends to have largely male producers and receives most appreciation from male audiences; but so does most architecture, abstract painting and geometry. All may result from right-hemisphere orientation.

These patterns took on new meaning when Frank Farley, a University of Wisconsin psychologist, found that male sensation-seekers or novelty-seekers have "rather high testosterone levels." Farley named these types Big T's and called the other extreme, those who want stability, little t's. (Middle-T's, of course, exist, too, and, I assume, many fuzzy cases...)

Farley found the biggest Big T's among males in general and young males especially (made up of the highest testosterone group in any society.) Big T adolescents tend to show extraordinary creativity or proneness to delinquency, or sometimes show both tendencies (like the charming and terrifying Harry Lime in *The Third Man.*) Farley also found the Big T's, whether creative or criminal, exhibit more inclination than average males to self-destructive behaviors like drug abuse, smoking and alcoholism, and have twice as many auto accidents as little t people.

Little t types, Farley says, "cling to certainty and predictability, avoiding risks and the unfamiliar...neither creative nor criminal—they're grey."

There even seems to have been a migratory pattern in Big T genes through American history. The Western film, especially the Clint Eastwood film, portrays a Big T explosion, and many of its traits still linger. As Michael Hutchison points out in *The Anatomy of Sex and Power,* people west of the Rockies tend to die at younger ages, more of them die by violence, they have more car accidents, and they statistically use more drugs and booze than Easterners. He thinks this means we have always had more Big Ts out here, from the Wild West days to the present, and I tend to agree.

Balancing this, on the creative side of the Big T profile, California has more Nobel prize winners in science *than all the other 49 states combined,* and sociologist Rodney Stark has found more adherents of deviant "cults" and wild ideas (scientific, pseudo-scientific or outright dingbat) in the West, along with less attendance at orthodox churches. Amusingly, the West also has more anti-smoking laws than the East, and more smokers, too.

Similarly, in the California Medfly war—in which the State has insisted of spraying millions of citizens with malathion, a pesticide that some claim may prove as dangerous to humans as to insects—Professor William Jordan of University of California at Davis recently wrote, "the high command of pest control is hooked on the pesticide equivalent of saturation bombing." Having worked on the malathion program himself, Prof. Jordan describes this high command as "husky men in their late 50s or early 60s (with) sagging jowls...deep, coarse voices...deep creases of experience and, yes, of courage, toughness, endurance... This is the portrait of a warrior... In the study of animal behavior this would be called an alpha male."

The alpha male represents the animal form of the extreme Big T or high testosterone male. He also, of course, exemplifies the Male Chauvinist Pig denounced in all Feminist polemic—the guy they think all of us "really are."

Colin Wilson has a lot of evidence, in his *Criminal History,* that, at most 5% of all males exhibit the "alpha" qualities of criminality, leadership, or artistic/scientific temperament. 4 out of those 5 alphas, however, either compete in politics, business or art, because only one of them—one per cent of all males—ever lands in jail, and half of that one per cent lands there for non-violent "crimes-by-definition," i.e., dissident behavior, nowadays usually drug-related.

As we have come to understand the biochemical roots of Big T-ism, we also come closer to understanding how to modify such types. Science writer Harold Rheingold reports that one unnamed Feminist biochemist has told him she would like to promote "a more peaceful humanity" by altering prenatal testosterone or "readjusting hormone levels at puberty." The totalitarian implications of this chemical pacification of unruly males seem obvious and ominous; but we must also remember that victims of rape and other violence would be very happy to support any program likely to decrease those particular Big T behaviors. Can we do this without also diminishing a lot of creativity, art and mathematics?

Frank Farley, who first observed the Big T/little t profiles at opposite extremes of the male psyche, also noted that whether Big T's become Creatives or Delinquents depends largely on non-chemical factors—*the kind of socio-economic class into which their parents' income places them, for instance.* (Colin Wilson, similarly, has much evidence that juvenile gang leaders have the kind of personality that would become an explorer, entrepreneur or genius, *in a better environment*.)

A much more important factor, according to neurophysiologist James Prescott, lies in the kind of child-rearing a society practices. Studying infancy in 49 societies, Prescott concluded that *"the root cause of violence is deprivation of physical pleasure"* in the early years. Theft, child abuse and customs of "killing, torturing or mutilating the enemy" appear seldom or not at all in nurturing cultures where infants receive much love and pleasurable stimuli. They increase sharply in cultures where infants experience repression or denial of love. *In 73 per cent of all societies, Prescott discovered, the amount of pleasure infants receive predicts how much physical violence will appear in adulthood.*

In other words, to get the best out of our middle-to-Big Ts, we should rear them in a loving, pleasure-oriented ethos, like the liberal/bohemian fringe in every civilization, rather than in a repressed, punishing ethos, like that of Feminism and Fundamentalism. Big Ts might not all become Einsteins or Beethovens, but they would probably compete ferociously in business, science or art—not crime—and we would all profit from that.

Meanwhile, let us note that the eastward-to-westward migration of Big Ts in U.S. history, noted by Hutcheson, seems part of the much bigger historical/evolutionary process discussed in *Cosmic Trigger II: Down to Earth*. To summarize the evidence presented there, briefly:

The Bronze Age began in Thailand/Cambodia about 5000 years ago. This outburst of aggression and creativity created a series of Sun Kingdoms (large agricultural societies, unlike previous tribal groupings) each ruled by a "divine" or quasi-divine alpha male. These despotisms introduced female subjugation, constant warfare, imperial expansionism and slavery. They moved steadily Westward ("and mildly northward," as Bucky Fuller says) across Asia, into Egypt and Greece and, in the Roman Empire, formed the largest power-and-information system achieved until the time of Christ.

According to statistics by French economist George Anderla, if we count all the information bits acquired by humanity by 1 C.E. (3112 of this cycle on the Mayan calendar) and consider this mountain of information as one unit, then—

Information doubled to two units by 1500 C.E. (5500 A.L.); and the center of power and "knowledge" had shifted from Rome northward to the banks and universities of Florence and a few similar city-states. This unleashed the first two Protestant revolutions (1517 and 1534) and demolished the Authority of Rome over the Occident.

The next doubling, reaching 4 units, happened by 1750 C.E. (2934 y.C.) and power and knowledge had centered in the British Isles, north and west of the previous hot center. This unleashed forces more radical than Protestantism, including free thought, democracy, socialism, feminism itself, anarchism and industrialism.

The next doubling, bringing us to 8 times the knowledge of the best educated Roman, occurred by 1900 C.E. (29 E.P.) and power and information, in a more gigantic heap than ever, had moved West again and centered around New York and Boston.

Information has doubled again by 1950 to 16 units, by 1960 to 32 units, by 1968 to 64 units, by 1973 to 128 units, and now appears to double every 18 months; the Westward shift of power has followed this information revolution to California, Japan and the emerging culture called The Pacific Rim. Industrialism meanwhile faded into the post-industrial Information Age.

Most of the information superhighway runs at least occasionally through satellites in outer space, so the East-West trajectory has become an expanding "omnidirectional halo" carrying information into a unified field around Earth.

Some see only the brutal, imperialistic side of this evolutionary vector. A few optimists, even today, see only the creative and beneficial side (e.g., the spread of Enlightenment ideas after 1750, the increase of life span from less than 30 years average to 75 years average in the same period, a few dozen horrible diseases vanquished, while the *average* living standard of ordinary working people in the most advanced nations now ranks higher than that of early kings.)

I think we should see both sides, and also exercise our intelligence in producing the artistic, scientific and innovative Big Ts and not the thugs and hoodlums. We should also realize that this information-enrichment has fractal (unpredictable) aspects, and not imagine that we can precisely predict its next direction from its previous trajectories.

Principle references:

The Anatomy of Sex and Power, Michael Hutcheson, William Morrow Co., New York, 1990.

The Three Pound Universe, Hooper and Teresi, Macmillan, New York, 1986.

Critical Path, Buckminster Fuller, St Martin's Press, New York, 1981—the North/West trajectory of information

Los Angeles Times April 23, 1990—Prof. Jordan quote.

TWENTY-TWO

BENEATH THE PLANET OF THE PRIORY OF SION

In Which the College of 'Pataphysics Offers New Clues via Mr. Michael Lamy

> Who the hell wants to see a movie
> about Adolph fucking Hitler?
> —*Chaplin*
>
> Adolph *who?*
> —*One, Two, Three*

In 1989, finding myself in Paris again, I wandered down to the ancient streets of the *rive gauche* and dropped by the College de 'Pataphysique.

M. de Selby greeted me warmly, as ever. I noticed that he looked older and grayer than he had when I last visited, and then with a faint shock realized that I also looked older and grayer. So subtly does the Ancient Enemy creep up on all of us...

We had some Portuguese Espresso and enjoyed some hash mixed with tobacco—a Continental custom that all the cancer warnings in the world hasn't abolished yet. You have to go North Africa, or come back to the States, to find straight hash without nicotine poison added.

De Selby reacted with caution when I mentioned my researches into the murky Priory of Sion. "Ah, *oui*," he said dubiously. "Everybody wants to know more about them, except me. I'd rather know less, thank you. Some things should not allow themselves to become known, I think...but have you seen Lamy's book yet?"

I confessed that I hadn't seen the book or even heard of it.

"Oh," he said happily. "This you will enjoy immensely." And he went rummaging through the archives, shelves, desk drawers and general rubble, until at last he produced the book: *Jules Verne: Iniate et Iniateur*, by Michael Lamy.

"Do you know this man, Lamy?" I asked.

"Nobody does," he said darkly. "Some say he doesn't exist. The name may be a mask for the C.I.A., the K.G.B. or even the Priory itself, for all I know. Some actually claim 'Lamy' is another front for UMMO. In this post-modern world...well, you know your Jarry and Nietzsche..." Then he excused himself, retiring to the computer room. "You will want some time with this," he said. "It is, as the Irish say, enough to make a bat grin."

I picked up the book and started to browse, doubting that I could read it all in one afternoon. I soon found that M. Lamy's text surpassed all Priory of Sion literature I had seen to date; it would not only make a bat grin, as de Selby said—it might even make an owl laugh out loud.

According to my notes, Lamy spends a lot of time discussing the origins of the vampire legend in general and noting curious parallels between Christ and Dracula: especially the details of rising from the grave and instituting cannibalistic rituals—only symbolic cannibalism in the Christ case, according to Protestants, but real cannibalism *disguised* as symbolic cannibalism, according to Catholics. (It depends on whether you believe the bread *literally* turns into the flesh of a dead Jew. Catholic dogma claims it does.)

I suddenly saw the synecdoche: how could I write this book on the counterfeits of reality and the reality of counterfeits without taking note of a widespread masque in which believers claim to consume flesh and blood, swilling it down with the gusto of Hannibal Lecter, where unbelievers see only bread and wine? From a phenomenological, or even a 'pataphysical, point of view, if the participants in a social rite fervently believe they have enjoyed a cannibalistic feast, then those words describe their *experience* accurately. The detached observer who sees no flesh or blood has not entered the participatory gloss of the group, their reality-tunnel, and merely brackets the experience differently, seeing the external acts but not the internal meaning—like a deaf man watching but not hearing a symphony orchestra.)

M. Lamy takes off, then, from Christ's "walk through Hell" in Catholic art (an event not mentioned in the Bible itself) to underworld journeys in general, and, of course, the hollow earth theories of Symmes, Blavatsky, Shaver *et. al.* By the time I decided that Lamy intended, like de Sede, to do a lot of hinting and very little real explaining, he finally came to his title character, the uncanny Verne.

Why and how did this unique man describe so many events that occurred nearly a hundred years later in ordinary time? Lamy lists some of the more eerie details, e.g., the first "real" moon landing took off from the same part of Florida as the first fictional moon voyage in Verne. (To fit the theme of the present book better, I recall that a popular film, *Capricorn One,* shows how the government could have faked the "real" moon landing, if they wanted to.)

Lamy, after trying to sell Verne as a mutant prophet (a pre-cog in current sci-fi jargon) examines Verne's politics, which he defines as Orleanist or aristocratic-anarchistic. (Americans not familiar with French politics can replace Orleans with Howard Hughes, and will get the general idea, although not the historical context.) Lamy then does his own riff on the Illuminati theme: Orleans, not Weishaupt, served as the real Grandmaster of the Illuminati; the Orleanist-Illuminati conspiracy recruited Verne in his youth; all of Verne's heroes and/or hero-villains have the same aristocratic-anarchistic attitudes that Lamy identifies with the Illuminati. Verne's novels, M. Lamy wants us to believe, serve as subliminal Illuminati propaganda for most readers and also double as cloaked recruiting manuals for those who can read between the lines. The Priory of Sion, similarly, acts as a masque to befuddle the unworthy and lead the proper persons into the Illuminati.

We then go back, one more time, to that "accursed" church of Mary Magdelene (the one that actually announces its accursed status on the door, remember?) The real secret has nothing to do with treasures of gold or genealogies of Jesus and Ms. Magdelene: the church itself contains the treasure and the secret.

Yes: if you go down to the cellar of the church, Lamy assures us, you will find a carefully hidden sub-cellar; and, beneath that...the tunnels to the inner worlds of the Earth described in Jules Verne's *Voyage to the Center of the Earth.* And at the center. you will find...not Shaver's sadistic Deros, but super-human, godlike immortals, who act as the Inner Heads of all true occult orders and manage the long-term project of educating humanity for the day when it can handle the responsibility of also becoming immortal and godlike.

I liked that a lot. I had never thought before that the mysterious lore of the "Inner" Heads might actually contain a plain geological meaning.

My beeper buzzed and I realized I had to catch my plane for Zurich. I bade a hurried goodbye to de Selby and took off. Only later did I realize that my notes did not include the publisher of Lamy's book. When I wrote to de Selby about that, he replied that he had had the book on loan from a Bavarian woman named Anna Sprengle, who had returned and claimed it. It has evidently gone out of print already.

But here I must insert another inconclusive little anecdote. Mr. Frederick Lehrman, dean of Nomad University, Seattle, told me a while back about a curious visit he made to the Magdelene church in Rennes-le-Chatteau. Here, Lehrman says, he met a French researcher who has found a completely new clue—one of the statues of Magdelene had a hollow space at the bottom. The Frenchman, according to Lehrman, managed to open it—and found a German newspaper for 1904.

Dean Lehrman, alas, could not remember the exact date. Only romantic fantasy, and a taste for these games, underlies my hope that the paper actually says June 16, 1904.

Anyway, whatever the precise date, the researcher told Lehrman that some words in the newspaper have heavy underlining. He intends to work on the code until he "cracks" it.

Will it tell us more about the hollow earth? The married life of Jesus and Mary Christ? Those intrusive blokes from Sirius?

Or will it just say "Noon blue apples" again?

TWENTY-THREE

ANDROPHOBIA

In Which We Examine How Old
Group Stereotypes Have Gotten Shifted
To New Scapegoats in Recent Years

> Okay—we'll take the niggers and the chinks,
> but the Irish have to go somewhere else.
> —*Blazing Saddles*

> What we have here is a failure in communication.
> —*Cool Hand Luke*

Around a year ago, I finally came out of the closet. I admitted my true nature and openly joined forces with others in the same despised minority as myself, braving all the contempt and loathing I knew this would bring down on my head. I joined the Men's Movement.

Worse, I began speaking and writing about "Men's Issues." The chapter on testosterone represents just part of my growing rebellion against the new Hate Cult (enshrined in Academe and almost equally entrenched in the mass media) which places males in the "low other" position (as sociologists call it) formerly reserved for either Blacks or Orientals.

This "defense of the indefensible" should surprise nobody, since I have never had much common sense. I have written controversial articles and books since 1959 and have had the honor of seeing myself called every possible nasty name in the English language by every gang of fanatics that infests this planet, from Christian Crusade to CSICOP. Joining the Men's Movement just indicates that at 62 I still do things as undiplomatic as I did in my 20s; I have graduated from a Perfect Young Fool to a Perfect Old Fool without ever passing through Maturity or Pragmatic Caution.

Curiously, most of the amusing and usually quasi-illiterate hate mail I have received for my current defense of men comes not from women but from other men. I would say about 90% of it, in fact, comes from men. Even after profound study and meditation, I cannot understand this. I can only think of the Jews who have become leaders in the American Nazi Party—several cases have gotten into print, and one committed suicide when a New York newspaper documented his Jewish family tree. (Another Jewish Nazi changed his name when a Chicago paper exposed his Hebraic ancestry.)

Like those Jews, who hated their "Jewishness" more than the original Nazis had, some men evidently hate themselves and other men even more than the Radical Feminists do. I recall the insane but totally convincing character of "Buffalo Bill" in Thomas Harris' brilliant *The Silence of the Lambs*—the fellow who wants to escape malehood so desperately that he tries to make a female skin to hide in, when he can't get a sex-change operation. Maybe Harris understands male self-hate better than I do.

In all the hate mail I have received for writing and speaking about androphobia, nobody has attempted to refute my central point: after nearly 100 years of Intelligence Testing, no psychologist has proven any IQ difference between females and males. High and low IQs appear equally in both genders. Alleged male inferiority, like alleged black inferiority, remains pure fiction, without one jot of experimental evidence to support it. In continually insisting on the mental deficiency of men, Christine Craft, Carol Hemingway and other Radical Feminists merely copy Hitler's technique of the Big Lie.

Of course, I know that, like the Nazi Big Lie, male "inferiority" will go on getting repeated endlessly, no matter how much scientific evidence contradicts it. Politics does not rest upon scientific validations. Politics rests upon passion and prejudice; otherwise, this planet might become suddenly stark staring sane.

To put it mildly, men who hate men, like women who hate men, seem to be working on inner psychological problems, not on scientific research.

In this connection, I have found much food for thought in the Rodney King case.

That crescendo of barbarities, which unleashed the most violent riots to shake the U.S. in the 20th Century, perfectly illustrates the neurological grid, or reality-tunnel, that maintains androphobia. The media can *see* (i.e., can perceive or recognize)—and, according to polls widely quoted in *Time* and on TV, the majority of ordinary citizens can *see*—that Rodney King suffered that terrible beating, and the jurors acquitted the perpetrators, because of the lurking and vicious racism of our society.

A conditioned self-censorship "built into" our brains by three decades of Radical Feminist intimidation, however, blocks an equally elementary perception. Nobody on the airwaves or in print can see, or can allow themselves to notice, that the Rodney King atrocity also owes a great deal to the equally vicious sexism which the androphobes have infiltrated into all the media in the past 30 years.

Nonetheless, those who at least *try* to think honestly and *try* to transcend the prejudices of their times, might feel a distinct Shock (or "Awakening" experience) if they sincerely attempt two simple mind exercises:

1. In memory, re-run the infamous video one more time, and try to see it with Rodney King as a female. Does this savage beating still seem possible? With 21 other officers watching *and none objecting?*

Think about it and really *try* to get beyond conditioned perception. Police violence against Black women does occur, of course, but I can recall no case where the brutality reached the same level of sadistic frenzy as in this case, and female officers watched impassively. Can you?

2. Imagine that incredible Simi Valley jury watching this video, with Rodney King still as a woman. Would even those rednecks have acquitted the cops in that case? Could they look at

the video tape and convince themselves that what they saw did not constitute excessive force?

"Sociopaths" and "drunks" commit violence against women, and we all experience horror and revulsion. But every day allegedly normal people commit violence against men like Rodney King, and many of us, like the Simi jury, can still find reasons to "excuse" such atrocities. Both Dan Quayle and Bill Clinton have had to answer charges of cowardice for having enough elementary sanity to avoid the war in Vietnam, but nobody accused Geraldine Ferraro of the same metaphysical "crime" for not volunteering to go over and get her arms or legs blown off in that hellish bout of national lunacy.

Similarly, in the Michael Hay case in Singapore, the overwhelming majority of Americans supported the barbaric caning of this young man, by a martial arts expert (a guy who really knows how to hurt you) even though (a) Hay never had a jury trial (b) Singapore justice has a notorious reputation for proceeding from accusation to punishment without many legal niceties (c) Hay claimed his confession had resulted from torture; and supporting evidence came from others who said the Singapore police regularly obtain confessions that way.

I can only conclude that Americans have suffered so much brainwashing by the Radical Feminists that any man anywhere now has a "presumption of guilt" instead of the traditional Anglo-American "presumption of innocence."

But just change the gender and try to believe the same result. If the Singapore authorities decided to have young American female caned by a martial arts professional, without even a jury trial, how many Americans would have supported this with equal enthusiasm?

Would our government have limited itself only to tepid protest in a polite and conciliatory language?

Would Feminists have remained silent, as they did when Hay got caned, or would they have howled to high heaven, if it happened to a girl his age?

As the sociologist Lawrence Diggs has said, racism remains totally visible whether from whites against blacks or from blacks against whites, but sexism remains totally invisible if it comes from women against men. We would think it pathetic but perfectly "normal" and natural if Danny Quayle or Bill Clinton had to spend their lives in wheelchairs like Ron Kovic, but it only becomes *monstrous* and *unthinkable* if you imagine it happening to a pure, noble, female creature—like Tonya Harding, say...

We only regard our allegedly sub-human males as expendable, like laboratory animals. Women we see as truly and fully human, and hence not mere "cannon fodder." Even today, after 30 years of Radical Feminist agit-prop women have hold any rank in the Army—except front-line combat which we still reserve for our "sub-human" males.

Consider this little irony: Diggs, the sociologist cited above, says that when he writes about this, certain people always accuse him of defending the "white male power structure."

Lawrence Diggs does not belong to any "white" power structure. He has black skin—in Aristotelian language, he "is" Black—and he merely reports what he has seen first hand of the neuro-psychological damage that the combination of racism and sexism has done to young black males in this country. Damned for their blackness and damned again for their maleness, these boys and young men represent the Heart of Darkness for our times.

George Bush took the negative archetype, *Black Male*—two terror signals in one image—gave it the name "Willie Horton," carefully repeated the negative conditioning hour after hour on TV, and frightened the masses into electing him, just as similar anti-Semitic stereotypes put Adolph Hitler into power 50 years earlier. The police who beat Rodney King probably never "saw" him in an existential sense; they *saw* the Monster that Bush had invoked and called "Willie Horton." The Giant Black Male, with a half-image of King Kong in the psychic background.

If this point still seems obscure (or deliberately perverse), try one more Reality Check, to determine whether you've suffered brainwashing or I have:

Try to think of how many movies you have seen in the last ten years in which the heroine attacks a man, bops him upside the head with a blunt instrument, punches him in the face or the gut, shoots him dead, or commits similar violence against several men in succession. Then try—really hard, now—to think of *any* movies in which the leading actress does not at least slap one man's face. Can you recall even one such film? Made since 1970?

A while back, I thought I had, in fact found one happy case of nonviolence toward males—*The Fisher King*. But then I looked at it again, and saw that in the climax, the heroine slaps the hero as hard as she can—a major assault—before they kiss. He, of course, doesn't mind being smashed in the face like a slave in the Old South, and acts merely grateful for the kiss. Males, in the new mythos, must be bashed, at least a little, in every film and TV show. And, of course, they never show pain. The directors evidently wish us to think *they don't even feel pain, like other inanimate objects.*

Feminists, of both the Radical and the rational varieties, complain rightly about the violence against women in movies. But they don't *see*—they can't see or won't see—the much more prevalent violence against males.

And nobody except Lawrence Diggs, Dr. Alfred Ehlenberger and Warren Farrell has ever discussed the statistical fact that, in real life just as in films, all men (not just black men) suffer violence, both from women and from other men, much more often than women do. This fact remains censored by as many taboos and "systems of denial" in our society as homosexuality did in the Victorian age, or alcoholism in a dysfunctional family.

As psychologist Kathi Cleary writes (*Men In Crisis*):

> Most women are very aware of a man's sexism but totally blind to their own... When you find yourself becoming uncomfortable with male-bashing jokes, comments and conversation, you'll also find yourself more aware of other women's sexism. Point it out... (But) you may end up laying some friendships on the line. For some reason, women seem to feel that an acknowledgment of their sexism toward men will send feminism back to the dark ages.

Dr. Cleary can *see* female sexism (or androphobia, as I call it) because she has a sane attitude toward feminism, as a crusade for justice and not just another Hate Group. To repeat one of my favorite lines, *just as Marx called anti-Semitism "the socialism of fools," I think anti-andrism will appear (in a saner future) as the feminism of imbeciles.* It has nothing to do with any legitimate struggle for women's rights, anymore than Nazi anti-

Semitism helped Germans resolve any of the real injustices piled on them after World War I.

Psychologists like Dr. Farrell have just begun to calculate the total damage androphobia has inflicted on men; they show us statistics of the suicide rate of young males (*six times* that of females); the rapidly rising male heart attack rate; the graphs showing equal life expectancy for men and women from the dawn of statistical science until the 1920s and the dizzying decline to the present where men have seven years **less** life expectancy than women, etc. One could almost predict such statistics *a priori*: No group can live normal, healthy lives in a society which hates their guts, and tells them so daily.

The highest suicide rate, incidentally, appears in white males, who make up 72 per cent of all suicides. I think this results from the fact that our official Opinion Makers have selected white males, like the "witches" in medieval Europe, to become the one group so Indisputedly Damned that not even the most wild-eyed libertarian dares to defend them.

The most frequent charge against any of us who oppose androphobia says that in defending all men we perforce defend those indefensible white men, which our society's mythos simply does not allow. Diggs speaks of hearing this constantly, despite his Negritude. Like the Jews in Germany again, white males always appear rich, robust and comfortable in the popular media; only other people (non-white, non-male) might pass as poor, sick or troubled.

My father, although white and male, remained a poor working man all his life. He not only earned less money than Rockefeller; he learned a hell of a lot less than any of the Radical Feminists who write blockbuster best-sellers about how all men have exploited them. He never hit my mother, or me, and tried to prevent her from beating up on me. He gave her his whole pay check every pay-day, and never drank except on holidays, when he drank a little but never enough to get drunk. At least, that's my memory. I must have hallucinated, of course. All white males have great wealth and a vicious streak a mile wide. Therefore, my father never existed, I guess. I just emerged from the void.

Yeah, sure.

Under the cha-cha pent-house where Robin Morgan and a gaggle of other Radical Feminists hold a cocktail party to complain about their exquisite emotional sufferings, way down in the dark, in the alley, among the discarded condoms and the rubbish, you will find our new Jews: a group of males, some of them white, sleeping in the freezing rain. A rat bites one and he cries out, briefly, in his sleep. But the exquisite ladies do not hear that, up in the pent-house where the Intelligentsia meet to manipulate the media and mold the lines of thought and image that control social perception.

The rain continues to fall on the homeless men. Their bodies and minds destroyed in Vietnam, these dehumanized creatures remain beyond pity and beyond compassion, beyond the perimeter of the human commonwealth, because of the shape of their genitals. We must not consider Radical Feminism a crazy Hate group, of course. We must accept it as chic; and as ultra-modern; and as *Politically Correct.* Only the people who hate on the basis of nose-shape or skin-color deserve the label of bigots, of course. Of course.

TWENTY-FOUR

VIRTUAL REALITIES WITHOUT COMPUTERS

In Which We Discover That People
Who Don't Exist Can Influence Those Who Do

> If I put something in my mouth, I want it to be the best.
> —*The Fabulous Baker Boys*

> You cock-sucker!
> —*Glengarry Glen Ross*

When Swift arranged to have his most famous (and explosive) work delivered to the publisher the way spies deliver Military Secrets in the dark of the moon, he acted partly out of prudence (censors could imprison or even kill in those days, and the book constitutes a gross and obscene libel on the state, the church, the law and humanity in general)—and partly, perhaps, out of the mad logic required of a truly creative counterfeiter. Thus, disguised as fact, the 18th Century received its most subversive fable, and horses who had *humanitas* where they should have had *equinitas* befuddled our literary tradition forever, together with malodorous primates called Yahoos who didn't have *humanitas* at all: a most amazing anticipation of Darwin. Scientific Lem Gulliver also described the two moons of Mars

161

before astronomers "discovered" them. Art and magick have strange linkages: and great masques always include odd little details like that, to linger on as puzzles when the major hoax has collapsed.

Here, said Mr. James Joyce to the Paris intelligentsia of 1922, *I offer you a shockingly realistic novel.* And everybody nodded sagely, appreciated the genius of Joyce's prose, and swallowed the realism claim like art dealers grabbing up Elmyrs before 1968. After all, in what previous "realistic" novel, did the hero defecate, urinate, and masturbate? And the heroine fornicate, menstruate and urinate? In the 72 years since then, we have gradually noticed that the ultra-realistic *Ulysses*, parodies every other realistic novel, parodies romantic novels and epics also, even parodies itself, and contains 102 synchronicities, three cases of ESP, one case of precognition, one ghost walking in the broad daylight of a Spring afternoon and more uncertainty than quantum equations. Like the first perusers of *Travels in Remote Parts of the World*, by our boy Lem, most readers simply had mistaken satire (or something else...) for objective reporting, just because they believed in labels—"travel book" or "realistic novel" respectively.

The "hoax" or "counterfeit" element in the art of Swift and Joyce does not register merely a peculiarity of the Celtic temperament. Every college by now has suffered the phantom student prank, or a good attempt at it. In this Swiftian invasion of the *infobahn,* a notational student appears on all relevant records, and, in successful cases, proceeds smoothly from registration, to excellent marks in most courses, to triumphal graduation, without the necessity of existing in consensus reality at all, at all.

She or he exists only as pure information, in the sense that money or kilometers exist as pure information. (Or the sense in which I exist as pure information, now that Internet has had the assurance of some **Experts** or of some bold frauds—if you still think you can see a difference—who claim that the villains who killed me have also replaced me with a Virtual RAW...)

The notational student, we may assume, derives from the notational agent, a widespread practice in the Intelligence Community for some decades (and the plot gimmick of Hitchcock's hilarious thriller, *North by Northwest.*) The notational agent, created out of nothing, like modern (printing press) money, immediately begins acting real. A paper trail, and supporting evidence, shows that the Agent owns clothes, toothbrushes and all the necessities of a real person, has a passport and wallet with credit cards, "flies" in real airlines, "stays" at real hotels, and exists in almost every sense that you or I exist, except that he or she never manifests in the sensory world. Like the "normal" person, or even more like the "normal" world of CSICOP's pious belief, or even more like the phantom student, the notational agent lives only in Virtual Reality. (And we have heard the same claimed for all those rocks which, according to some Fundamentalists, appear 4 billion years old because the first Artist whimsically included them to make His work appear more than 6000 years old. Does this theory make God an "artist" or a "counterfeiter" in your estimation?).

For two decades, mathematicians wondered about the brilliant but reclusive Nicholas Bourbaki. He wrote one dazzling mathematical paper after another, not in one field but in more areas of math than anyone since the 19th Century super-genius, Gauss. Everybody wanted to meet this stellar intellect, but Bourbaki never attended mathematics conferences and his vita always showed him on extended sabbatical from his last university post. At last, when his papers had his peers convinced that more than a new Gauss, they had a new Leonardo among them, somebody got suspicious.

Nicholas Bourbaki, like Lemuel Gulliver, the phantom student and the notational agent, never existed outside the information system. His brilliant papers covered so many unrelated areas of math because a committee of whimsical European mathematicians had produced them in collaboration.

The Gulliver hoax served a serious purpose ("human liberty," Swift said on his tombstone.) The phantom student serves a purely psychic or ritual purpose; such jokes release energy, anger and rebellious creativity in safely formalized manner: the Big Ts adapting to the bureaucratic little t world, but mocking it. The notational spy serves to confuse the enemy and send them on snark hunts. Bourbaki? I don't know. Ask the perpetrators.

What purpose would you attribute to the UMMO and Priory of Sion committees, if you accept them as human game-players?

And now that we have "unmasked" Gulliver and Bourbaki, or at least found the mask behind the mask, what of Jean Paulhan?

According to Reliable Sources, including **Expert** Testimony, M. Paulhan exists in the same world as you and me, and President Clinton, and O.J. Simpson, and Madonna. Proof of his existence? Many Reliable Sources claim to know him; he allegedly edits the *Nouvelle Review Francaise;* he certainly has standing as an **Expert** in literature. He even wrote the preface to *The Story of O*, that classic of porno-masochism. (Some claim he wrote the book, too.)

Nevertheless, for decades now, the College de 'Pataphysique has claimed that Paulhan doesn't exist.

Some kind of 'Pataphysical humor or paradox? Or do they know something we don't know? And why do I recall "noon blue apples" and the famous warning:

DADA IS NOT DEAD

WATCH YOUR OVERCOAT

In this context, consider the following document, allegedly received by an applicant for an instructor's position at the University of California:

> Dear Dr. _____
>
> Thank you for your application for the assistant professor opening #279-923 in the Anthropology Board of Studies at the University of California, Santa Cruz. Enclosed you will find an ethnic identity card that must be completed and returned.

Germany in the 1930s or California in the 1990s? Political Correctness or a bit of guerrilla ontology again? "Real" or satire? (I will give the answer a bit later.)

And, because I often speak at Libertarian conventions, I have met quite a few people who have adopted the method of art (i.e., the method of the counterfeiter) in dealing with the Control System. Some of them pick up extra 1040 forms every year, fill them out with false names and addresses, then add them up incorrectly, so they show high income and incredible deductions, like a crude attempt to "cheat." They then mail these gross frauds to IRS; God knows how much time the Agency wastes looking for these notational taxpayers to collect the huge sums these unpersons "owe."

Other anarchists, less bold, merely write a different Social Security number on every form the Government or the

Corporations impose on them. I presume the computers of the Control System have different folders for Joe Smith 171-32-7123, Joe Smith 181-42-6123, Joe Smith 161-56-1761, and all the other semi-fictitious Joe Smiths the real Joe has left in his anarchistic wake.

Somewhere or other, the painter Wyndham Lewis said that when alleged "objectivity" becomes a cult, parody becomes an irresistible urge. I would say, rather, that when inflexible Authority exists, the satirist and counterfeiter express two variations on, fundamentally, the same strategy for coping in such a world. The manufacturers/sellers of the "Guaranteed Drug-Free Urine" widely advertised these days exemplify the practical, as distinguished from artistic, mode of this insurrection.

Most of the "Guaranteed Drug-Free Urine" I have seen advertised comes from Boulder, Colorado. I can't imagine how anybody can find even a molecule of guaranteed drug-free urine within a hundred miles of Boulder, and I suspect the managers of this fraud have defrauded those who use the product to defraud the piss-police. Someday, somewhere, a seemingly obedient troll of the Corporate State, successful in hiding the symbolic rebellion of an occasional joint on Saturday night before love-making, will to his horror show positive for hoof-and-mouth disease, and the managers will have him "put down" before he can infect the rest of the herd...

When we contemplate UMMO and the Priory of Sion, we deal with projects that increasingly look more like serious frauds than mere pranks. But a good prank of this sort would *have to look somewhat serious*, and somewhat sinister, to function as a good prank, wouldn't it?

How about the Federal Reserve, then, which has convinced millions that the paper it prints "is" "real" "money"? Prank or fraud? Or perhaps some species of magick that only other sorcerers can understand?

Did the Priory, UMMO or even Lem Gulliver ever try to sell a yarn comparable to the National Debt of $4,000,000,000,000 (four million million) that we allegedly "owe" to the people who print the paper and/or those who wave the magick wand that makes the paper "real" "money"?

Elmyr said it most bluntly: "Without the **Experts**, there would be no forgers."

Principle Sources:

"Who Is Bourbaki?" by John Kobler, *Saturday Evening Post*, February 26, 1966.
The Counterfeiters, Kenner, *op. cit.*

TWENTY-FIVE

THE CARDINAL AND THE STRIP-TEASE DANCER

In Which A Churchman's Death May Unveil Links Between P2 and the Priory of Sion

> No matter how elaborate a philosophical system you work out, in the end it's going to be incomplete.
> —*Crimes and Misdemeanors*

> He meddled in the domain of God.
> —*Bride of the Monster*

On 20 May 1974 Cardinal Jean Danielou died in the apartment of a young strip-tease dancer named Mimi Santini. Because high Catholic officials do not normally die in the apartments of young ladies who take off their clothes in public, and because the Cardinal had a "large sum of money" (*New York Times*, 25 June 1974) on him, the case attracted a certain amount of curiosity. Nothing, alas, ever emerged with any great clarity, except that Cardinals sometimes visit strippers and sometimes carry hefty wads of the long green. Medical examiners pronounced that the old man had died of a heart attack.

Only those with nasty anti-Catholic minds will conjecture about what a Cardinal and a stripper might have done together to bring on the heart attack.

Cardinal Danielou had served on the Academie Francaise, which almost certainly means he had known André Malraux and Jean Cocteau, two prime suspects in the Priory of Sion caper. It certainly doesn't mean that the Cardinal must have co-conspired with them in that group art-work—or hoax, or heresy, or last ditch stand of individualism, or whatever we identify the Priory as.

However, in December 1983, two strange new events cast the Cardinal's death, and the whole P2/Priory mystery in a weird new light. First, on 16 December, Pierre Plantard de Saint Clair resigned as Grandmaster of the Priory of Sion, after a cryptic interview with Baigent, Lincoln and Leigh (the *Holy Blood* blokes) in which he said the Knights of Malta had infiltrated the Priory to an extent he found worrisome.

Second, a pseudonymous *Scandals of the Priory of Sion* came to leading Priory investigators in ordinary mail, just like a new bulletin from UMMO.

Scandals, signed "Cornelius" (does that help at all, at all?) claimed that Cardinal Danielou had been involved with the Priory of Sion since he met Cocteau in the 1930s. (The Cardinal, at that time, did compose a Latin translation of Cocteau's *Oedipus ...*) The Cardinal had also acted a middleman in many shady financial transactions involving the Priory and Michele Sindona, this pamphlet further asserted.

Michele Sindona, to refresh your memory—by volume three, I assume, some of the Machiavellian labyrinths of our tale may prove confusing to the plain blunt reader in Kalamazoo for whom I intend all my works—Sindona, as I say, started out as a Mafia lawyer, got inducted into P2, soon collaborated with Roberto Calvi and Archbishop Marcinkus in major drug laundering operations, founded his own Franklin National Bank in New York and then, ka-boom, it all came tumbling down. Franklin National went bankrupt, Sindona got convicted of 65 counts of stock and currency fraud in New York, got convicted of murdering a bank examiner in Rome, and died in a cell while awaiting trial on charges that he and Calvi and the P2 crowd in general had conspired toward a fascist *coup* in Italy. Like the deaths of Calvi and several others in this yarn, Sindona's death remains in the shady area where nobody has quite proven either suicide or murder.

Scandals further alleges that Sindona did *not* kill the bank examiner, Giorgia Ambrosoli. That murder, the pamphlet claims, intended to cover up the links between the P2 conspiracy in Italy, the Priory conspiracy in France and the Grand Loge Alpina in Switzerland. The Priory of Sion itself ordered the hit on Ambrosoli, *Scandals* says.

Baigent, Lincoln and Leigh (who, as I pointed out, may not act as independent investigators at all, but as propagandists for the Priory) allege that they checked all of these allegations and could find no proof of any of them. They just *claim* that. They don't offer us any of their evidence.

This threesome, who always seem to know a little more about the Priory than other "outsiders" and who, by and large, sound less crazy than most writers on this subject, do, however, provide a lot of evidence indicating close, and long-lasting, links between the Priory of Sion and the Knights of Malta.

That mystic brotherhood, often considered the Vatican's secret police, works closely with the C.I.A., according to Baigent, Lincoln and Leigh—and other sources listed in our *Cosmic Trigger Volume II*. (Look back and check.) Messrs. B.L & L also note that Francis Cardinal Spellman acted as a major architect of the C.I.A./Knights of Malta alliance.

I find that passing strange. Cardinal Spellman also worked closely with Senator Joe McCarthy, J. Edgar Hoover and Roy Cohn in concocting the anti-communist hysteria in this country during the '50s. All four—McCarthy, Hoover, Cohn and Spellman—met often at the Stork Club, a cocktail restaurant owned by Mafia boss Frank Costello.

"Cornelius" in *Scandals* claims the Mafia has long worked in cahoots with both the Priory of Sion and the P2 lodge.

Somehow I think all this indicates something more than just a high-level game or prank. I begin to suspect that the terrible word "conspiracy" actually fits at least some of the capers we have followed in these books.

As a singer of strange songs wrote:

> To his bride said the keen-eyed detective,

"Can it be that my eyesight's defective?
Has the east tit the least bit
The best of the west tit
Or is that a trick of perspective?"

References:

New York Times, 9 June and 25 June, 1974—Cardinal Danielou's death, the stripper and the money.

Cornelius, *Scandals of the Priory of Sion*, 1983, no publisher listed.

Baigent, Lincoln and Leigh, *Messianic Legacy*, Henry Holt, New York, 1987—Knights of Malta and CIA links.

Anthony Summers, *Official and Confidential: the Secret Life of J. Edgar Hoover*, Pocket Books, New York, 1994—Hoover, Cohn, Spellman, McCarthy links.

TWENTY-SIX

THE BARD AT BAY

**In Which Shakespeare Gets Politically Corrected and
Professor Taylor Locks Horns with Professor Bloom**

> He's a legitimate target.
> —*The Crying Game*

> Atmospheric conditions in outer space
> interfered with transmitting.
> —*Plan 9 From Outer Space*

The world may not yet have become ready for a *monstre gai* like
Will Shakespeare. The 18th Century tried, frantically, to purify
the Bard's "barbarous" style. The 19th Century attempted, nervously, to improve his morals; and, surveying the pitiful results,
Leo Tolstoy at the end of the century pronounced Sweet Will
still morally corrupt beyond all hope of redemption. Now the
20th Century wants to dump Stratford's butcher boy on the
grounds that he belongs to the condemned species of DWEMs
(Dead White European Males) and appears egregiously guilty of
every possible Political Incorrectness.

Perhaps the critics of the 21st Century, or maybe the 23rd, will
have evolved enough to have the large minds and larger hearts
that can accept William Shakespeare, all his barbarity, immoral-

ity, political incorrectness, deadness, whiteness, maleness and monstrous genius notwithstanding?

A strong argument against such a possible Futuristic Shake-spearean age appears in *Reinventing Shakespeare* by Gary Taylor, a masterpiece of fundamentalist post-modernism. Shake-speare has no future, as Professor Taylor tells it: the current academic orthodoxy has seen through him, smelt out his guilt and shame; he can never again deceive the educated. The Bard, quite simply, reeks of maleness, whiteness and other stigmata of the Beast. We have done with him, and good riddance.

Taylor feels exhilaratingly righteous about dumping Sweet Will, and quotes with delight the opinions of those who compare his Politically Correct allies with adolescent "rebellion against parental authority" or "the Young Turks versus the Old Guard." Shakespeare represents "phallocentrism" and the ever-accursed "Patriarchy," and this, like the unknowable Sin Against the Holy Ghost, we can never forgive, not in this century nor in any time to come. No way back exists and no way forward exists, for us. We live in a Politically Correct box with no exit.

To quote Taylor's own words,

> But I, here in my present, could see all the ways in which my thinking is typical of this period only if I could somehow get outside of our paradigm, if I could rise above it and look down upon it... But if I could rise above our [Politically Correct] paradigm, I would no longer be in it.

In simpler words, Taylor means that he cannot escape the P.C. paradigm because he lives at the present time. This seems too absurd to require rebuttal. Millions alive today, all over the world—Europe, Asia, Australia, Africa, the Americas—still love Shakespeare. What Taylor means to say, I think, amount to: you cannot escape the P.C. paradigm *if you want to hold a university job in the U.S. today* .

Outside of such pragmatic cages, a paradigm that you "cannot escape" intellectually has the sci–fi horror of Philip K. Dick's Black Iron Prison, a place that exists *nowhere and everywhere*, but a place where you must remain as long as the Control System convinces you the Black Iron Prison exists *and that you live in it.*

But this becomes even clearer if we state it this way: the majority of critics, for nearly 300 years, have claimed

Shakespeare "is" the greatest writer who ever lived. The P.C. paradigm claims Shakespeare "is" just another Patriarchal White Man, that all artistic standards "are" relative, and that the Shakespeare mystique "is" a mask for White Male Imperialism.

On the opposite side, still able to survive in the Groves of Academe, although he sounds harassed and thinks of himself as part of a dying culture,[1] Professor Harold Bloom defends Shakespeare with fire and eloquence in his *The Western Canon*.

Denouncing Taylor, Alice Walker, and the P.C. crowd in general as "the School of Resentment," Bloom gallantly defends the old-fangled idea that it makes sense to describe a book as esthetically "more than, less than or equal to" another book (a notion so archaic that re-stated now, here in America, it seems suddenly revolutionary again, as Taylor's PC dogma sounds smugly conformist) Going beyond even that Heresy of Hierarchy ("more than, less than..." contradicts the P.C. axiom that no difference exists between anybody), Bloom even tries to resurrect the Canon, and puts the Upstart Crow from the Stratford butcher shop at the pinnacle of it:

> Shakespeare's eminence is, I am certain, the rock upon which the School of Resentment must at last founder... If it is arbitrary that Shakespeare centers the Canon, then they need to show why the dominant social class selected him rather than, say, Ben Jonson, for that arbitrary role... (H)ow much simpler it is to admit that there is a *qualitative* difference, a difference in kind, between Shakespeare and every other writer, even Chaucer, even Tolstoy...

As for the Foucaltian (or New Age) Marxoids, Bloom writes with a fine Johnsonian scorn:

> If the social energies...of the English Renaissance somehow wrote *King Lear,* then the singularity of Shakespeare can be called into question. (But) in a generation or so "social energy" as the author of *King Lear* will seem about as

---

[1]He writes, "The unhappy truth is that we cannot help ourselves. We can resist, up to a point... I recall one of us, doubtless with irony, telling a *New York Times* interviewer that 'We are all feminist critics.' That is the rhetoric suitable for an occupied country, one that expects no liberation from liberation."

enlightening as the surmise that the Earl of Oxford or Sir
Francis Bacon wrote the tragedy.

Frankly, I would rather accept Bacon as the author of *Lear* than
give the credit to "social energies," because Bacon at least has a
front name, a hind name and an address and I have no clear sense
of where to look, in space-time, for any "social energies" that
can use a pen to write.

Let me enlarge on that point, since many don't seem to
understand it. Applying the same standards to political *shmeer-
meisters*, I find Senator McCarthy's "list of 205 card-carrying
communists" in the State Department more meaningful than
Newt Gingrich's "about a fourth" of non-card-carrying pot-
smokers in the White House. The Baconian theory and the
alleged list of 205 may not have any verifiable truth content, but
they at least counterfeit what truth generally looks like.
Undefined and undefinable "social energies" and an unlisted and
nameless "about a fourth" sound just like the noises people make
when they don't even know how to counterfeit a meaningful
slander.

But if spooks climb, ghosts of ladders will serve them, as
Charles Fort once said. A great poet may have written,

> A rose is a rose is a rose

But a greater semanticist wrote,

> Whatever you say a thing "is," it *isn't*.

Both positions, Taylor's and Bloom's, collapse—lose their
absoluteness, become *opinions*, not matters of fact—once we ask
what function the "is" of identity serves in our judgments and
what, if anything, such an "is" means. We will explore that
further in a short while.

Meanwhile, I assure you, with a straight face, that a prominent
Feminist scholar has proven that Newton's *Philosophiea
Naturalis Principia Mathematica* consists of more rape fantasies,
just like Beethoven's music. I even assert that she called that
marvelous mathematical poem "Newton's Rape Manual." What
do you think? Does this represent another tasteless bit of
adolescent satire on my part, or does such an assertion, by a
Feminist, actually exist, in print, today?

I will answer that when I answer the similar puzzle, about ethnic cleansing at UC-Santa Cruz.

Sources:

Reinventing Shakespeare, Gary Taylor, Weidenfeld and Nicolson, New York, 1989.

The Western Canon, Harold Bloom, Harcourt Brace, New York, 1994.

TWENTY-SEVEN

BILL O'DWYER RESCUES A QUEEN

**In Which a Former Mayor of New York Rescues a
Victim of Police Harassment and Receives a Rich Reward**

> Pay no attention to that man behind the curtain!
> —*The Wizard of Oz*

> Do you believe in Justice, judge?
> —*And Then There Were None*

Those of you who can remember all the way back to *Cosmic
Trigger II: Down to Earth* will recall that I grew up in a family
in which everyone believed that the Democratic Party consisted
entirely, or almost entirely, of Irish Catholics who took care to
see that other Irish Catholics didn't get shafted by those rich
Dutch-and-English Protestants (Orangemen all) who run the
Republican party.

William ("Bill") O'Dwyer served as mayor of New York in
those Paleolithic times, and he could well serve also as the model
of that kind of Democratic politician. His administration had one
graft-and-corruption scandal after another, but he spread the
booty around—just like an Irish chieftain of pagan days, I
realized when I learned more about his, and my, genetic roots.

Bill O'Dwyer fits the "Irish politician" stereotype in so many
ways that even Richard Daley of Chicago didn't equal him, and I
only saw Bill's psychic twin when I moved to Ireland and
studied the career of Charlie Haughey (a very meaningful archetype to every reader in Ireland, and totally meaningless to all the
rest of you, alas...)

Bill finally left office under a bit of a cloud (some of the graft
seemed to track back directly to his office) but soon had an even
better job. His fellow Democrats arranged to make him U.S.
Ambassador to Mexico. Having lived in Mexico myself once, I
would like it very much if the U.S. government made me an
Ambassador and paid me a humunguous salary to stay there. It
suits me better than a poke in the eye with a sharp stick, as they
say in Dublin.

In 1956, O'Dwyer's term as ambassador had just expired, but
he lived on in Mexico D.F. (*District Federale*) practicing law —
which consisted mostly of using his connections to negotiate
Americans out of trouble, whenever they got themselves in Deep
Doodoo with the local authorities. One day a Hungarian noble-
man named Baron Louis Raynal came to see him, saying he had
previously consulted the American and English ambassadors and
they had recommended Bill as "the man who gets things done
down here."

Baron Raynal looked like a rich old Queen—exactly the type
Bill's Irish Catholic conditioning taught him to dislike—but Bill
had become cosmopolitan as he climbed the international
political-legal ladder. The Baron obviously had money: you
could see it by his expensive clothing and his genuinely
aristocratic manners.

Baron Raynal's problem? He had once attended a party given
by a rich local homosexual, who later had the bad taste to get
murdered. Now the police insisted on calling the Baron in for
questioning on a regular basis, even though he could tell they
didn't seriously suspect him. They would only let him out,
however, after he paid a suitable bribe. And the bribe only
worked for a month or so, or, lately, only for a few weeks; then
they would haul him in for questioning again. The whole business had become financially draining and emotionally harassing.

Bill understood that kind of case. He happily informed Baron
Raynal that he would settle the matter quickly, which he did.

Within a week he called the Baron and told him the *right people* had received the bribe money this time, and the police would not bother the Baron again.

Baron Raynal came to Bill's office to settle accounts. When he saw the bill—bribe money plus Bill's fee as "arranger"—he frowned and confessed that he had a small cash-flow problem that month; but before Bill could put the muscle on him, he quickly added that he had something better than money to offer. He had an original Renoir, bought by his father from Renoir himself.

Like all Irish Catholic politicians, Bill O'Dwyer secretly nursed a lacerating anxiety that some people might consider him a barbarian. A Renoir hanging in his living room would settle their hash. He agreed—but, of course, as a lawyer, he wanted the painting authenticated.

You can guess the rest, *amigo*. O'Dwyer found some **Experts** *;* the **Experts** examined the canvass, did mystic Cabalistic analysis; and **Expertly** pronounced that Renoir himself, and nobody else, had painted it.

Everybody felt happy. O'Dwyer had a real, honest-to-God Renoir hanging where every guest had to see it, Baron Raynal did not get harassed by the *Federales* any longer, and the **Experts** had again proven their necessary role if we wish to maintain civilization as we know it.

Years passed. Then came the calamity of 1968-69, when Paris art magazines, *Look* magazine in America, and soon the whole international press took up the Elmyr *scandale*.

Bill O'Dwyer no longer had a Renoir hanging over his fireplace. He had an Elmyr. And if he had stopped to think he might have noticed that Louis Raynal does not sound like a Hungarian name at all, at all. Elmyr had arrived in Mexico with a stolen Canadian passport, and in keeping with his lifestyle stuck a "Baron" before the "Louis Raynal" when introducing himself.

And Clifford Irving still believed, or pretended to believe when he wrote *Fake!*, that Elmyr de Hory (?) had a genuine Baronetcy before the Nazi invasion of Hungary. But in Orson Welles' *F For Fake,* we learn that Elmyr de Houry (?) came from the common folk, just like Bill O'Dwyer, but had achieved Top Dog social status with much less labor than poor Bill. He simply *declared* himself Noble; and in the chaos after World

War II, if he stayed out of Hungary, nobody he met knew enough about Hungarian bloodlines to contradict him...

By a similar but braver process, Joshua Abraham Norton declared himself Emperor of the United States in 1859. Later, he added Protector of Mexico and King of the Jews. He didn't go on to forge paintings, like Elmyr, but he did issue his own currency. Every dollar he printed now has a commercial value over a hundred times its face value, because any relic of Norton has become a Historical Curiosity.

Moral: Hang on to your Elmyrs, folks. They, too, may become Historical Curiosities. And remember: a counterfeit dollar, hung in a museum as found art by Andy Warhol, will have a value in the hundreds of thousands, whereas a "real" dollar, blessed by the Wizards in the Federal Reserve, will retain its meager face value until inflation reduces it even further.

And let us ask again why a Federal Reserve dollar has more initial value than a Mafia dollar printed on the same paper with the same design? Earlier I suggested one possible explanation: the Fed owns a magick wand and blesses their paper with it. I also suggested, more recently, that we might regard these magick tickets as part of either a prank or a deliberate swindle. Please write in care of my publisher if you can suggest a more plausible fourth theory.

TWENTY-EIGHT

HOW TO FAKE A FAKE

In Which the Magic of Orson Welles
Meets the Mystique of Madonna

> So back we go to these questions—
> friendship, character, ethics.
> —*Miller's Crossing*

> You are beautiful in your wrath,
> O woman of the Tartars.
> —*Genghiz Khan*

My favorite scene in *F For Fake* occurs when Elmyr explains his comparative innocence and the deep treachery of the Paris art dealers who exploited and betrayed him. "There is no crime in painting in another man's style," he says; indeed all students *begin* by painting in the styles of many Masters. Plausibly launched, Elmyr plunges ahead with confidence. "The only crime occurs when a false signature is put on the canvass. I never did that." Pause. We become aware of a clock ticking in the background.

Orson has shot this scene, uncharacteristically, in close-up. ("The only actors who worked best in close-up," he once told Bogdonovitch, "were Rin Tin Tin and Lassie.") Now, suddenly, he goes to montage, a technique he also usually avoided. As the clock ticks on, growing subtly louder (lke the bomb-tick that opens *Touch of Evil*) we see several close-ups alternating between Elmyr and Cliff Irving: Elmyr perhaps looking brazen, Clifford Irving possibly looking dubious, Elmyr probably looking inscrutable, Irving maybe looking unreadable, Elmyr seemingly looking abashed or embarrassed, Irving looking guilty (maybe?), Elmyr looking amused (I think), Irving looking sly (or cryptic?)...*and the clock ticks on* ...until Irving finally speaks.

"The paintings had signatures," he says, sounding unsure.

Quick cut to Elmyr hitting his head and looking disgusted or angry. Or betrayed?

This marvelous sequence appears *just like* one of those "moments of truth" that *cinema verité* directors seek so earnestly to capture by avoiding art, and it almost certainly represents actually another very artistic fake-within-a-fake. Welles, in fact, fills the movie with hints of what he later told BBC: "Everything in that film was fake." You repeatedly see him, Orson, sitting in the editing room with a moviola; he shows how the moviola works, taking a speech by Irving and moving it to a different sequence in the "story;" he doesn't ever let you forget for more than two or three minutes that he sits there, selecting and arranging what you will see on the screen out of raw material you usually do not see.

And in one brazen sequence, Elmyr in Ibiza stops in mid-sentence, searching for a word, and Orson, in a scene we have come to recognize as a gallery in Paris, prompts him: Elmyr *miraculously* hears Orson's word and uses it...an effect that echoes Welles' earliest experiments with wit as editing strategy (people in one scene of *Kane* who seem to reply to people in another scene, ten years earlier)

But this later bit of bilocation-by-editing (Welles in Paris prompting Elmyr in Ibiza) also blatantly reminds you of what the editing room suggests: Orson has orchestrated *everything* to create, not a "normal" documentary, but a satire on the mind-set that believes in documentaries. Just like the "war of worlds" satirized those who believe in official media versions of the news.

In the "revelation" scene (Who forged the signatures? and do we really see a self-incrimination here?) the clock's ticking, of course, convinces the naive that what we see has transpired in real time. It probably actually results from Welles' conspiracy with the sound mixer. You can create a similar "revelation" scene by taking ten or twelve close-ups from half a year of filming, putting in a sound track with a tick-tock clock, and then just using your imagination to make the opening and closing dialogue seem to refer to each other. All the close-ups in between will then appear as reactions to the two lines of dialogue which can come from a scene, or two scenes, having no real link to the spoken words.

Similarly, the Russians discovered, in the 1920s, that an actor ordered to show no emotion as he looks out a window will seem to show any emotion the director wishes, if in the editing we, the audience, see something outside the window. Do we see a dying child? The expressionless actor seems to project grief so deep it cannot find expression yet. A dog playing? The same actor with the same non-expression seems to project quiet amusement...

Another of my favorite bits in *F For Fake* uses a woman's high heels clicking down a street the same way the "signatures" sequence uses the clock's ticking. Oja Kodor, Welles' last wife-or-mistress (published reports still differ about the legality of their love) walks down the street, looking absolutely stunning in a mini-mini-skirt. Orson's voice, on the sound track, informs us that we will now observe the traditional male art of "girl watching." A montage of male faces appears, all of them (as far as I can judge after many, many viewings) registering the most noncommittal or ambiguous expressions Orson could find in Paris that week. The sound of Oja's heels, and increasingly tight close-ups on her pelvis swinging as she walks, convinces the unwary that every male face registers a reaction to that very sexy little lady. (Whose name you can pronounce as OY-a.)

I have frequently shown this sequence at my seminars and people all see a great deal of lechery, or lusty appreciation, or male chauvinism, or some erotic response in every male face. Since the heel clicks function to "sell" us this kind of response, I take Orson's "everything was a fake" rather literally here. I imagine that not one single male in that sequence ever saw Oja Kodor. They all, probably, registered such emotions or thoughts as *Two weeks to tax day and I don't have the money yet—Where in hell* did *I leave that toothbrush?—I think I'll use a line from*

Molière to open my lecture—About time to stop and have some coffee etc.

Every time I see this wonderful film, I find more room for "interpretation" (or guessing) about *how much* Orson faked, since his statement that he faked everything seems like hyperbole. (Elmyr and Irving and Ibiza, for instance, really did exist and two of them still do.) I sometimes wonder how far Orson carried his antic humor here. Swift made everything in Lilliput exactly 1/6 the size of English equivalents, with scientific care; did Orson extend the Law of Fakery even to his own magic tricks?

I mean, man, like we all know Orson had great skill as a stage magician (I saw him work once, and know his superb craftsmanship from more than hearsay) and had a membership in the Magic Castle (which admits professional magicians only), but...in a fake movie about a fake biography of a fake painter, why not fake the magic, too? Did Orson perhaps do every stage magic trick in the film without any real stage magic (his own hands and props), just using camera magic (editing)? Would he stoop to *faking* his own magic in the interest of artistic unity?

At the end of the film, Orson "confesses" that it contains seventeen minutes of fakery; but that seventeen minutes, once recognized as fiction, throws varying degrees of doubt on many other scenes which depend to some extent on the fictional segment passing as truth.

In short, like all truly post-modernist art, *F For Fake* forces you to think like a fuzzy logician, or at least a non-Aristotelian. "Everything" in the movie, contrary to Welles' BBC interview, does not rank as fakery; you can actually find Oja Kodor, although you won't find her "Hungarian grandfather." But many segments logically connected to the seventeen minutes of admitted fakery remain in enigmatic suspended judgment. We cannot say "yes" or "no" to this film but must consider most of it in the "maybe" state where von Neumann and Finkelstein (among others) locate quantum systems. (Many pivotal scenes in Welles' earlier, less experimental films also have this "maybe" quality, if you look at them more than once.)

I accept that Elmyr existed and faked a lot of paintings, and that Welles, Irving, *LOOK* magazine *et. al.* did not invent this pixie-ish fellow.

I do not accept Oja Kodor as Hungarian or "very rich," as the film claims. I tend to suspect she comes from Yugoslavia (as various journalists claim) and does not yet have as much money as the film implies. (Otherwise Orson would have directed a lot more movies...)

I think Welles deliberately exaggerates the extent to which all of our museums have Elmyrs hanging in their modern art wing; but I do not dare to guess *how much* Welles exaggerates. Every Picasso now exists for me in a "maybe" state—maybe Picasso, maybe Elmyr.

I feel entirely unable to even assign a probability figure to some of the Howard Hughes stories in the film, especially Hughes' alleged use of Kleenex boxes as shoes, and the tree with the ham sandwich hidden in it...

And so on. I love this film because it forces the viewers to think as I believe we must all learn to think in this post-quantum age: not in Aristotelian either/ors, but in probabilities.

And, curiously, I only know one film that follows Welles' lead in this discovery of how to make post-modern "documentary" cinema—Madonna's *Truth or Dare* .

And, even more curiously, in all the controversy about that off-kilter and amusing film, only one critic I have found—E. Diedre Pribram, in her sly "Seduction, Control and the Search for Authenticity: Madonna's *Truth or Dare"*—recognizes that every scene in that alleged "documentary" about one of Madonna's concert tours deliberately provokes the same uncertainties that Welles always took as his *métier*. (And even Pribram doesn't mention *F For Fake* as a model for the strategies of Madonna's film.) Every other critic I have read, without exception, believed—like the mass audience for the "war of worlds" in 1938—that something that looks or sounds "documentary" must literally reflect some unrehearsed "moment of truth."

("If it looks like a duck, and walks like a duck, and quacks like a duck, I say it *is* a duck."—Senator Joe McCarthy.)

And yet Madonna's videos, where she has as much control as in *Truth or Dare*, all exploit ambiguity and never seem the same to any two viewers. Only in her studio films (where others have final cut) does a Madonna emerge almost as simple (and simple-minded) as the Madonna of the mass media; just as only in Orson's one studio film, *The Stranger,* do you find a simple-minded "hero," a simple-minded "villain" and a simple-minded script.

In *Truth or Dare* you see Madonna at her mother's grave and get a "moment of truth" starkly revealing the extent to which the shock of the mother's death still dominates the actress. Considering the lighting of that scene and Madonna's proven acting ability (in her videos more than her Hollywood films), do we *dare* accept that "moment of *truth*" at face value, or do we suspect shtick? Who edited this film anyway?

(Madonna acted as producer and co-editor...)

Later we see an encounter with Kevin Costner, who seems a remarkably intelligent and sensitive actor to most of us. Here he appears surprisingly shallow, and Madonna appears even cruder and ruder than her media image. Marvelous—two actors boldly avoid acting and show us the "truth." Does anybody but a San Jose newspaper critic believe this at face value, without some doubt? Even if Joyce and Welles had never lived, could any reader of Swift take the Madonna/Costner scene as a "revelation" and not wonder about it a little bit?

How many times do *you* think Kevin and Madonna might have rehearsed this scene before shooting?

What about Madonna's sexual confessions in this film? She once declared herself a Lesbian (on the Letterman show), then later "confessed" that she had made up the Lesbian yarn as a joke. Which confession do we believe?

I do not, in the least, insist that any given scene in *Truth or Dare* results from Wellesian trickery; I merely indicate that, as Pribram notes, with an artist whose *ouvre* frequently seems intended to puzzle and provoke, it seems hasty and unsophisticated to assume that the "documentary" parts of the film emerged out of less irony and ambiguity than the "staged" song and dance numbers, which all parody conditioned gender-and-caste rules. Whether we like it or not, many of our pop artists today play post-modernist games with their audiences.

Another film comes to mind in this connection. Directed by actress Louise Lasser (best known as TV's "Mary Hartman") this movie appeared on *Saturday Night Live* only once, I think. At least I only saw this short short once, about twenty years ago, so I don't remember the title.

In Lasser's little jest, a half dozen actors sit in a luncheonette making small talk. Nothing happens; nothing interesting gets said. One notices only the director's scrupulous adherence to the rules of Method Acting and *cinema verite:* a "chunk of life" and nothing more seems to unfold. Then an actor blows his (or her) lines. Lasser enters, as the director, of course, and suggests that everybody take a break and try again.

During the break, the actors and director talk, and we become aware of professional and sexual elements in their relationships. Then another actor blows her (or his) lines and somebody else— the "real" director—enters and suggests they take a break and try again. We realize that this "real" sequence had as much scripted acting as the previous sequence, which also seemed "real" until a line got muffed...

Another conversation just barely begins, and the movie fades to black. The end.

I think that if you continued Lasser's structure four or five steps further, you would approximate the Buddhist concept of Awakening.

References:

F For Fake, op cit.

The Madonna Connection, edited by Cathy Schwichtenberg, Boulder, CO, 1993—for Pribram's "Seduction, Control and the Search for Authenticity: Madonna's *Truth or Dare.*"

TWENTY-NINE

THE WARRIOR LORD

In Which We Learn Terrible Secrets of the PATRIARCHY and See the Priory of Sion in a Sinister New Light

> No, I don't think I'll ever get over Macho Grande.
> —*Airplane II: The Sequel*

> O Dragon-God, we bring men for Wanga.
> —*Wild Women of Wanga*

Another book revealing the "real" inner secrets of the Priory of Sion has come my way. Some of you will probably feel relieved to learn that it doesn't involve a hollow Earth, the wife and son of Jesus, or those rambunctious E-T's from Sirius. It merely explains that the Priory acts as the Brain or Power Elite of the dreaded, blood-splattered, terrifying, cosmically evil PATRIARCHY depicted in Radical Feminist mythology.

Inside the "Men's Club:" Secrets of the Patriarchy by Hawthorne Abendsen traces the Priory back to the first all-male secret societies of the first Stone Age tribes. (Some students of occultism want to trace Freemasonry that far back, too...) According to Abendsen, at the beginning of the Bronze Age, when both war and trade shook up many remotely deployed societies and brought them into frequent contact, these magick brotherhoods began to amalgamate, and today they have all joined together into the Priory of Sion.

The basic "secrets" of the Priory—the mystical doctrines underlying THE PATRIARCHY— Abendsen claims, have nothing to do with that Head of Satan on the Coat of Arms of Steny, or the frogs falling out of the sky there, or the accursed Magdelene church in Rennes-le-Chatteau, or any of the data we have already heard. Every bit of that represents counterfeit or, as the English say, red herrings—to hide the real truth.

The real truth, Abendsen tells us, consists chiefly of two long-guarded secrets:

1. The Priory identifies the True God of Judaism, Christianity and Islam as the God who appeared to Abraham and gave his name as *Al-Shaddai,* "the Lord of Battles." In other words, the Priory serves a divinity cognate with the Roman Mars, the Egyptian Ra-Hoor-Khuit, the Greek Ares, the Teutonic Wotan— a god of war and bloodshed, pure and simple.

Worship of this god consists of making war (what does a war god most desire?) and of various grisly human and animal sacrifices of the type Protestant Fundamentalists and *MS.* magazine have attributed to a Satanic conspiracy. Satanists actually have nothing to do with it, according to Abendsen: holy war and ritual bloodshed represent the earliest and truest form of the Judeo-Christian-Islamic faith. Later, more humane images of divinity—i.e., the "god of love"—represent conscious fraud, intended to keep the majority from knowing the true purpose and meaning of what our rulers do.

Of course, Bob Shea and I suggested a very similar theory in *Illuminatus!* , but that book, like the travels of Mr. Gulliver, did not mean exactly what it said; in fact, it meant to satirize various quasi-paranoid movements by taking some of their rhetoric literally. Abendsen does not appear to have a satirical bone in his (or her?) body, or even her (or his) head. He/she means what she/he writes, and means it literally—or so I believe. (But then maybe, like some of the first readers of Swift's fabulous voyager, I don't always recognize a jester when I read one…?)

2. A central part of the cult of *Al Shaddai,* god of war, consists of homosexual rituals, affirming male bonding and maintaining the magick subjugation of women as second-class citizens.

Sort of sounds like the *Protocols of the Priory of Sion,* doesn't it?[1]

I must admit that Abendsen (whose first name does not clearly reveal gender: hence my weird pronouns) has made a more concrete image of THE PATRIARCHY than most Feminist writers. The usual fanatic denunciations of THE PATRIARCHY, especially from jargonized academic sources, fail utterly to give us front names, hind names or addresses of any of the major culprits, and hence sound like smoke and flashing lights, not substance. Usually, THE PATRIARCHY in most left-academic writing resembles Gingrich's "about a fourth" (of alleged dopers in the Clinton administration, accused by an anonymous and therefore uncheckable "intelligence officer") more than it resembles the professionally wrought paranoia of a true artist like Joe McCarthy with his clear and definitive "205 card-carrying Communists" (in the Truman administration) which meant something specific, even if Senator Joe never proved it.

Abendsen, in other words, has thrown up a rope of speculation and hauled down the androphobia of Radical Feminist theory from the realm of airy academic abstraction (the realm logical positivists long ago rejected as meaningless) and now places it in a concrete and meaningful context here on Earth. Just like Hitler, who took the vague anti-Semitism that had infected Europe for centuries and pinned it down to the *Protocols'* specific theory of high crimes committed by specific bankers, allegedly Jewish, Abendsen ties THE PATRIARCHY down to a specific occult order. If the Abendsen theory catches on, Rush Limbaugh's insulting term "Feminazis" will have a lot more truth in it: instead of Hitler's Jewish conspiracy to exploit Aryans, we now

---

[1]*The Protocols of the Elders of Zion*, a forgery long discredited by historians, depicts a similar conspiracy behind all wars. In that case, 13 Rabbis start the wars to get nations into debt and thereby increase the profits of the International Banks they allegedly control. No matter how often this Granddaddy of kook literature gets refuted by scholars, it continues to circulate. I have over the years received three or four copies of it from people wishing to enlighten me about what they consider the One Real Conspiracy Behind Everything. (On the other hand, according to the Church of the Sub-Genius, the One Real Conspiracy consists of a sinister alliance of extra-terrestrial cattle-mutilators and *Interstellar* Bankers...)

have a Jewish-Christian-Islamic-male conspiracy to exploit
everybody else, but especially to exploit women.

I don't think this charmingly literal Feminist myth will catch
on, because of Abendsen's point two (the homosexual rituals of
the Priory) which will annoy Gay men—and I use the word
"annoy" as ironic understatement. The Rad/Fem crowd have an
alliance with Gay Lib and will not endorse a book that makes it
sound as if all wars and serial killings derive from a homo-
conspiratorial early Old Testament cult. Now, if Abendsen had
said a *hetero*-conspiratorial Old Testament cult, the book could
easily become the Bible of Radical Feminism...

Abendsen's evidence does not require much discussion; the
book has virtually none, and what it does have proves very little;
it does not support its major thesis at all. It appeals only to those
who have never discovered the important differences between
assertion and demonstration.

But now we have the Priory of Sion linked, by various sources
(1) to important persons bridging the French art world and the
French aristocracy (Malraux, Cocteau...), (2) to hollow Earth
theories, (3) to extra-terrestrial invasions, (4) to P2 and Mafia/
CIA drug operations, (5) to vampires and the precognitive talents
of Jules Verne, and (6) to the dreaded PATRIARCHY (which
seems as real to Radical Feminists as the Thesis, Antithesis and
Synthesis seem to Marxists, or Transubstantiation to Catholics.)
Somebody or some group has gone to a lot of trouble to create
this group art-work, if we still want to call it that.

And if we do not want to call the Priory "a group art-work,"
what in the name of all the pot-bellied gods of Burma shall we
call it?

Well, while we ponder that pretty puzzle, let me note that the
"human and animal sacrifices" which Abendsen attributes to the
Al Shaddai cult (and *MS.* and the Fundamentalists attribute to a
Satanic cult) have firmly entered modern American mythology.
Sociologist Jeffrey Victor has chronicled 33 "rumor panics" of
substantial size in the past decade, all dealing with alleged cults
allegedly engaged in human and animal sacrifices.

A typical case: the McMartin hysteria in Manhattan Beach,
California, 1983-1990. Over 100 teachers and one clergyman,
accused of Satanic sacrifices, child molestation and running a
pornography ring, all suffered mob hostility, loss of reputation,

police investigation, harassment etc. and most of them lost their jobs. (All this before any of them got convicted of anything, or even stood trial, or even got arrested.)

The police investigated extensively and finally arrested seven of the over-a-hundred accused—i.e., even before going to trial, 93 per cent of the accusations seemed mere hysteria to professional investigators.

The D.A. brought only two of the five arrested persons to trial, finding the evidence too weak in the other five cases. 98 per cent of the accusations now seemed unsound. The two remaining suspects stood trial. The juries refused to convict. Some of the accused have since collected over a quarter of a million in libel suits against the accusers. (For further details, see my *Chaos and Beyond,* Permanent Press, San Jose, 1994.)

The other Satanic panics have the same structure: wild charges against large numbers of people, not enough evidence to convict anyone. The FBI Behavioral Science Unit (remember them from *The Silence of the Lambs*?) has investigated extensively and dug into dozens of alleged "mass graves" without finding a single body, or even a big toe.

Despite this lack of evidence, similar panics continue to erupt periodically, and now have started in England also. Abendsen has not drilled in a dry hole, obviously. Such horrid "rituals" may not happen in the sensory-sensual world of ordinary space-time, where police officers must work, but they occupy a secure place, now, in the imagination and the nightmares of millions, i.e., in our collective psychic space.

MS. has endorsed the witch hunt and two Santa Cruz writers, Ellen Bass and Laura Davis, continually incite the anxieties of the gullible, and regularly *use the word "accused" exactly as Joe McCarthy used it*—as if it means the same as "arrested, prosecuted by a professional, defended by another professional, judged by a professional, and convicted by a jury that heard all the evidence."

If Ms. or Mt. Abendsen had only left out the homophobia, she/he might have the new *Mein Kampf*, which could unite Radical Feminists and all the other nut groups in the country into a unified witch-hunt against THE PATRIARCHY and its evil minions...

But they would still argue, I suppose, about whether the God of this monstrous cult has the name "Al Shaddai" or "Satan."

One further point seems worthy of note:

Since almost all (about 90%) of the wealth of this country belongs to 60 families, and most of those families have female rulers or partners—the men dying off of heart attacks seven years earlier than the women (on average) and leaving the stocks, bonds and other goodies to their wives—THE PATRIARCHY does not seem like a very accurate term to me, especially since it implies that *all* men, including the lowest-paid workers and the homeless wretches begging on the streets, share equally in the economic clout. No: the correct, traditional term used in political science for societies in which a small minority of rich families makes all the decisions, *Oligarchy*, fits our situation much better. In fact, it fits all post-tribal societies I know anything about, including the allegedly "communist" nations. *Patriarchy, a theoretical form of society in which* all *fathers have equal power—"one bloody man, one bloody vote"—has never existed anywhere.*

Oh, incidentally, the letter from UC-Santa Cruz demanding ethnic qualifications for a teaching job—I found that in *U.S. News and World Report*, December 1994, which vouches for its authenticity.

The claim that Newton's system of mathematical physics represents a rape fantasy derives from Sandra Harding, an embattled Delaware foe of the fearful and loathsome PATRIARCHY. I saw it quoted in Christine Sommers' *Who Stole Feminism?* and in the same *U.S. News* cited above.

Neither of these notions seem to have any satiric intent, anymore than the Nazi decision to ban Relativity as "Jewish science" represented an unexpected sense of humor in Hitler. As I said in *Cosmic Trigger II: Down to Earth,* when describing a trip I made through East Germany before the Wall came down, totalitarianism always looks like a parody of itself.

Reference:

Inside the "Men's Club": Secrets of the Patriarchy, by Hawthorne Abendsen, A-Albionic Research, Ferndale, MI, 1989.

THIRTY

THE ASTRONOMER WHO ABOLISHED GRAVITY

> The normal is what everybody else is and you're not.
> —*Star Trek: Generations*

> My mind is going. I can feel it, Dave.
> —*2001: A Space Odyssey*

If anybody possesses all the qualifications necessary for a fully ordained Expert in America today, Carl Sagan certainly has that dizzying eminence. Through frequent appearances on TV and in *Parade* (a news magazine circulated through hundreds of newspapers in their jumbo Sunday editions), Dr. Sagan has issued Expert verdicts on every possible controversial issue in science, and in politics, and even in theology, for three decades now. And, like the Experts who authenticated hundreds-to-thousands of Elmyrs, he has never once admitted he ever made a mistake.

You may wonder how a man who only has qualifications in astronomy can also function as an **Expert** on everything in general. Well, I think it requires that Sagan have a lot of raw courage, in the first place, and a strong, well-founded confidence that those who don't believe his dogmas have much less access to the media than he does; if they answer him back, however effective their arguments, very few of his large, gullible audience will ever hear about it.

Let us see how **Expert**ese works, by examining Dr. Sagan's long series of polemics against Dr. Immanuel Velikovsky.

First of all, in every page Sagan has written about Velikovsky, he only once calls him "Dr. Velikovsky" as I just did. Thus, most people who know Velikovsky only through Sagan's attacks have never learned that Velikovsky had scientific training. [1] The contest thus seems a struggle between "Dr." Sagan, the learned scientist, and "Mr." Velikovsky, the ignorant layman. Little tricks like that go a long way in deluding the naive, and Sagan never fails to use every dirty trick he knows.

In what follows, I reverse this process, just for the hell of it. Sagan I will call Sagan and Dr. Velikovsky I will call Dr. Velikovsky. Sauce for the goose can serve, after all, as sauce for the gander.

Sagan continually states bluntly, and falsely, that Dr. Velikovsky intends his cosmic catastrophe theory to revive the old-time religion: "It is an attempted validation of religion..." "Velikovsky attempts to rescue not only religion but also astrology." (*Broca's Brain*, p 126) We can only conclude that Sagan either reads very carelessly or engages in deliberate lying. Any close reading of Dr. Velikovsky shows numerous expressions of skepticism about both religion and astrology.

In addition, Dr. Velikovsky's theory of cometary near-collisions offers a naturalistic, scientific explanation for many events or alleged events in ancient history, which the religious prefer to explain supernaturally, as miracles. Nobody who suggests a *natural* explanation for allegedly *supernatural* events offers real support to religion, in either the judgment of the religious themselves or of those of us with agnostic disposition.

Only Sagan—and a few others, who seem to never have read Dr. Velikovsky and obtained their "knowledge" about his works from Sagan—think of the comet model as "validating" religion,

---

[1]Velikovsky studied ancient history at Moscow University before acquiring an M.D. there. Later he studied psychoanalysis with Freud in Vienna and edited an international scholarly journal of Jewish studies to which Einstein contributed. (Einstein also became a lifelong friend and continually opposed those, like Sagan, who tried to slander Dr. Velikovsky without actually examining the evidence for his later, controversial comet theory.)

since Dr. Velikovsky uses a hypothetical comet to replace a hypothetical god in explaining huge reported floods, and other catastrophes. Most of us think of Dr. Velikovsky's theory as one which, if proven, would knock one more leg from under the edifice of Bible Fundamentalism. Nobody seems likely to worship Dr. Velikovsky's comet, but millions still worship the Bible's god.

In the 30 years or more that Sagan has engaged in diatribes against Dr. Velikovsky, somebody must have pointed out this fundamental confusion to him—mis-identifying a naturalistic theory with a supernatural theory. Evidently, he has a lot of trouble hearing or remembering such corrections. You become a leading **Expert** by acting as if everybody else's opinion deserves no attention and never even deserves the courtesy of an answer.

For instance, to leave Dr. Velikovsky for a moment, consider Sagan's hilarious theory of "nuclear winter."[1] Briefly, Sagan's theory holds that nuclear war could result, not just in the horrors we all know, but in a freeze that would probably abolish all life on this planet. (He published this notion in *Parade*, where his mass audience could see it and gasp.) His refusal to accept valid criticisms of this sci-fi story led to the following summary in *Science*, official journal of the American Association for the Advancement of Science, "News and Comments" section, Jan 16, 1987:

> Sagan's refusal to acknowledge merit in the NCAR [National Center for Atmospheric Research]'s analysis—known as "nuclear autumn"—sends some people up the wall. One wall-climber is George Rathjens, professor of political science at M.I.T..." (Sagan's) claim that the original nuclear winter model is unimpeached [he says]...is the greatest fraud we've seen in a long time"... Russell Seiz, a fellow at the Harvard Center for International Affairs...gibes at [Sagan and his co-authors] for mixing physics and advertising.

---

[1] "Hilarious" represents my own subjective judgment, of course. But I really doubt that anybody can read Sagan's woolly theorizing on the subject, then read the scientific rebuttals, then read Sagan's blithe reiterations of his theory (all written as if he had never heard of the rebuttals) without laughing out loud or at least snickering. As I said, Sagan knows that he has a bigger audience than any of his critics, so he can afford to bluff. Cf. Elmyr on **Experts**.

Most scientists I have spoken to about Sagan share this dim view of his use of publicity to represent his pet notions as Scientific Truth even when—or *especially* when—a large segment of the scientific community has severe doubts about these notions.

(Similarly, in *Broca's Brain*, Sagan rejects data on so-called "out of body experiences" among near-dead patients because, he says, nobody in that state has reported anything they couldn't have heard while unconscious. But the literature of OOBE has hundreds of cases of such reports, including numerous incidents in which the subjects reported things in rooms far away from the operating room. Once again, we can only wonder if Sagan habitually lies through his teeth or just doesn't read any of the literature on the subjects upon which he claims **Expert**ese.)

But returning to Dr. Velikovsky, and Sagan's crusade against his ideas:

Sagan likes to quote a "distinguished professor of Semitics" who told him no Semitic scholars take Dr. Velikovsky seriously. Like the "intelligence officer" who told Newt Gingrich about dope in the White House, this "distinguished professor" remains anonymous, and thus Sagan's hearsay about him would get thrown out of any civilized court. Three distinguished professors of Semitic studies, however, have all shown cordial support for Dr. Velikovsky: Prof. Claude F.A. Schaeffer, Prof. Etienne Droiton, and Prof. Robert Pfeiffer. Look them up in any Who's Who of Semitic studies, archeology and Egyptology. They have a lot more prestige in those fields than Sagan's Prof. Anonymous, who doesn't have a single entry under his name anywhere in the scholarly journals (although elsewhere he receives credit for many olde ballads and almost all bawdy limericks.)

Another choice bit of Sagan's **Expert** testimony: he accuses Dr. Velikovsky of believing that ancient cultures had a calendar of ten months of thirty days each and 360 days in the year. Of course, 10 x 30 = 300, and this gives Sagan a chance to gibe at Dr. Velikovsky's inability to handle simple arithmetic. Very good, wouldn't you say? The only trouble with this brilliant analysis consists of the simple fact that, once again, Sagan has either consciously and deliberately lied or accidentally revealed again that he doesn't read carefully. Dr. Velikovsky says specifically "the month was equal to thirty-six days" (*Worlds in Collision*, p. 344.) 10 months of 36 days each = 360. See?

According to Dr. Velikovsky's model, the year changed to 365 days (plus a few hours) after the cometary near-collision. Whether he has proven that or not, he did not make a crude mistake in arithmetic. Sagan either made a crude mistake in reading, or followed Elmyr's formula for **Expert**-ness: "sheer bluff."

Consider next the high temperature of Venus (480° C.) As Dr. Roger Wescott and others have pointed out, Dr. Velikovsky predicted a temperature in this range for Venus when astronomical orthodoxy believed that planet much, much colder. Sagan tries to avoid giving Dr. Velikovsky credit for this confirmation of his model by claiming "many" had predicted a high temperature before the Venus flyby. Actually, he only names *one* other who had made such a prediction, Dr. Rupert Wildt, and Wildt's work did not win general acceptance. (Others try to get around Dr. Velikovsky's correct estimate in this and other instances by describing him as a "lucky guesser." That seems mere cage-rattling to me. One could as well call any scientist who made many correct predictions a "lucky guesser"...)

As Harry H. Hess, president of the American Geological Society wrote in a published letter to Dr. Velikovsky:

> Some of these predictions were said to be impossible when you made them. All of them were made before proof that they were correct came to hand. Conversely, I do not know of any prediction you made that has since been proven to be false.

But the final joker came on page 153 of *Broca's Brain* where Sagan writes (and this really deserves caps):

ONE NOW FASHIONABLE SUGGESTION *I FIRST PROPOSED IN 1960* IS THAT THE HIGH TEMPERATURES ON THE SURFACE OF VENUS ARE DUE TO A RUNAWAY GREENHOUSE EFFECT.

(all emphasis added, and deserved)

First, Sagan claims that Dr. Velikovsky does not deserve credit for predicting high temperatures on Venus because everybody knew it, although historical fact shows that *only* Dr. Wildt had made the same prediction before Dr. Velikovsky. Then Sagan either tells a double lie or else suffers an alarming memory lapse that may require neurological consultation, claiming that neither Dr. Wildt nor Dr. Velikovsky had made this prediction (which they had, and he had noted earlier)—and then he brazenly claims he had originated it himself. Quite a performance, wouldn't you say?

Now do you know how to become an **Expert**? Keep a straight face and make sure the mass media gives you more coverage than it gives those who try to correct your mis-statements.

I could go on and on, for hundreds of pages, but instead I eagerly refer you to Charles Ginenthal's book, *Carl Sagan and Immanuel Velikovsky*. (Synchronistically, it is published by New Falcon Publications, 1995; when I wrote this chapter *I did not know Falcon was publishing Ginenthal's book*; nor did *they* know I had read it and was writing this chapter. Really!) Ginenthal does spend hundreds of pages documenting one fallacy after another—literally dozens and dozens of them—in Sagan's smear campaign against Dr. Velikovsky. I will conclude only with the most dramatic, and funniest, of Sagan's goofs:

In several places, Sagan has published a mathematical proof that several near collisions between a comet and a planet have odds against them of "a trillion quadrillion to one."

$$(1,000,000,000,000,000,000,000,000,000 \text{ to } 1.)$$

Sounds pretty damned improbable, doesn't it?

The problem here lies in the fact that Sagan considers each near-collision as an isolated or haphazard event, thereby ignoring gravity. In fact, any two celestial bodies, once attracted to each other, *will tend to continue to approach each other periodically*, according to Newtonian laws unmodified by Einstein. This periodicity will continue until some other gravitational force pulls one of the bodies away from the gravitational attraction of the other. Ask any physics or astronomy professor about this, if you think I'm pushing too hard here. As Dr. Robert Jastrow of NASA's Goddard Institute of Space Studies wrote (*New York Times* 22 Dec 1979),

> Professor Sagan's calculations, in effect, ignore the law of gravity. Here, Dr. Velikovsky was the better astronomer.

Robert Bass wrote, even more harshly,

> This Sagan assumption [ignoring gravity] is so disingenuous
> that I do not hesitate to label it a deliberate fraud on the public
> or else a manifestation of unbelievable incompetence or
> hastiness combined with desperation. [cited by Ginenthal]

Well, I always had doubts about Sagan's ability to pronounce
verdicts outside astronomy. When he does calculations *inside*
astronomy and then ignores or forgets gravity, I begin to wonder
about his competence in general. Perhaps the misfortunate man
needs a guide or keeper, to lead him about and ensure that he
doesn't bump into buildings.

As far as I can see, Sagan's greatest area of ability lies in one
truly well-proven and absolutely undeniable talent—for getting
himself promoted in the mass media as an authority on everything in general, even though he seems to have no competence at
anything in particular.

Sagan serves on the Board of Directors of the *Committee for
Scientific Investigation of Claims of the Paranormal* (*CSICOP*),
the neo-Platonist cult mentioned earlier, who believe that the
"normal" not only exist somewhere but that it exists everywhere.
Guess what? They have in their whole career performed only *one*
scientific investigation, which resulted in the statistician quitting,
claiming they had changed his figures to suit their prejudices.
That happened in 1982 and they prudently haven't attempted
another scientific investigation since then. They still use
"Scientific Investigation" in their title, however. Would you call
that "hastiness," "desperation," "incompetence" or—deliberate
fraud?

References:

Carl Sagan and Immanuel Velikovsky, by Charles Ginenthal,
    New Falcon Publications, Tempe, AZ 1995.
"Starbaby" by Dennis Rawlins, *FATE*, October 1981—on the
    statistical study that led CSICOP to abandon scientific
    investigation. Told by the statistician (Rawlins).

THIRTY-ONE

THE ONLY TRUE
TRUE RELIGION

In Which We Examine the Claim That Some Dogmas
Should Never Suffer Critical Re-Examination

> Nothing is true, all is permitted, nothing
> is true, all is permitted, nothing is true,
> all is permitted, nothing is true...
> —*The Adventures of Omar Khayyam*

> You can't wait to shove that thing
> up your ass, can you?
> —*The Road to Wellville*

Several chapters back, you may remember, we mentioned
*Higher Superstition: The Academic Left and its Quarrel With
Science* by Gross and Levitt. This book claims for current mainstream science what only religious zealots have previously
claimed for their faiths, namely that in a certain *correlation of
formulas* (ideas contain no more than that) humans have created
a True Picture of Reality (*All* Reality) which we should adore in
humility and never dare to doubt or to question. As regular
readers of my works know, I refer to that kind of faith, whether
in religion or science (or philosophy...) as Idolatry, because it

asks us to worship *a representation of the experiential world*, and I do not think representations or maps (or masks) make satisfactory objects of worship.

However, the position of my books, and of post-modernism in general, which regards all representations, or maps, or models, as probabilistic and relative to their social context, Gross and Levitt dismissively call "perspectivism" (a good word in my estimation, so I cheerfully accept it). Gross and Levitt see *perspectivism* as an insidious threat to their One True Faith and a pathway downward to the bottomless abyss of nihilism.

My way of understanding the relationship of absolutism to "perspectivism" I learned many years ago from psychologist O.R. Bontrager, Ph.D. Every student in the class had to make a certain kind of drawing (even those who claimed they didn't have any artistic talent). Each drawing showed the classroom *as it looked from that student's position* in the room, so naturally each looked a *little* different from those drawn by students close to it and *vastly* different from those drawn further away. Taken together the drawings gave us approximately 40 different views of the same room, all "true" in one of the usual meanings of the word "true"—"true" to experience, or "true" to perception.

This represents the kind of insidious "perspectivism" you will find in all my novels (and in the works of my great teachers, Mr. J. Joyce and Mr. O. Welles.)

Then Dr. Bontrager would have us all make a drawing of the room as shown in an architect's blueprint, i.e., an abstraction of the view looking directly down from the ceiling. These, of course, all looked very much alike—*almost* exactly alike (i.e., as close to absolutism as most scientific work ever gets.)

Many very interesting points emerge from this exercise, and I leave it to the reader's contemplation (or, better, to experiments with friends) to find them. Here I only want to stress one point. Gross and Levitt believe the current scientific model (i.e., the most popular one...) stands above all other perspectives, in the way one might claim the architects' view "stands above" the other drawings of the room. I hold to the contrary that *we must at least partially remember, at all times, that the "absolute" or architect's blueprint has its own kind of relativity, its own "perspectivism," or else we risk going totally mad.*

For instance, if you try to believe in the "absolute" view and ignore your own situation in the perspectivist world, you will at least start bumping into things, falling over things, banging your nose against walls, maybe breaking legs or hurting yourself seriously, etc. and at worst start to believe you have achieved "astral projection" when you have merely entered into a kind of self-hypnosis. (From the point of view of Finnegan's 'patapsychology, *each perspective represents another 'patanormal event*—"an event, unique and non-replicable, but encountered and endured"—in the infinite 'patanormal' continuum of experience. The "absolutist" blueprint represents *the abstract or so-called "normal" view invented by the logical-mathematical mind*, which has many uses but never occurs in actual human experience. [1])

In other words, the blueprint view has many functions, but they all relate to abstract and technological purposes (in this case, architectural purposes.) You in your daily life remain in the "perspectivist" position, and if you want to shift to the absolutist or blueprint position you must remember the *purpose* of doing this—e.g., solving a real problem in architecture, or just getting the thrill of a novel view of the room. If you forget the purpose, and think the absolutist view has *all* the truth and the *only* truth, you have mistaken the map for the territory. When I call this "crazy," I do not think I exaggerate. The only form of Idolatry (symbol-worship) loonier than this which I can imagine would occur if you ate the menu instead of eating the meal.

Worse yet, scientific models, like people and cattle and insect species and mountains and all things known, have a lifespan. Mountains may survive geological eras, but scientific maps, like people and birds, have short lives. None has ever lasted more than a few hundred years, at present. To believe in any such mask with the fervor of Gross and Levitt contradicts all known facts of scientific history. Every theory they worship will someday get junked.

---

[1]Even if you tied yourself to the ceiling with ropes and looked down, you would not see what the architecturally correct blueprint shows. You would see some degree of perspective (three dimensionality), and the perspective would vary depending on what part of the ceiling you looked down from. If the whole class tied themselves to the ceiling, their drawings would have as many different perspectives as the drawings made from ground level.

But even in their robust age of maximum utility, before senility sets in, scientific theories only refer to the current scientific masque, or paradigm—the reality-tunnel of a few technicians among us.

For instance, the chair in which you sit reading this—or perhaps the floor you stand on, to avoid any nit-picking here—consists mostly of *empty space* in the modern quantum view. In this almost total void a lot of little thingamajigs [1] bounce around constantly in unpredictable patterns. They move so fast, in fact, that you, and every other human, and every critter with an opinion, perceive the chair or the floor as *solid.* The scientific view, or absolute view (of emptiness with sparkles) has more usefulness in science than your ordinary view, but it remains relative to such scientific uses. If you imagine that this scientific model (or this "mask," in my current jargon) contains "all" truth and the "only" truth, you can try banging your head into this empty space for a half hour or so. You will eventually get a headache and learn that in the relative world of our senses, things still behave as the perceived *solids* we imagined before we learned the scientific model portraying the universe and all "things" in it as 99 per cent emptiness with one percent jumping quantum gizmos buzzing around.

In short, scientific models have wonderful uses in science—*they work,* as Gross and Levitt exclaim with the ardor of all missionaries explaining Truth to the ignorant heathen—but they only have these uses, and they only *work,* in that special context. *In ordinary contexts, your subjective perspective has more to tell you about how to avoid bumps, headaches, sudden shocks, falls, charges of sexual harassment and broken arms.*

Scientific maps (or masks) function as useful perspectives for one class of humans: workers in science—but other perspectives function just as usefully for other classes of humans, working in

---

[1] These thingamajigs act like waves part of the time and like particles part of the time. This basic paradox has remained all through the 94 years of development of quantum mechanics and gives great comfort to those of us who believe no one model or perspective ever shows *all* the truth or the *only* truth about anything. For further details see my book, *Quantum Psychology*, New Falcon Publications, 1990.

other fields[1]. The absolutist One True Faith came out of the Dark Ages and should get sent back there. *We live with varying perspectives, especially if we have to deal with people of varying cultures.*

For example, Gross and Levitt have the kind of "mental imperialism," as John Michel once called it, which just can't resist ridiculing all non-Western cultures and their non-Western sciences. They dismiss all alternative healing, especially from the Orient, with a hoity-toity arrogance only equaled by Christian theologians writing about Oriental religions; and this seems especially narrow and provincial in 1995, since the American Medical Association, once a hotbed of that kind of prejudice, has grown increasingly open-minded in the past 20 years and prints more and more studies in their *Journal* in which researchers investigate alternative therapies scientifically, instead of just dismissing them with racist jokes like Gross and Levitt. (The A.M.A. has even printed studies in which alternative medical theories *seem to work* (!), although of course this research requires replication before it will become generally accepted.)

Gross and Levitt also show the mental imperialist slant in their use of Oriental titles to mock scientists whose theories they don't like, calling Dr. Rupert Sheldrake, for instance, a "guru or shaman", as if those honorable Third World titles made him a clownish figure, beneath contempt. (In fact non-Western cultures do not recognize one as a guru or shaman without as much training and study as a scientist undergoes in our culture.) This kind of arrogance and prejudice appears especially pathetic to me when I remember that the only three scientific tests of Dr. Sheldrake's morphic resonance theory published so far all support Sheldrake.[2] I might even write that these experiments have "proven" Sheldrake's model, except that I know that it

---

[1]For instance, the scientific view of the sun as a molten rock worked for 18th Century science, but Blake's contrary view of the sun as a band of angels singing "Hosanah to God in the Highest" worked for him as a poet. (Note also that the scientific view never remains constant. Modern astronomers do not regard the sun as a hot rock but more as a nuclear furnace.)

[2]For a brief summary of these three experiments, see my book *The New Inquisition: Irrational Rationalism and the Citadel of Science,* New Falcon Publications, 1991.

takes more than three tests to prove a new theory. Meanwhile, as we await further light on the Sheldrake matter, I note only that I have yet to see a single study that refuted the morphic resonance hypothesis, and no amount of sneering at Dr. Sheldrake's alleged "guru"hood will refute him until such studies have appeared.

Now, I don't want it to seem that I stand at the opposite side of an either/or debate with Gross and Levitt. As indicated several times already, I don't think most issues in the sensory-sensual space-time world (the world of experience) actually reduce to such two-valued logic. And, frankly, I identify more with artistic post–modernism (the art of perspectivism) than with the academic post-modern theorists Gross and Levitt assault. Most of the post-modern Feminists and Multi-Culturalists Gross and Levitt criticize have indeed made egregious errors, in my opinion, and richly deserve criticism.

The chief fault of most academic theoreticians of post-modernism, as Gross and Levitt emphasize, lies in never applying perspectivism to themselves—i.e., in holding an oxymoronic position that always implies "everything is relative except my own dogmas." I do not make that error habitually, and I like to think I never make it at all. (I sure *hope* not, but as a Cosmic Shmuck, I assume I have slipped into it on occasion. [1]) I see the universe as Puzzle to Work On, Joyce-Welles fashion, and not as Puzzle Solved. The academic post-modernists always start with the World as Puzzle view and unobtrusively slip into the Puzzle Solved view. The latter, the solution to the puzzle, always curiously resembles the works of a second-rate German ideologue named Karl Marx, whose theories, having failed notoriously in practice, live on only among these academics (and, I must admit, in China and Cuba: two excellent countries to live in, if you want to have Political Correctness hammered into you 24 hours a day.)

However, I do find myself in sympathy with academic post-modernism on the issue that arouses the most rage in Gross and Levitt—the existence of social forces that shape the scientific

---

[1]The Cosmic Shmuck Law, as stated in several of my books, holds that if you occasionally notice that you have said something or done something that qualifies as Cosmic Shmuckery, you might become, in time, less of a Cosmic Shmuck; but if you never notice any Cosmic Shmuckery in your own thinking/doing, you will become more and more of a Cosmic Shmuck every year.

models of a given time and place. I do not say that social forces *create* scientific theories—an idea as absurd as the academic post-modernists' notion that social forces wrote *King Lear*—but social forces, I think, clearly play a role in determining which masks (scientific, artistic or philosophical) predominate, at least in a given decade, sometimes for a given generation, sometimes for even longer.

As a concrete and specific example, consider the scientific fate of Dr. Timothy Leary. Gross and Levitt, typically, dismiss Dr. Leary's scientific work (nearly 50 years of research now, published in more than 40 books) as "vaporous posturings." Now that refutation of 40 books does not really contain a valid scientific criticism, as any text on methodology will tell you; it hardly qualifies as a particularly witty example of mud-slinging. But what social factors have contributed to Dr. Leary's controversial career? Let us look again at that matter (a major theme of the first volume of this trilogy, but one still new to many readers who just picked up this volume...)

1. Some of Dr. Leary's work has achieved general recognition throughout the psychological community. Specifically, the Leary Interpersonal Test ranked as the number one (most used) psychological test in the country when I wrote volume one of this series. I do not know if it still ranks that highly, but it still continues in wide usage; I frequently meet young people who have taken it at university or at job applications, and it still routinely gets administered to all convicts in the California penal system.

2. The work on Behavior Modification with LSD for which Dr. Leary has received unanimous condemnation among non-psychologists and especially among the pundits of the mass media has *not* suffered universal criticism from those best qualified to judge—other psychologists. Many of them have said, off the record, that they suspect Leary will achieve vindication in a less hysterical age. On the record, when Dr. Leary got out of prison, he immediately received an invitation to give the keynote speech at the Association for Humanistic Psychology, strongly suggesting that those in his own area of psychology did not consider him a nut at all, but a gifted researcher condemned by irrational prejudice.

3. The controversy about Dr. Leary's Behavior Mod work continues and will continue because no later research has either confirmed or refuted him. This point I consider most important of all, and I will enlarge upon it. I may even relapse into boldface and capital letters...

None of Dr. Leary's most important studies have either suffered refutation or enjoyed confirmation, because *enacted law—statutes enacted after and because of Dr. Leary's research—makes it a crime for any other psychologists or psychiatrists to replicate such research.* I know you've heard that the Inquisition ended in 1819, but in many areas of psychotherapy and medicine, the U.S. government has taken up where the Vatican left off.

Maybe you didn't get that. I feel sure, somehow, that Gross and Levitt didn't get it and don't want to get it. Let me say it again, in leaner English. *ANY PSYCHOLOGIST OR PSYCHIATRIST WHO TRIES TO REPEAT DR. LEARY'S EXPERIMENTS WILL GET THROWN IN JAIL.*

Dig? When one speaks of "social forces shaping the scientific models" of a decade, of a generation or even of a longer time period, one does not merely refer to vague "prejudices" or "vested interests" or the notorious "conservatism of the Head of the department"—*although all of these play a role* as social forces shaping scientific models. In some cases, "social forces" means the very terrifying threat of imprisonment, in a prison system where mayhem, murder, rape and corruption play a larger role than in any slum on the outside. Now I would say that counts as a quite concrete and clear-cut example of how "social forces" have shaped the psychology *of the last three decades.*

Researchers don't do certain kinds of research *because they don't want to get thrown into San Quentin*, as happened to Dr. Leary.

Can anybody dismiss the Leary case as an isolated example?

Recall the "vaporous posturings" of Carl Sagan in his diatribes against Dr. Velikovsky (if I may borrow a lively phrase from such talented gutter fighters and Gross and Levitt, and apply it where I think it really belongs). Has anything solider or more scientific than Sagan's flapdoodle appeared refuting Dr. Velikovsky? If it has, I haven't seen it.

What do Gross and Levitt offer on the matter? In their one reference in 314 pages, they describe Dr. Velikovsky as "the notorious crank Immanuel Velikovsky." Note that this does not constitute argument but more name-calling, like their reference to Dr. Leary; note also the repetition of Sagan's tried-and-true technique of never giving Velikovsky the courtesy of his full title, Dr. Velikovsky. I would say that this kind of thing, not confined to Sagan and such gents as Gross and Levitt, has represented a significant "social force" acting over 40 years—two breeding generations—to influence what areas young scientists think it safe to investigate if they hope to acquire tenure.

Amusingly, Gross and Levitt admit that many social scientists have written on the social implications of the Velikovsky case, and that these researchers found the scientific community narrow-minded and intolerant in this matter. For instance, Dr. Roger Wescott, an anthropologist and polymath, has written several pieces on the prejudice that prevents research on Dr. Velikovsky's comet model. Gross and Levitt do not mention Dr. Wescott by name, and I wonder if they realize that his enormous academic qualifications would make their adjacent slur against social scientists look rather silly. (They claim all social scientists who found bigotry behind the banning of Dr. Velikovsky's work started out with that view, and just sought evidence to confirm it; but they do not inform us how they acquired such the high degree of ESP and mind-reading ability that allows them to know what all the social researchers secretly thought before they researched.)

Oh, well, if Gross and Levitt did mention Dr. Wescott by name, I bet they'd leave off his doctorate...

As a third example of "social forces" influencing which scientific models prosper and which get starved out, consider the case of Dr. Wilhelm Reich. Dr. Reich, an M.D. trained in psychiatry by Freud and an associate and collaborator with Dr. Bronislaw Malinowsky, a great anthropologist, and A.S. Neill, a great educator, had *all his books burned in an incinerator* by U.S. marshals in 1957. I would say that constituted a "social force" discouraging others from working in the areas that got Dr. Reich in so much trouble.

(You may not believe that in this country, with our first amendment, the government literally *seized Dr. Reich's books and burned them all*. They did. See any book on the Reich case. See, for the best in-depth coverage of the scandal, *Fury on Earth*, by Dr. Myron Sharaf, St. Martin's Press, New York, 1983.)

Only 18 scientists in the whole country had the intellectual integrity to protest this book-burning when it occurred in 1957. You can decide for yourself whether the silence of the rest of the scientific community represents hundreds of thousands of unrelated individual cases of moral cowardice and insensitivity to civil liberties, or if it collectively represents a "social force."

Frankly, I see it as a "social force." Before coming to this country (in naive pursuit of scientific freedom...) Dr. Reich had successively gotten expelled from the International Psychoanalytical Association for sounding too Marxist, expelled from the Communist Party for sounding too Freudian, expelled from the Socialist Party for sounding too anarchistic, fled Hitler for having known Jewish genes, and then got driven out of Sweden by a campaign of slander in the sensational press (for doing the kind of sex research that later made Masters and Johnson famous.) I would say Dr. Reich touched on a lot of hot issues and annoyed a lot of dogmatic people of Left and Right, and this created a truly international "social force" for the suppression of his ideas.

Perhaps we might decide, comfortably, that Dr. Reich held such extreme and unsound views that he deserved all this condemnation? Well, his work on character armor[1] has vastly influenced all modern psychology; his pioneering techniques of body work in conjunction with psychotherapy has inspired numerous others to copy his techniques outright or to develop similar techniques (e.g., Dr. Christopher Hyatt, Dr. Fritz Perls, Dr. Ida Rolfe, Esalen in general, the Primal Scream school, etc.) Dr. Reich's *Mass Psychology of Fascism* underlies, quite clearly, such works as Fromm's *Escape From Freedom* and Adorno's *The Authoritarian Personality*.

---

[1] Based chiefly on the proposition that a neurotic or psychosomatic symptom does not exist in isolation but functions as part of the defense system of a "armored" personality.

What of Dr. Reich's later, even more controversial works on
the orgone/bion theory, in which he attempted to bridge psycho-
biology and biophysics? Although the U.S. government threw
him in jail for this, and smashed the scientific equipment in his
laboratory with axes, and burned all his books, his theories have
never lacked scientific defenders. You can check that for yourself by writing to Dr. James De Meo, Natural Energy Works, PO
Box 1395, El Cerritos CA 94530. Send him $5 or $10 to cover
his costs and ask for his Orgone bibliography. This lists over 400
scientific papers by over 100 authors, most of them possessing
the M.D. or Ph.D. These papers cover the period 1934-1986 and
include 18 Master's dissertations or Ph.D. theses, 38 papers on
the bion experiment (including a confirmation reported to the
French Academy of Sciences by a Prof. du Tiel) 50 confirming
papers on Reichian weather control experiments, etc.

In opposition to these 400+ confirming papers, the Estab-
lishment which condemns Dr. Reich has never published a single
experiment refuting his results; they "know intuitively" that his
ideas have no merit, you see, so they don't have to experiment.
Personally, I find it hard to distinguish this intuitive "knowledge" from ordinary pig-headed prejudice, but it still rules the
U.S. government and most of the A.M.A. I would say this
represents a case of social forces influencing psychology and life
sciences for over 60 years, or around three generations.

Incidentally, Dr. De Meo acquired his Masters from the
University of Kansas for a study of the Reich cloud-buster (one
of Dr. Reich's weather control devices.) Everybody expected his
experiments to refute Dr. Reich, De Meo said in a letter to me,
and seemed very annoyed when the experiments once again
confirmed Dr. Reich. De Meo wanted to do further work on Dr.
Reich for his doctorate, but the University would not allow for
the chance of further heretical results; he got his doctorate for a
study of the effect of deserts on human psychology.

More recently, the University of Marburg, Germany, accepted
a Ph.D. dissertation on the orgone accumulator, a fraudulent
device according to leading American **Experts** who have never
experimented with it. The dissertation, using randomized double-
blind methodology, found that those in accumulators had the
psychological and physical sensations reported by Dr. Reich
(sweet, melting sensations, higher temperature, some tingling or

"wired" feelings); and those in similar-looking, non-orgonomic devices did not have these reactions. Since these tests had double-blind and randomized controls, suggestion could not have influenced these results.

You can also get a copy of this dissertation in German from Dr. De Meo, at the above address, but remember that he can't afford to operate a charity. Send him a decent sum to cover costs.

The FDA anathema against Dr. Reich only included his medical-psychiatric research, and that remains *verboten*, but they forgot to include other aspects of the orgone/bion theory. Thus, Dr. De Meo continues to do research in Reichian weather control, but he does not dare do Reichian mind-body therapy. Nobody dares to do that—or if they do, they dare not publish their results, because like Dr. Reich *they can land in jail for it.* (I received some Reichian mind-body work from a certain psychiatrist a while ago. He did not publish or publicize his results, with me or with any other patients, and stayed out of jail.)

In short, Dr. Leary and Dr. Reich both landed in jail for psycho-physical clinical work with revolutionary implications for personal and social health. Anybody who repeats their work will also land in jail. Do you think Gross and Levitt really, deep down, believe their claim that science, unlike any other human endeavor, really stands above social prejudice and never, never, never suffers both subtle control (the conservatism of the profession itself) and brutal overt control (imprisonment, book-burning etc.)?

Well, I think they really *might* believe it. I've met hundreds of people who believe very ardently in much, much weirder Faiths, including Lourdes water and Creationism.

Reference:

Higher Superstition, by Paul Gross and Norman Levitt, Johns Hopkins Press, Baltimore, 1994.

THIRTY-TWO

THE VAGINA OF NUIT

In Which Ley Lines Open Up a
Shocking New Secret of the Priory of Sion

Please! Not in front of the Klingons!
—*Star Trek VI: The Undiscovered Country*

Peggy, you know what a penis is...
Stay away from it!
—*Peggy Sue Got Married*

As every student of New Age literature knows, any number of ancient European monoliths taken together with any number of medieval churches will form a significant occult symbol if you connect them with straight lines. If not, you will find an interesting pattern using curved lines. If this doesn't yield any promising results keep trying until you find lines that seem to work. Good results will appear quicker and become increasingly clear and undeniable if you use a very small map and a very thick pencil.[1]

---

[1] The book that started all this, or the New Age way of interpreting the diagrams so obtained, John Michel's *View Over Atlantis*, used only straight lines. Later, others discovered that you can get even prettier and more mysterious diagrams by using curved lines. Eventually some will try broken lines and find that Ancient Astronauts left us messages in Morse Code.

There cometh now before this Court a book called *Genisis*, by one David Wood. The title does not represent a misprint but a Joycean bit of language play: Gen-Isis. Get it? The secret goes all the way back to Egypt...and even earlier...

Mr Wood has taken that ever-accursed church of Mary Magdelene in Rennes-le-Chatteau—the one where another investigator recently found a German newspaper hidden in a hollow statue, remember?—and has drawn some amazing lines connecting it with all sorts of other churches and some ancient megaliths in southern France. He has found a variety of interesting patterns, especially when he uses curved lines, and he has even found one he calls "the vagina of Nuit"—something really new and different in Priory mysteries once again.

I have looked at this diagram with great care and it doesn't look like Nuit's vagina, or anybody's vagina, to me. It looks like some overlapping circles and triangles and an off-kilter pentagram. Maybe Mr. Wood, or Picasso, once saw a woman with a vagina like that, but I never did.[1]

Taken together Mr. Wood's diagrams all cumulatively prove that either all the medieval churches and all the ancient megaliths of Langue d'Oc region have followed a secret code from the Stone Age to the early Renaissance, or else that Mr. Wood has a most lively and whimsical way of organizing straight and curved lines to make interesting patterns. More briefly, he has either discovered a truly great secret or mis-used a talent that should have gone into abstract painting.

As usual, people will decide that issue by gut intuition— because we cannot decide it rationally, since we don't know what data would prove relevant. We can, however, give some

---

[1]Of course, you can see a vagina in all these lines if you try hard enough. I can also see the assassin in the bushes on the Grassy Knoll, if I try really hard; and a Mr. Bill Cooper can see the real assassin, a secret service man in the front of the car, turn around and shoot JFK; after Cooper shows the famous Zapruder film about five times, telling you to look closely, most of the audience can see it that way, too. Prof. Finnegan once sent me a computer-enhanced photo of the alleged "face on Mars" which he insisted any objective observer would recognize as the late Moses Horowitz, whose intellectual influence we must now regard as interplanetary. However, I think Finnegan intended to make a Gaelic joke, unlike these other **Experts** at seeing things invisible to the common herd like you and me.

sort of probable value to the "code" that Mr. Wood has deciphered in all these circles and polygons.

Briefly, Wood claims that these diagrams offer a true history of Earth, and reveal the astonishing facts that—

1. The first inhabitants of Southern France came from the lost continent of Atlantis.

2. The human race did not evolve from animals but resulted from genetic manipulations by an extra-terrestrial named Satan. (Hey—this might explain how Satan got on the Coat of Arms of Stenay...)

3. The Priory of Sion worships the Egyptian sky-goddess Nuit and regards Mary Magdelene as a "coded" version of Nuit inserted into the Christian mythos. (Hence, the importance of the Magdelene church in all Priory literature.)

4. Initiation into the Priory requires bobbitization; the penis of the candidate gets sliced off and preserved in a special vessel where the Priory preserves all their old, useless penises.

That last point sort of contradicts Abendsen's notion of homosexual orgies in the Priory, I guess. Or maybe I still don't know enough about the possibilities of weird sex. Maybe they use gerbils?

At this point some will say the Priory of Sion has replaced Shakespeare as "the happy hunting grounds of all minds that have lost their balance." I, personally, will believe sooner in Abendsens' war–worshippers (if any evidence for that ever appears) than I would in a cult that has survived since Atlantis even though it requires members to hack off their wongs. I just don't believe that the Priory could find enough men who want to chop off Little Willy, generation after generation, in all those millennia. Lorena Bobbit became a heroine only to the craziest Radical Feminists, not to men (and not to any sane women I know, either.)

As I prepare to send this book off to the publisher, I just encountered an advertisement for a new book by Mr. Wood— *Geneset*. The ad (*Fortean Times*, Dec. 1994/Jan. 1995) says,

> The book that discovered the greatest threat to mankind coded in the geometry of a landscape in South West France! This timely book explores the origins of man—the enigma of the mind—Who is God?—The codes of Jules Verne...

Jules Verne again, eh? Sounds like "the beat goes on." And I suppose that the SET in *Geneset* like the ISIS in *Genisis* indicates more Egyptology in the mix. Both Set and Isis, like Nuit, play important roles in Crowley's occultism (see volume one) and Al-Shaddai also plays an important role, according to Crowley's magick "son" Frater Achad, as you can see if you find a copy of Achad's usually out-of-print but very interesting *Liber 31*.

Crowley and the O.T.O. have as many plausible links to the Illuminati as the Priory of Sion does... I begin to suspect that somebody has seeded the mask with some real clues, for those shrewd enough to find them. But I also suspect that the joke, or disinformation, component will hide the real clues from most of us for a while yet...

Nonetheless, I can't quite regard the Priory of Sion as a mask in exactly the same sense as the Elmyr *ouvre*. By now, I think the evidence tends to support the notion that the Priory of Sion predates Surrealism (contrary to my goodwyf's guess) and may even date to the middle ages, as it claims. I also think this masque, or conspiracy, or brotherhood of sages and jokers, has encouraged a lot of false leakage in the last two decades because it no longer intends to act secretly. It plans, I imagine, to surface soon, at least to the extent that Aleister Crowley's Ordo Templi Orientis (which also has a mystique about Nuit and Isis and Egypt and the Knights Templar...) has surfaced.

But I wonder—

When the Priory of Sion does surface, will it reveal some wonderful secret we all needed to know, without even knowing we needed it, or will it unleash the greatest hoax of this century?

Reference:

GENISIS, David Wood, Baton Press, Kent, 1985.

THIRTY-THREE

BEYOND ISNESS AND ALLNESS

In Which We Attempt to Apply Fuzzy Logic to Our Neurolinguistic Habits

Licorice! *Mmmm*!
—*Adam's Rib*

Crucifixion? *Good!*
—*Life of Brian*

As I mentioned once, and some of you might have noticed on your own, I wrote this entire book without any form of "is" or "was" or "be" or any cognate verb asserting identity. I will now explain this stylistic innovation, and I beg those readers who have encountered the theory before (e.g., in my book, *Quantum Psychology*, New Falcon Publications, 1990) not to skip this section. (*Skim* if you must, but don't *skip* entirely. I will put it in a new context and explain it, I hope, better than I have before.)

Back in 1933—*Lawdee*-me, doesn't that seem like the Dark Ages now?—both von Neumann and Korzybski proposed non-Aristotelian logics, as I mentioned many chapters ago. Von Neumann just allowed for a "maybe" (1/2) between true (1) and

216

false (0); Korzybski extended the "maybe" as far as you want—or as far as data allows you to calculate probabilities.

In other words, von Neumann gives you a three-valued logic of true (1), false (0), and maybe (1/2); but Korzybski offers an infinite-valued logic, which may reduce to 0 (false) 1/4 (most of the evidence runs the other way), 1/2 (even-steven), 3/4 (most of the evidence supports the idea) and 1 (proven true); or we can extend this to 0, 1/10, 2/10. 3/10 etc...to 10/10 or 1 (true); or, calculating with more data, we can extend to 0, 1/100, 2/100 etc. etc...to 99/100 (almost proven) and 100/100 (1/1) or absolutely proven true for all time.

Since then Sir Karl Popper has argued, plausibly I think, that no proposition can ever reach the level of *absolutely proven true for all time* (1/1) because that would require an infinite number of experiments and we haven't done that many experiments yet, nor does it seem likely that we can do them in any foreseeable future. Any of our theories, however, can reach the level of *proven false* (0) very quickly, since any failed experiment raises doubt, and a long rigorous series of failed experiments must either indicate that (a) the theory has no relation to experimental/experiential data, or else (b) some god or demon has rigged the results just to mislead us. The latter choice does not rank as a meaningful proposition in science, although it might keep theologians (or some academic multi–culturalists) busy with debate for centuries.

The theories that survive this process of repeated experimental challenge longest we may call "scientific relative successes," just as the species that survive long periods of natural challenge rank as *evolutionary relative successes.*

From a post-Aristotelian perspective (based on von Neumann/Korzybski and others who came later) most of the mysteries and masks explored in this book obviously exist in the *maybe* state. Calculating of probabilities will have to remain subjective, or intuitive, at this time due to the prevailing lack of hard data. For instance, I rank hollow Earth theories at less than 1/100, and Dr. Velikovsky maybe as high as 1/2 (middle maybe), chiefly because, due to the slanders, polemics and disinformation about Dr. Velikovsky circulated by Sagan and his ilk, the catastrophic scenario has just not had a fair scientific hearing yet.

I avoid making sentences with "is" or its relatives in them because all such sentences have definite semantic defects, the first of which consists in the fact that they make it appear as if one has reached the unreachable 1/1 of proven truth, when in fact one usually only has strong maybe, and (especially in politics and Ideology) sometimes only a weak maybe.

English without the use of "is" and its cognates, called English Prime and abbreviated E-Prime, has many other proponents besides me. For instance, Count Korzybski, who urged this reform (but didn't always practice it); David Bourland, who named it E-Prime and does consistently practice it; Dr. Edward Kellogg III, who has used it for decades and now says he *talks* as well as writes in E-Prime [1]; Dr. Albert Ellis, who has rewritten four of his books on Rational Therapy in E-Prime; etc. I find that E-Prime avoids some of the emotionalism of either/or debate; limits statements to what one has actually encountered and endured; cuts off all indeterminate or meaningless jargon before one can utter it; and generally leads to saner, clearer writing. I hope it will even lead me to somewhat saner and clearer thinking, eventually.

As Korzybski used to say, "Whatever you say a thing is, it isn't." On a primitive, childish level (which we sophisticates ignore at our peril), the word "ashtray" does not serve to extinguish cigarettes safely; if you try to use the word "ashtray" here on this page for that purpose, you might set this book on fire. The word "umbrella" will not keep you dry if you walk in the rain; the words "steak and lobster, with a baked potato" will not feed you if you need food; the word-phantom "formless spiritual essences" gave great satisfaction to Irish author A.E. (George Russell) but never clothed the naked, fed the starving, visited the sick, or (for that matter) broke a leg or gave a bully a black eye.

Everybody knows all this, of course? If you think so, walk into a Gay Leather Bar and ask "How many of you guys are fairies?"; walk into a Nation of Islam mosque and enquire "How many niggers come here regularly?"; walk into *MS.* magazine and demand to know "Which of you cunts is in charge of this place?"

---

[1]Dr. Kellogg did talk in E-Prime on the one occasion when we met. I listened very closely.

Nowadays, these admittedly tasteless jokes can get you jailed in some states, and sued in any state.

Do people only re-act as if words really equal things ("sticks and stones may break my bones, and names can also hurt me") in such "touchy" areas? Try opening two restaurants and have the menu in one say "Chef's special: Tender, juicy filet mignon" and have the other menu say "Chef's special: a hunk of dead meat hacked off a castrated bull." Both phrases describe the same non-verbal event, but see which sells better.

Thus when we say something "is" a good word or a "bad" word, people who claim they never confuse words and things will nevertheless react as if the word affected them as the thing would. Almost all words become "fighting words" in a contest over physical or "mental" territory (possessions or dogmas.)

Take an extreme case, where E-Prime seems overly pedantic: instead of "This is a chair," I write "I call this a chair, and use it as a chair." The is-ness statement tends, to a greater or lesser degree, to make you forget what the E-Prime statement helps you to remember: the non-verbal space-time event called a "chair" can have many other names, and many other uses—e.g., an aggressive weapon in a dysfunctional family, a defensive weapon if a burglar breaks in, kindling wood in some Ice Age situation, a scratching post for Kitty, etc. Similarly, "This is a rose" encourages you to forget that the non-verbal Gizmo "is" also a botanical specimen, a structure created by DNA out of other other molecules, a source of pleasant aroma, a gift for a loved one, a subject for a painter, a mass of electrons, etc. etc. etc.

These neurosemantic issues have many practical and urgent applications.

To illustrate: consider, first, the current debate about abortion, and the series of terrorist murders it has provoked. The whole controversy always whirls around the question: what "*is*" the fetus? In E-Prime one *cannot even ask that question*. One's opinion, in E-Prime, also *sounds like an opinion* and does not masquerade as a Law of Nature of a Proven Theorem. The best I can come up with for the two opposed positions would read:

"I classify the fetus as a human person."
"I don't classify the fetus as a human person."

These could only achieve further clarity and sanity by amending them further, thusly:

"Due to the philosophy I hold at present, I currently classify the fetus as a human person."

"Due to the philosophy I hold at present, I currently do not classify the fetus as a human person."

This hardly represents an isolated case of how the "is" perpetuates dogma and hostility (what psychologist Edward de Bono calls the I AM RIGHT, YOU ARE WRONG syndrome) and how the use of E-Prime *tends* (at least) to lessen the dogma and the hostility. Very few forms of fascism, racism or sexism (even those most fashionable in P.C. circles) can survive in E-Prime. For instance—

"I tend to see all Hispanics as fundamentally the same, and equally obnoxious." "I tend to see all Asiatics as fundamentally the same, and equally obnixious" "I tend to see all men as fundamentally the same, and equally obnoxious."

While one may not want to associate with the persons who might utter such statements, such persons do not seem quite as holpelessly nutty as those who tells you what all Hispanics "are," or what all Asiatics "are," or what all men "are," etc.

"I *tend to see* all X's as Y" and similar meaningful and obviously self-referential propositions in E-Prime do not incite people to violent prejudice (and violent acts) like the scientifically and existentially meaningless is-ness statements—"All Italians are gangsters," "All Presbyterians are kooks," "All plumbers are thieves."

Of course, **Expert**ese cannot survive in a world conditioned to "This looks like a Picasso to me." **Expert**ese demands "This *is* a Picasso." Elmyr understood that, which explains his paradox that the **Experts** create the forgers. And, similarly, **Expert**ese cannot survive "At present, this looks like unsound science to me"; **Expert**ese demands a flat "This *IS* pseudo-scientific and vaporous posturing and its inventor *IS* a shaman, a guru and a notorious crank"

The "is of identity" encourages dogmatism and in many more cases than the one we mentioned (Dr. Reich) even escalates prejudice to the point where book-burning and outright fascism become inevitable. Remember again that none the murders recently committed at Planned Parenthood clinics resulted from "In my system of philosophy, I do not see a distinction between fetus and child." The murders resulted from "The fetus IS a child," and "The abortionist IS a murderer" as clearly as the success of Elmyr resulted from "This IS a Matisse" and "This IS a Modigliani."

And so by a "culious vicus of recirculation" we come back, again, to the quasi-religious Canon and its critics, and confront once more the question, "Is Shakespeare the greatest writer who ever lived?" to which Prof. Bloom still gives a resounding YES and Prof. Taylor and his cohorts in Multi-Cultural Feminist Post-Modernist Academia shout an emphatic NO. In E-Prime, we cannot even ask the question. We can ask, however, "How do *you* rank Shakespeare among the world's writers?"

My answer to that would read, "In my present mixed state of literary knowledge and literary ignorance, Shakespeare seems the greatest writer I have ever read"—because I like to reinforce E-Prime by stating my limitations clearly within any statement of my judgments (as a scientist will state the instrument used within a statement of the measurement obtained.)

Frankly, I do not know enough Italian to compare Dante and Shakespeare adequately, or enough Greek to compare Gentle Will meaningfully with Homer, etc. I emphatically do not know enough Persian, Arabic, Chinese, Hindustani, Sudanese etc. to have more than a vague idea of the merits of Rumi or Li Po or Shiki or Samba Gana or many other non-Occidental writers (who have, however, impressed me tremendously in translation.)

Prof. Bloom will probably think I have had my mind ruined by multi-culturalists, because I state my personal opinion as a "mere" personal opinion. Prof. Taylor will think I have had my mind ruined by Tradition, because I still like Shakespeare better than Alice Walker.

Well, at least they'll both agree that my mind has gotten ruined somewhere, and I value persuading two such dogmatic gents to agree about *anything* as no small achievement.

Meanwhile, my willingness to admit that somebody writing in a language I don't know may have surpassed Shakespeare does not compel me to rush in haste to join Prof. Taylor and the School of Resentment (as Bloom calls them) in their effort to promote any writer over Shakespeare if that writer happens to lack white skin and male genitalia. Such a nonwhite female super-genius may exist, I stipulate; but I will not *assume* her existence until I discover her works and personally find them superior. Meanwhile, I think the attempt to dump Shakespeare because of his skin-color and gender illustrates the kind of blatant racism and sexism that once marked "the ragged and the golden rabble"; and I do not see why such racism and sexism, reversed but still foolish, have become the Dogma of our totally-indoctrinated and half-educated neo-Left Wing.

All "is" statements expressing judgment become more accurate (describe the instrument used to make the evaluation) when rephrased as "seems to me" statements: "Beethoven seems better to me than Punk Rock," "Punk Rock seems better to me than Beethoven," "Abstract Expressionism seems like junk to me," "Abstract Expressionism seems to me the most important innovation since Cubism" all speak a "truth"—in the sense of the *truth of experience* or the *truth of perception*—even though different people will speak them. (Ah, alas, Gross and Levitt detect sinister "perspectivism" rearing its head again...)

On a broader scale, beyond artistic/academic feuds, E-Prime immediately answers many Zen *koans*, such as "Name the Great One who makes the grass green!"

(If that puzzles you, I offer a hint: Moses got the name from a burning bush...)

In psychology, for instance, consider how much time learned people have wasted debating such questions as "Does the patient do this because he is in Oedipal rebellion or because he is still following early conditioning?" In E-Prime, this question becomes "Does the Freudian model help us to understand this patient's behavior more than, as much as, or less than the Pavlovian model?" One can still have lively debate, but the debate will remain scientific and not drift off, unaware, into medieval theology or demonology.

In physics, recall the time and energy once wasted by brilliant theoreticians debating "Is the electron a wave or a particle?" In E-Prime this becomes "Does the wave model of the electron model tell us more than, as much as, or less than the particle model?" Once stated that way, it would not have required the genius of Bohr to find the answer, which appears nowadays as

"Usually, *as much as*; sometimes, in special cases, *more or less than*." (Insofar as Bohr admitted the influence of the pragmatist James and the existentialist Kierkegaard, both of them also obvious influences on E-Prime, Bohr had the spirit, if not the letter, or E-Prime, when he realized physics could usefully model the electron both as wave and as particle in different contexts: a triumph of perspectivism that, curiously, does not arouse the fury of Gross and Levitt...)

In economics, "The Marxist model seems better to me than the Monetarist model" states a fact (about the nervous system of the speaker, if I must make the obvious even more obvious.) "Marx *is* true and the Monetarists *are* refuted" states an opinion disguised as a fact. The former encourages intelligent discussion; the latter virtually incites emotional conflict.

FLASH! A FASTBREAKING STORY FROM VIENNA... IMMEDIATE P.C. REACTIONS IN AMERICA

On December 17, 1994—Beethoven's 224th birthday—Associated Press revealed that a lock of Beethoven's hair, removed from his head by his sister-in-law Johanna van Beethoven, and presently held by the Huettenbrenner family, will soon settle the racial rumors about the composer. A fragment of the hair, given to scientists, will undergo DNA testing to determine if Beethoven did, indeed, have "Negro" or "African" genes, as many have speculated.

This scientific study may yet rescue Ludwig from the abyss into which P.C. has consigned him. If evidence of partial African ancestry appears, then the ever-controversial Beethoven will no longer fit the negative stereotype of the DWEM (Dead White European Male) and may qualify as a DAEM (Dead African-European Male) or DBEM (Dead Black European Male.) It might then become permissible to enjoy his music again.

"If Beethoven is even partly Black, I'll be able to buy all the Nine Symphonies again," said Prof. Mary La Puta of UC-Berkeley Music Department "I've really missed hearing them since I had to throw them out three years ago."

Other Experts expressed doubts. "If no Black genes are found," said Prof. Leckarsh of UC-Santa Cruz, "Beethoven is

done for. His stock will just continue to drop, and even the Gary
Oldman movie won't help."

In anthropology the debate about whether humanity consists of
three races or five wasted incredible time and energy earlier in
this century, and the Eugenicists continue to waste energy on the
question of the superiority or inferiority of one race over or
under all others. In E-Prime, we can only ask, "What heuristic
advantages do we obtain from a three-race model? A five-race
model? What heuristic advantages might we find in Buckminster
Fuller's one-human-race model? What kind of evidence indicates
statistical superiority, and in what areas? What kind of evidence
indicates that those inferior in one area score as superior in other
areas? Do we have any tests yet that approach these questions
without any cultural bias?"

In everyday life, consider the time, energy, emotion, shouting,
yelling, physical violence etc. that result from sentences like
"That *was* the dumbest thing I ever saw." "You *are* a liar!"
"Dammit, Tom Mix *was* a hell of a lot better than Gene Autry!"
"You and your whole damn family *are* crazy!" Consider how
much misery, and how many psychotherapy bills, result from
internal sentences (thoughts) in such forms as "I *am* really
hopeless." "I *am* a fool, and everybody knows it now." "I *am*
depressed again and I don't think I'll ever get over it this time."
"What the fuck does she think I *am*, some kind of *putz?*"

Elsewhere, I have argued for the introduction of the word
"sombunall"—meaning *some but not all*—because "allness"
makes as many problems as "isness." In human relations, group
prejudices continually get reinforced by habitual use of "all"
along with "is:—e.g., Hitler's "all Jews are usurers," Brown-
miller's "all men are rapists," etc.

"Sombunall" might not miraculously cure this highly
contagious neurolinguistic disorder, but it certainly seems to
alleviate it.

Note how the spirit of sombunall permeates the average social
scientific report—more relevant than physical science here
because we now consider human relations—"In this study,
subjects consisted of 57 white males, 52 white females, 33 black
males, 30 black females, 40 Asiatic males and 17 Asiatic
females...54% of the whites, of both genders, showed the

behavior expected, as against 40% of the black males and 34% of the Asiatic females. Black and Asiatic females, however, showed a different pattern…"

Regularly reading and/or writing that kind of precise prose (even if it sometimes sounds over-finicky or more technical than required for the subject [1]) conditions the reader/writer to the kind of antisepsis against over-generalizing that I hope to popularize with "sombunall." In ordinary non-scientific cases where you do not have exact percentages available, you must admit that sombunall fits what you know, where "all" pretends you know more than you possibly can. Recall an old and childish joke:

"All Indians always walk Indian-file."

"How do you know?"

"Well, the one I saw was walking that way."

How many generalizations in daily use have no more statistical basis than that one?

As Korzybski said once (violating his own ideal of E-Prime) "Allness is an illness." In fact, the F-scale, invented by Adorno and used to measure fascist tendencies, does show a correlation between heavy use of "allness" statements and the fascist personality. Can you imagine a full page by any fascist (or any red fascist) without reckless generalizations about *all* members of some scapegoat group?

Looking again at "internal sentences," consider how many so-called mental and emotional illnesses take the form of habitual self-hypnosis with "allness" sentences like "I always screw up," "They're all rejecting me," "They all know I goofed again," "They all hate me," "I never win" etc. etc. Allness certainly does have a remarkable correlation with mental/emotional illnesses, and probably with physical illnesses, too, because *your body "hears" everything you think.*

So: if you have tried to abandon sexist terminology and have seen some changes in your perceptions and human relations thereafter, why not try getting rid of "is" and "all" and see what happens? As Benjamin Lee Whorf stated, "A change in language can transform our appreciation of the cosmos."

---

[1] Defects usually caused by the social scientists' desire to sound more like the "real" scientists over in the physics department.

THIRTY-FOUR

THE BLACK IRON PRISON

In Which Another Sci-Fi Writer has a Donnybrook
With Those Intrusive Blokes From Sirius

> Every time one of those lights flashes,
> somebody is looking for a job.
> —*A Star Is Born*

> Every time you hear a bell ring,
> an angel just got his wings
> —*It's A Wonderful Life*

Between November 1951 and November 17, 1971 Philip K. Dick wrote the most mind-boggling fiction ever to escape from the surrealist underground into the domain of commercial science-fiction. After November 17, 1971, he came to live, more and more, in the world he had himself created.

On November 17, 1971—a date that the future may remember as we remember July 4, 1776—somebody broke into Phil's house, stole many of his literary files, and did enough "pointless" damage to leave a clear threat: malice, more than any commercial motive, had inspired the invasion.

Phil wondered and worried about this vandalism for a long time; I think you or I would wonder and worry equally if it happened to us. In fact, it reminds me of another writer I once knew slightly (so slightly that I have forgotten his name.) Bill, as I will call this fellow, met me because we both wrote articles, in the early '70s, for the *Berkeley Barb*. Later, Bill got an assignment to write a piece for a slick men's mag on the cattle mutilations that have so often occurred in the mid-west and south-west. After a lot of investigation, while working on the first draft of his story, Bill asked me to evaluate his favorite theory, namely that the mutilations resulted from the activities of a Mithraic (neo-pagan) cult within the U.S. Army. (The historical Mithrists, in ancient times, killed bulls in their rituals and used bull penises as amulets.) I told him that made a good story, and he should use it if he believed it, but I found the evidence far from overwhelming.

A few nights later, Bill came to see me, very shaken. His house had also suffered a break-in and he had the creepy feeling that this indicated that the cult knew about his investigations. We discussed it, and gradually he grew more calm. He had no evidence that anything more than an ordinary Berkeley burglary had occurred. I emphasized that worrying about remote possibilities would only wear him down. He left, less shaken, and I only saw him once or twice after that and learned no more about the cattle mutilators or the burglars.

In Bill's case, ordinary burglary certainly seemed the most reasonable explanation, but I do not think his reaction indicated "New Age" gullibility or neuroses. You simply cannot investigate certain weird subjects and then have a break-in without thinking some very unpleasant thoughts. I consider that an immutable law of investigatory psychology. As Nietzsche said, if you gaze into the abyss, the abyss gazes into you... [1]

Phil Dick had more to worry about than poor Bill. His break-in bore no traces of burglary, as ordinarily understood. Somebody or some group wanted to scrutinize his private files, and also to frighten him, or to warn him, or at least to harass him. Phil

---

[1] Another writer whose name I do remember, Ed Sanders, also wrote an article about the mutilations for a slick magazine. He then received a cow's tongue in the mail, and got even more weirded out than poor Bill. Some of Ed's books: *The Family* (about the Manson cult), *Shards of God* (novel), *Fuck God Up The Ass* (poems).

suspected various persons and groups at various times, but never did solve the mystery.

I *think* I have solved it. (Remember: that wording intends to avoid the "rush to judgment" implied in "I have solved it.") In Anthony Summers *Official and Confidential: The Secret Life of J. Edgar Hoover* (*op. cit.*) we read on page 480, discussing Nixon's super-secret secret police called "the plumbers" (the group assigned to clandestine operations which Nixon didn't want Hoover's FBI to do, since Hoover might blackmail him later):

> Some believe Watergate was only the tip of the iceberg. During the Nixon administration, unidentified intruders invaded the homes and offices of numerous people... There were at least a hundred such break-ins... Radicals...were regular targets... But so were respected reporters (including) Dan Rather, Marvin Kalb...Ted Szulc...So were prominent politicians—Democratic Party Treasurer Robert Strauss... Senator Lowell Weicker...etc.

I suggest that Phil Dick, known throughout the San Francisco Bay Area in the 1960s and early '70s as an active "Radical" (i.e., a supporter of equal rights for black Americans and an opponent of the Vietnam war) might have seemed a threat to G. Gordon Liddy and his equally paranoid cohorts in the "plumbers" unit. At least, no other group seems more likely candidates for the Phil Dick break-in, and in "over a hundred" such invasions, it doesn't seem likely they would overlook a writer/activist of Phil's stature.

Phil did consider this possibility himself (among many others) but it all took on a new, more *outré* aspect after his *gnosis* experiences of February/March 1974. Since Phil always referred to this transvaluation of all concepts by the date 2-3/74, I will call it that in this chapter.

The experience began with a tooth extraction, during which Phil received sodium pentathol. Later, in his more secular moments, Phil wrote a great deal of speculative prose about whether the gnosis resulted from the sodium pentathol, from the LSD he had taken in the '60s, from the megavitamins he took in the '70s, or from some combination. He never did decide, but I guess all of the chemicals played some role, although hardly the only role.

After the tooth extraction, Phil began to have unique perceptions. All the usual masks collapsed, and he saw hundreds, thousands of alternative reality-tunnels. "The entire universe blew up in his face," as he wrote in a novel.

In the 8 remaining years of his life, Phil, who had once written 17 novels in five years, wrote only three more novels (although I consider them among his very best...) Most of his time went into work on the *Exegesis*, a kind of neuro-psycho-philosophical diary in which he attempted to understand what had begun to happen to him. This eventually reached over 8000 pages, of which only part has received publication so far.

At the beginning, when Phil fell into the whirlpool he called "orthogonal time"—defined as "real" time, at right angles to our spurious linear time—he experienced events in ancient Rome and modern America almost simultaneously, and he had great difficulty in remembering whether the tyrant who misruled that segment of Hell had the name Nero or Nixon.

In the early *Exegesis*, Phil experimented with the theory that what really had happened consisted of a transmigration of his late friend, Bishop James Pike, who had all the languages and historical details to make the Roman visions accurate. In other words, Phil thought Bishop Pike, after death, might have entered Phil's aura and now co-existed with him—two people in one brain, sort of like the Catholic three persons in one god...

At other times, Pike seemed an inadequate explanation, and Phil thought he had begun to remember a past life as one Thomas, a Gnostic mystic. (*The Gospel of Thomas*, sometimes credited to the twin brother of Jesus, remains a favorite with esoteric Christians. I personally find it the most congenial of early Christian writings.)

As the experience broadened and deepened, Phil found both Pike and Thomas inadequate to explain the multi-dimensional new world order he now perceived. He considered the possibility that Soviet parapsychologists had attained "mental telepathy" with extraterrestrials, and he, somehow, had gotten into the interstellar *infobahn* by accident. (At one stage, he saw a history of human art, lasting about eight hours in linear time, and partially glimpsed Soviet scientists transmitting it to their Space Brothers.)

Later, in hypnopompic and hypnogogic visions, Phil began to perceive and/or conceive the experiences in terms of three-eyed extraterrestrials from Sirius trying to help humanity escape the Empire and the Empire's Black Iron Prison.

"The Empire never ended"—an urgently meaningful message to Phil, and one repeated several times in *VALIS*, my favorite of his novels—sums up this aspect of the Experience. On one literalistic level, this means that the Roman Empire never fell; it still governs the world, but it has inserted nearly 2000 years of "false memories" into our brains to keep us from remembering that we live in the Messianic Age when all miracles have become daily possibilities. The Black Iron Prison became Phil's metaphor, or masque, for the 2000 years of delusion we have suffered in linear time, while our orthogonal selves still live in "real time"—Eternity.

On another level, the Empire literally never ended. We still live in nations where, under the mask of "democracy" or "socialism" or whatever, a small oligarchy rules and the masses live in overt or covert slavery. (Thus, the break-in signified that Nero, or Nixon, or some agents of the Empire feared Phil's awakening to the horror of the situation.) The Black Iron Prison, similarly, represents not only the "nightmare of history" from which Joyce tried to wake us, but the illusion that "material things" possess both the solidity of "matter" and independence of "things." As Phil dramatized it in *VALIS*, humanity did not "fall" due to moral error, but due to the ontological error of "taking the phenomenal world as real," i.e., confusing the map with the territory.

Later, Phil attributed his experiences alternately to "Zebra" and "VALIS." *Zebra* denotes an intelligence so huge that it, insect fashion, remains invisible, because we normally see it as the environment—the whole entire environment. *VALIS* means "Vast Active Living Intelligence System," usually conceived as a space satellite left in orbit around Earth by explorers from Sirius to guide our evolution from animal through human to superhuman.

Sometimes—in fact frequently, as the years passed—Phil admitted to himself (in the *Exegesis*) that both Zebra and *VALIS* constituted sci-fi metaphors, congenial to his sub-culture, for a kind of super-mind that earlier ages would simply call "God."

Just as often, Phil considered, impartially, the theory that he had simply gone schizophrenic. He never did make up his mind about that.

In fact, when I met Phil around 1977 (I don't keep diaries and archives, as he did, so I can only estimate these things) he questioned me very closely about my own "mystic" experiences of 1973, in which I also thought at times that I had contacted a Higher Intelligence from Sirius. (I had published *Cosmic Trigger I*, recounting these experiences, in 1976.) Phil did not tell me, on first meeting, about his 2-3/74 experiences with Sirius, and I think he questioned me so closely to see how "crazy" I seemed to him. If I seemed sane, he could stop worrying about himself, maybe; but if I seemed nutty, he had to face again the possibility that he must classify himself as another nut from the same pecan tree.

I guess we both passed the test in Phil's judgment, at least tentatively.

Nietzsche said that mystics never practiced the kind of ruthless honesty, or skepticism, which he dared. He would have had to withdraw that condemnation in the case of Phil Dick (and also, I think, in the case of Aleister Crowley.) Phil never did stop questioning, doubting and seeking alternative models (masks) to contain-or-explain his 'patanormal perceptions.

The only novels he wrote in those last eight years take three different approaches to the personal experiences recorded and analyzed in the *Exegesis*. In *VALIS*, Phil sits on the fence like an agnostic owl, bending a little each way but never leaving the fence. In the next one, *The Divine Invasion*, Phil presents his wildest sci-fi and Gnostic ideas as absolutely true (but, remember, he published this as a work of fiction.) In the last and funniest and saddest, *The Transmigration of Timothy Archer*, Phil leads us up to a revelation in which Gnostic and Buddhist reincarnation theories both appear justified, and then deconstructs his own story with rationalistic skepticism, showing that the transmigration always remains uncertain to some degree and urging that our real job, as writers and philosophers, should look straight at the real and undeniable suffering of the poor and hungry of the world and seek a solution for it.

Three different answers...and in the *Exegesis* he went on wondering and seeking new answers until his final stroke killed him. I loved Phil Dick for his books, and I loved him as a man of genius when we met; through the *Exegesis* I have come to know him as a philosopher so honest that even Nietzsche would have to admit he did not hesitate to challenge all his own ideas. What pleasure I find in writing about this open-minded, ever-questioning, intensely alive person, after the hours devoted to creeping around dark dogmatic caves with troglodytes like Sagan, Gross and Levitt...

As for me, after working with the ideas that my experiences resulted from telepathic assistance by real adepts on Earth, or similar adepts on Sirius, or from my own Poetic Imagination (as Blake called this faculty) I now tell people, when they ask about this aspect of my career, that I currently attribute it all to the *pookah*, a six foot white rabbit with supernatural powers well-known in County Kerry. I like that model because I don't think anybody exists damnfool enough to take it *literally*...

References:

Divine Invasions: A Life of Philip K. Dick, by Lawrence Sutin, Underwood-Miller, Lancaster PA, 1989.

The VALIS Trilogy, by Philip K. Dick, Quality Paperback Book Club, New York, 1990.

In Pursuit of VALIS: Selections from the Exegesis, by Philip K. Dick, Underwood-Miller, Lancaster PA, 1991.

THIRTY-FIVE

LUCY IN THE SKY WITH DIAMONDS ⸹

In Which We Commence to Begin to Seek A Concluding Chord for our Fugue

> Oh, good—nobody here but people!
> —*Harvey*

> It can't all be chance…it must be Destiny…
> —*The Man Who Would Be King*

"What do you turn on when you turn on?"

I first heard that question from Dr. Timothy Leary back around 1968 or '69. He never did answer the question; he just wanted me to think about it. I started thinking about it for maybe the thousandth time when I began looking for the final set of metaphors that would resolve the rather non-Elgarian Enigma Variations that I have presented in this book.

Before delving into masks and masks-behind-masks, let us consider something a bit less complicated than human psycho-neuro-pharmacology. Let us consider an ordinary television set.

Pretending that we have the minds of imbeciles or academic philosophers, let us sit down and imagine we will conduct an extensive meditation upon the television.

Since somebody turned the set on before we entered the room, we do not conclude at once that the set belongs in the class of all inanimate objects. On the contrary, we clearly recognize quite lively animation. In a while we even learn that the major animated parts have names: Lucy, Ricky, Fred and Ethel. With further logical analysis we determine that Lucy dominates the others, and we pronounce Lucy the "mind" of the set and name the others "organs."

We can then spend years or decades or even longer, arguing about the exact logical consequences of this fundamental dualism between "mind" and "organs." E.g. would the "mind" die if the "organs" died? How many "minds" can dance on the head of an "organ"?

Skip ahead a few centuries. Empiricism has arrived and we now have the courage to experiment upon the set, or the world, or whatever we now call it. We actually try turning the dials. Assuming that the Inquisition or DEA or CSICOP or somebody like that doesn't burn us at the stake, we have not only turned on but tuned in, and we discover that the worldset or worldprocess contains not only the Lucy Complex, but also the Golden Girls (Dorothy = left brain, Blanche = libido, Rose = right brain, Sofia = old brain)...and an endless series of atrocities and catastrophes narrated by people who never show any emotion about these horrors (but always smile cheerfully before they sign off) ...and lots and lots of cops shooting at lots and lots of "bad guys"...and some charming folk living in the 24th Century in a ship called Enterprise...and an amazing horde of middle aged ladies who say their parents sexually molested them (with and/or without Satanic rituals) and want to talk about it on camera ...and various gents in funny suits orating about God...and two blokes who each want to become President and smile almost all the time except when they frown and denounce each other as lying scoundrels.

Obviously, the television set, since it contains so many people, has MPD—multiple personality disorder. Or, at least, so say the psychologists among us.

Not so, says another group of investigators who have created a different model of the multi-channel perceptual muddle. The set contains memories of many lives, because it has lived in other consoles before, they say; and, furthermore, you have lived many lives also, and you can remember them if you fast for a long, long time and sit staring at a blank wall... (Others mutter that you can do it quicker with certain Weird Chemicals, but almost everybody considers them Agents of Chaos.)

A third group has tried more dangerous and hitherto forbidden experiments. They have performed vivisection and removed parts of the set. They conclude that the set does not possess a "life force" at all and does indeed belong in the class of all inanimate (or at least mechanical) objects, because whenever they take out certain tubes the set goes black and dies, but if they put those tubes back in, the set comes back to life, just like the Frankenstein monster whenever Hollywood wants to make another sequel.

They have also discovered that if you pull the plug, the set stays dead no matter how many new tubes you put in.

Furthermore, if they remove certain small parts, only some functions of the worldset will die—e.g. they lose all the parts with English accents and, curiously, all the long stories without commercials, but they still have "Lucy" and other primitive functions. Ergo, the worldset consists of mechanical parts joined to other mechanical parts and we can understand it—this group says—as the sum of mechanical reactions in a mechanical continuum.

The most adventurous of this group even "explains" how the set appeared here. If you throw enough junk over the wall into a vacant lot, they say, in about 4 billion years or so... *by sheer chance*...some of it will organize into a television set. They have also collected evidence that the set first appeared 4 billion years ago, which helps make this scenario plausible. Indicating (perhaps) some inner uncertainty or anxiety, this group insists that the state should not allow any discussion of rival theories in public education—especially not the theories of a nut group who claim the TV has only existed for about 40 or 50 years and owes its existence to a Higher Intelligence named Czarnoff.

And as you know, other blind men examined the same TVelephant and came to other conclusions, so we can cross-cut to another parable at this point.

One young lady, tired of the debates between the rationalists and mechanists and others in the dark room, turned her back on all of them and discovered—a door. It stood opposite the TV and nobody had ever thought to look in that direction. Our heroine, who had the name Anna, walked to the door and opened it and stepped out of the room.

She had an out-of-the-TV experience (OOTE).

She found herself in a world much like the TV world, but also strangely unlike it in some ways. In fact, she quickly found a "TV studio," a place where some of the people from the TV, or their relatives, actually lived. These creatures, she decided, could not live in the TV because they stood much, much taller than their TV children.

The people in the TV now seemed, to Anna, like dwarfs, or shadows, of their relatives in the "studio."

As Anna watched, the Real People or the Big People or the non-TV People (she couldn't decide what to call them) went through a performance in which one of them died.

"Great, great," shouted another Real Person, who seemed in charge around here. "Perfect on the first take."

And then the corpse got up and walked away. He even lit a cigarette, which nobody in the TV could do.

Anna felt so confused that she ran all the way back to the TV room and locked the door behind her. She very carefully did not discuss her OOTE with any of the others in the room; she knew most of them would angrily call her "crazy" if she made that mistake.

The next day, she saw the same events on TV that she had seen in the other world, except that this time the corpse did not get up and walk away or light a cigarette and the Real Person in charge did not appear on screen.

Anna did a lot of thinking after that, and every time she felt sure nobody would notice, she went out the door again and investigated the Real World. Then she did a lot more thinking. She realized that if she told her experiences, some would not call her "crazy" but would say she had visited "heaven." If she predicted the ends of shows that she had seen in production, others would say she had the magick power of *psi* or "precognition." The religious would want to have her burned as a witch and the mechanists would want her locked up as a "psycho case."

One day, out in the Real World, Anna saw two lovers in a secluded park. They were Making Love. To her absolute astonishment, the lights did not go dim and drumming and pounding music did not start and the lovers did not just moan and roll around. They did things to each other which both of them appeared to enjoy.

Anna thought about that a lot, and about how easily you could tell the "good guys" from the "bad guys" on TV, even though you couldn't do that in the Real World, where sometimes the same Real Person would become two TV personoids, one "good" and one "bad," in rapid succession. She also noticed that, just as some people died on TV but remained alive in the Real World, some stayed alive on TV long after they died in the Real World.

She began to think of TVland as, not just a condensed electronic image or ghost of Reality, but a mask that had undergone considerable editing and rewriting to suit those in charge of Reality Selection for the whole society in which the TV existed. She realized that what the TV showed did not represent a simple Xerox of the Real World but a complicated social "game"—or tacit conspiracy—to pretend a certain set of programs contained all of the Real World.

Anna knew she had become a Mystic and that if she ever talked about what she had learned some people would praise her and some would condemn her, both in excessive language, but none of them would actually understand her until they also walked out of the door, *many times.*

After long years, Anna discovered that a few others sometimes slipped out the door and came back, usually looking as dazed as herself on first trips. She began to talk then, but only to those special star-eyed people. And gradually, as their group grew, and they compared notes, they realized that they had never found the Real World at all, but only another great Theatre of Fools.

Out there, beyond the door, all the "Real People" had scripts, and had to follow the scripts given to them, just like their shadows on the TV; and all of the "Real People" contained dozens of kinds of programming from a source unknown and "higher" or at least more mathematically complex...the Real World behind the "Real" World...

And Anna and her friends all wondered what might lie beyond that Real World beyond the "Real World" ...And some said we could only conceive it as pure Pythagorean geometry, but others said we could not conceive it at all except as a Void beyond words and concepts, and others said we could imagine it as a six dimensional spiral with cross-sections making a five dimensional sphere and a four dimensional circle (but everybody said those people had taken some of the weird chemicals of the shady alchemists), and some said we could almost visualize it if we thought of pure information as hidden variables without energy or form to limit them...

And they realized that even the ant who escapes the ant-hill and learns of the existence of a super-formican or meta-formican cosmos called the Back Yard (in which the ant-hill makes a very small part) will grow a bit groggy in trying to imagine the House that needs a Back Yard, or the mysterious "city" which contains hundreds and hundreds of thousands of Houses. And such an "illuminated" ant will find it even harder to grasp the genetic code that teaches ants to make hills and humans to make Houses and in similar fashion programs millions of lifeforms swarming over an entire planet, which exists as a mere speck amid billions of suns and galaxies, all organized by the same blueprint.

So they wrote, "The hardware remains local, but nobody can localize the software" to remind themselves of what they had learned, because otherwise such thoughts easily get forgotten or jumbled in all the babble and howling coming from the people still staring at the TV and arguing louder and louder about whether we could best understand Lucy as the "mind" or just as a set of electrons that randomly formed a "Lucy" every so often or as an Eternal Thought in the Mind of the Producer.

THIRTY-SIX

FROM RUSSIA WITH LOVE

In Which a Paper Rattlesnake Turns Around and Bites Us in the Ass

> Professor, you've got a bad case of Gogo on the Magogo.
> —*Spellbound*

> No ordinary tomato could do this, but—
> —*Attack of the Killer Tomatoes*

On April 24, 1989, when *glasnost* had already come to bloom but before the final break-up of the Soviet Union, a man named Ivan Vesalova in Cherepovetsk saw or imagined a craft of enormous size, bigger than any airplane, hovering about a thousand feet above the ground.

Just another UFO sighting. Nothing special. We all know that Vesalova might have actually seen an airplane distorted by lighting and weather, or a balloon, or a heat inversion. Those of us open-minded enough—or mad enough, as you will—to think he *might have seen* an alien spaceship do not need to rush in haste to the True Believer position of changing "might have seen" to a dogmatic and fervent "did see." We just don't know, and most of us prefer to remain dubious about such a case, where multiple earthly explanations seem quite likely.

On June 6, in Konantsevo, several children reported the landing of a luminous sphere in a meadow. They saw, or hallucinated—as you will—a headless person climb out. Then, like a special effect in a sci-fi movie, both the craft and the headless ginkus disappeared. Just faded away...

Well, maybe the kids had smoked some decadent Capitalist weed. Maybe they just wanted to hoax the grown-ups and invented it all. Maybe...maybe... We do not get beyond "maybe" in cases like this, unless we have a Dogma in mind and want to force the data to fit it.

On June 11 in Volagda a woman reported a fiery sphere crossing the sky, visible for about seventeen minutes.

Maybe she saw a meteor. Maybe she saw a space ship. You decide such maybes definitely only if you made up your mind long, long ago that you would always decide them that way.

For several days in October that year, in the town of Voronezh—an industrial center of about one million inhabitants—scores of witnesses reported landings of spherical craft. They also reported gigantic extraterrestrials (twelve to fourteen feet high) who got out of the craft and went walking around the city park.

They even saw or hallucinated several cases of seeming "teleportations"—people who vanished from one place and then re-appeared elsewhere.

The witnesses to all this weirdness did not number two or three, who might have hatched a good hoax between them. In most cases, witnesses consisted of huge crowds.

Kind of makes me wonder. George Lucas, as noted earlier, could fake this on film, but I don't know of any existing technology that would fake it in several parts of a "real," "solid" town.

The alleged extraterrestrials allegedly had three eyes, according to some witnesses. Others denied that and said the Visitors (let's not assume we know what kind of space they came from) had a strange bump in their foreheads that looked only a little bit like a third eye.

Many of the sightings had very large crowds of witnesses. For instance, a woman who saw a red-yellow-green globe maneuvering over her house called all her neighbors. Over 500 people later agreed they had seen it—or 500+ people all starting hallucinating at the same time, if you must dump the data instead of thinking about it.

Several Soviet scientists investigated and failed to convince themselves that all the reports derived from hallucination. They frankly felt stumped, as they told American researcher Dr. Jacques Vallee.

Just before Vallee finished interviewing the Russian investigators—as he prepared to fly back to the United States— one final report came from Voronezh. Another strange craft had flown over a nuclear power plant, and sent a beam toward the ground, which left a burn mark in the asphalt.

Witnesses described the craft, and garb of the giants who walked around the park, as decorated with a curious symbol. Perhaps the reader will recognize that symbol at this stage of our story:

$$)+($$

The sign of UMMO... By now, this group art work, or hoax, or whatever, must have cost its perpetrators about as much as a Spielberg film. What *can* inspire such spendthrift humor?

Reference:

Revelations, Vallee, *op. cit.*

THIRTY-SEVEN

MASK: MAP: METAPHOR

In Which We Offer a Final Philosophical Analysis
of Our Problems in Defining "Reality" and "Mask"
—or a Good Counterfeit of a Final Analysis

> Reality is the toothbrush waiting in a glass at home...
> a bus-ticket...a paycheck...and the grave.
> —*F For Fake*

> Huh?
> —*The Maltese Falcon*

We live, existentially and phenomenologically, in a universe of infinite aspects. Whether the model-universe of science, in its extensions in space-time, extends to infinity, or has finite boundaries, or fits the Einstein model of an unbounded but finite Reimanian geometry, the sensory universe of our *experience* remains stubbornly infinite, in the sense that we can never exhaust the number of things we may "see" in it or the number of ways we can organize our individual perceptions into models or reality-tunnels.

When Ahab told Starbuck, "All material things are but masks," he had in mind ancient Gnostic teachings, but he also anticipated most of the discoveries of recent neuro-psychology and brain science. "Material things" no longer appear solid ("material") to physics, and they no longer appear as *things* to the student of perception. They appear as abstractions, co-creations (combining external signals with our internal file-system), or as models, or maps, or metaphors (depending on which field of communication science we take our jargon from)—or as masks, in the language I have borrowed from Ahab.

We have manufactured all "material things" out of an ever-changing deluge of photons and electrons in an abysmal void. As Nietzsche first declared, "We are all greater artists than we realize." (Or, as the Zen *roshi* Hui Neng said, "From the beginning, there has never been a 'thing.'")

In the strip-tease, the dancer removes one article of clothing after another and then appears naked. This "tease," some think, derives from the myth of Ishtar, who descended to Hell and had to remove one article of clothing at each of its seven gates. At the last gate, naked, Ishtar entered Eternity. This symbolizes the removal of one mask after another until no masks remain. That state, as described by all who've lived it, transcends all words and categories: we cannot communicate the unmasked by any new mask.

Zen represents that "naked" state, not by Cross or Crescent or Eye in Pyramid or any other model, but by an empty circle; the emptiness, not the circle representing the unmasked, the unspeakable, the unconditional.

To borrow a metaphor from Einstein, the relation between events and our mental images of them does not correspond to that of beef and beef-broth. We do not extract the essence of events and make our mental image out of that, as we extract broth from beef. What happens in perception and thought resembles more the *assigned* (arbitrary) connection between our hat and the ticket we receive when we check the hat.

The world does not consist of words, graphs or mathematics, which make up the "tickets" or *pookahs* we most commonly use to file-and-index our experience. The world of experience consists of non-verbal, non-graphical, non-mathematical processes, encountered and endured, which *we* convert into words, graphs or math (or other, more arty *pookahs* or masks.)

Concretely, the word "water" will not make you wet; the equation $F = ma$ will not hit you like a physical force (although it means that force mathematically equals mass multiplied by acceleration); no scientific theory accounts fully for your feelings/perceptions at this moment; no philosophy or theology explains or predicts what will happen in the next 30 seconds.

Representations, as human brain products, have arbitrary, *culturally-biased*, connections with the non-symbolic (unmasked) events that trigger our brains to make the representations. Believing in any of them literally has the same fallacy as believing Picasso's wives and mistresses had giant bodies, three nostrils, or two profiles and a full face all visible at once, or that Robert Burns' lady literally looked like a rose—petals and stem and thorns included.

Since the human nervous system, including the human brain, encounters and endures literally hundreds of millions of electrons and photons every minute (at a conservative estimate) the masks or models which compose our experienced reality-tunnel always exclude more than they include. The world of masks, the social world, has limits and laws; the unmasked remains infinite and (as Nietzsche liked to say) abysmal.

All "paths of liberation" (brain-freeing schools) know that we cannot remain in the abyss of the nameless forever, unless we choose to become hermits. (Very few do.) Once we have returned from a school of brain-change to the ordinary world, we again must see and think in masks, or we will not have the ability to communicate with and deal with others.

But, after the unmasked or naked vision of Ishtar—the world experienced as infinitely more than all masks—we can never take any one mask (or any one *pookah*) as seriously as its Idolators. We can see many kinds of truth in many kinds of masks, and we can see the fallacies in all of them—chiefly, the fallacies of allness (the mask includes all) and Identification (the mask "is" all.)

If we try to write about this post-liberation experience, we perforce produce metaphysics. This can take the form of the incomprehensible and mind-boggling brands of philosophy normally called "metaphysics" or some new form, breaking the rules of ordinary literature, to jar "the" reader, or I should say a few readers, into the new perspective we wish to share. Joyce's prose, Yeats' poetry, the paradoxes of Charles Fort, the "occult" jokebooks of Crowley, all represent such grotesque masks, created to free us from believing in the more deceptive social masks. Like metaphysics, they mean more (and other) than they say, and never mean anything *literally*. As Wilde said, "The reality of metaphysics is the reality of masks."

EPILOGUE

[At the last moment, just before going to press, Dr. Wilson called New Falcon Publications and said it was essential that the following be included in *Cosmic Trigger III: My Life After Death,* as it has significance beyond our wildest...]

The latest *Fortean Times* just arrived, issue 77, Winter 1995, with a report on those 23 dead Rosicrucians and the others found dead elsewhere. It now appears that this cult intended to migrate to Sirius.

I knew they fit the mystery somewhere...

Robert Anton Wilson
March 20, 1995

TRAJECTORIES
The Journal of Futurism and Heresy
Edited by Robert Anton Wilson

In recent issues:

- Zen and Virtual Reality Hardware
- Japanese plans for hotel in space
- 832 PSI tests validated
- Nanotechnology and the Hillis Connection Machine
- Walt Disney as futurist
- The electromagnetic 'V' Effect and the 'Paranormal'
- The Immortalist Party
- Father Fox and Creation Spirituality
- Extraterrestrial theories of evolution
- 'Mind-Body' Relations and Recent Neurochemical Discoveries
- Psychics Smites CSICOP
- Mind Machines and Head Hardware
- Bucky Fuller's Global Energy Grid in Russia, Central America and Germany
- Cyber-Terrorism and Computer Pathologies
- Notes on longevity research
- Sex, Satanism and Sodomized Dogs in Southern California
- Interviews with *Dr. Linus Pauling, Norman Spinrad* and *Barbara Marx Hubbard*
- Contributions by *Dr. Tim Leary* and *George Carlin*

$20 for four issues (one year)
$35 for eight issues (two years)

Make checks payable to:

Permanent Press
P.O. Box 700305
San Jose, CA 95170

OTHER BOOKS FROM
ROBERT ANTON WILSON

COSMIC TRIGGER I
Final Secret Of The Illuminati

The book that made it all happen!
Wilson at his classic best. Explores
Sirius, Synchronicities, and Secret
Societies. Wilson has been called
"One of the leading thinkers of the
Modern Age." The critics rave!!

"A 21st Century Renaissance Man.
…funny, optimistic and wise…"
—*The Denver Post*

ISBN 1-56184-003-3

COSMIC TRIGGER II
Down To Earth

The LONG AWAITED SEQUEL to
the original *Cosmic Trigger*!! Wilson
explores the incredible Illuminati-
based synchronicities that have
taken place since his ground-
breaking masterpiece was first
published.

"Wilson is a Quantum Leap."

"Hilarious… multi-dimensional… a
laugh a paragraph."
—*The Los Angeles Times*

ISBN 1-56184-011-4

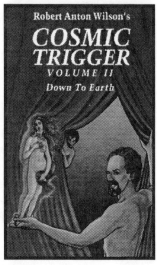

OTHER BOOKS FROM
ROBERT ANTON WILSON

PROMETHEUS RISING

Readers have been known to get angry, cry, laugh, even change their entire lives. Practical techniques to break free of one's 'reality tunnels'. A very important book, now in its *eighth* printing.

"*Prometheus Rising* is one of that rare category of modern works which intuits the next stage of human evolution... Wilson is one of the leading thinkers of the Modern age."
—Barbara Marx Hubbard

ISBN 1-56184-056-4

QUANTUM PSYCHOLOGY

The book for the 21st Century, complete with exercises. Picks up where *Prometheus Rising* left off. Some say it's materialistic, others call it scientific and still others insist it's mystical. It is all of these and none. (As Wilson says: 'I don't believe in anything!')

"Here is a Genius with a Gee!"
—Brian Aldiss, *The Guardian*

"What great physicist hides behind the mask of Wilson?"
—*New Scientist*

ISBN 1-56184-071-8

OTHER BOOKS FROM
ROBERT ANTON WILSON

ISHTAR RISING
The Goddess Obsession

The Return of the Goddess. Wilson provides a new slant on this provocative topic.
Exciting, suggestive, and truly passionate.
First published by Playboy Press as *The
Book of the Breast*. Updated and revised
for the '90s. All new illustrations.

ISBN 1-56184-109-9

SEX AND DRUGS
A Journey Beyond Limits

Both Sex and Drugs are fascinating and
dangerous subjects in these times. First
published by Playboy Press, *Sex and Drugs*
is *the* definitive work on this important and
controversial topic.

ISBN 1-56184-001-7

THE NEW INQUISITION
Irrational Rationalism &
The Citadel of Science

Wilson dares to confront *the* disease of our
time which he calls 'Fundamentalist Materialism'. "I am opposing the Fundamentalism,
not the Materialism. The book is deliberately shocking because I do not want its
ideas to seem any less stark or startling
than they are…"

ISBN 1-56184-002-5

OTHER BOOKS FROM
ROBERT ANTON WILSON

WILHELM REICH IN HELL
Foreword by C. S. Hyatt, Ph.D.
and Donald Holmes, M.D.

Inspired by the U. S. government seizure and burning of the scientific books and papers of the world famous psychiatrist Dr. Wilhelm Reich. "No President, Academy, Court of Law, Congress, or Senate on this earth has the knowledge or power to decide what will be the knowledge of tomorrow."

"Erudite, witty and genuinely scary..."   —*Publishers Weekly*

ISBN 1-56184-108-0

COINCIDANCE
A Head Test

The spelling of the title is *not* a mistake. *Dance* through Religion for the Hell of It, The Physics of Synchronicity, James Joyce and Finnegan's Wake, The Godfather and the Goddess, The Poet as Early Warning Radar and much much more...

"Wilson managed to reverse every mental polarity in me, as if I had been pulled through infinity."
—Philip K. Dick, author
of *Blade Runner*

ISBN 1-56184-004-1

BOOKS FROM
CHRISTOPHER S. HYATT, P H.D.

UNDOING YOURSELF
With Energized Meditation And Other Devices

Introduced by Dr. Israel Regardie
Preface by Robert Anton Wilson

"...the Energized Meditation system is fun and erotic and makes you smarter..." This *newly revised and expanded fifth edition* is extensively illustrated.

"*Undoing Yourself* is the latest attempt by the Illuminati Conspiracy to reveal the hither-to hidden teachings." —Robert Anton Wilson

ISBN 1-56184-057-2

SECRETS OF WESTERN TANTRA
The Sexuality Of The Middle Path

Introduced by Dr. J. M. Spiegelman
Preface by Robert Anton Wilson

Dr. Hyatt reveals the secret methods of enlightenment through transmutation of the *orgastic reflex*. Many explicit, practical techniques.

"This book is unique in the Tantric literature. Straightforward and honest, with no mystification..."
—James Wasserman

ISBN 1-56184-113-7

BOOKS FROM TIMOTHY LEARY, Ph.D.

THE GAME OF LIFE

*With Contributions by
Robert Anton Wilson*

Eagerly awaited and long out of
print, this new edition is already an
instant hit! Written in the 70's with
all the influence of the wild and
wonderful 60's, *The Game of Life*
reflects the depth of mind of one of
the unique human beings of this
century. In a beautiful 8 1/2″ x 11″
edition, extensively illustrated.

ISBN 1-56184-050-5

WHAT DOES WOMAN WANT?

Dr. Leary's first novel presents the
Quixotic saga of Dylan, a confused
by sincere minstrel and evolutionary agent. He has been assigned
to a primitive planet in the latter
years of the Roaring 20th Century
to perform those small but precise
jiggles needed to cause chaos in
the old, outmoded gene-pools.
Leary takes the reader across the
planet in his pursuit of the answer
to the seminal question: *What
Does WoMan Want?*

ISBN 0-941404-62-5

BOOKS FROM TIMOTHY LEARY, PH.D.

NEUROPOLITIQUE
A New Vision of Neuropolitics
With Robert Anton Wilson &
George Koopman

The first version of *Neuropolitics*
was written between 1973-1976
when Dr. Leary was in prison.
Several chapters were composed
during solitary confinement. Leary
explores the role of the dissident/
philosopher and offers a multitude
of brilliant observations on our
past, present and, especially, our
future. One of his best. Updated
and rewritten for the 90's.

ISBN 1-56184-012-2

INFO-PSYCHOLOGY
A Revision Of Exo-Psychology
"The Info-Worlds our species will
discover, create, explore and in-
habit in the immediate future will
not be reached from launch pads
alone, but also through our personal computer screens."

Dr. Leary explores the *real* issues
of our time: Space Migration,
Intelligence Increase and Life
Extension in this "Manual On The
Use Of The Human Nervous
System According To The Instruc-
tions Of The Manufacturers".

ISBN 1-56184-105-6

BOOKS FROM
CHRISTOPHER S. HYATT, P H.D.

THE TREE OF LIES
Become Who You Are

Introduced by Robert Anton Wilson

The Tree of Lies takes us on a walking tour of the prison erected by the lies that society tells us and the lies we tell ourselves. And then it provides the tools to tunnel out.

"Is it possible to use language to undo the hallucinations created by language? ...a few heroic efforts seem able to jolt readers awake... to transcend words."
—Robert Anton Wilson

ISBN 1-56184-008-4

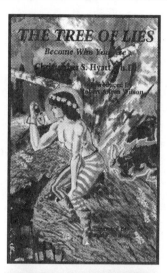

PACTS WITH THE DEVIL
A Chronicle of Sex, Blasphemy & Liberation

With S. Jason Black

Braving the new Witchcraft Panic that is sweeping America, *Pacts With The Devil* places the Western magical tradition and the Western psyche in perspective. Contains a detailed history of European 'Black Magic' and includes new editions of 17th and 18th century Grimoires with detailed instruction for their use. Extensively illustrated.

ISBN 1-56184-058-0

BOOKS FROM
CHRISTOPHER S. HYATT, P H.D.

UNDOING YOURSELF
With Energized Meditation And Other Devices

Introduced by Dr. Israel Regardie
Preface by Robert Anton Wilson

"...the Energized Meditation system is fun and erotic and makes you smarter..." This *newly revised and expanded fifth edition* is extensively illustrated.

"*Undoing Yourself* is the latest attempt by the Illuminati Conspiracy to reveal the hither-to hidden teachings." —Robert Anton Wilson

ISBN 1-56184-057-2

SECRETS OF WESTERN TANTRA
The Sexuality Of The Middle Path

Introduced by Dr. J. M. Spiegelman
Preface by Robert Anton Wilson

Dr. Hyatt reveals the secret methods of enlightenment through transmutation of the *orgastic reflex*. Many explicit, practical techniques.

"This book is unique in the Tantric literature. Straightforward and honest, with no mystification..."
—James Wasserman

ISBN 1-56184-113-7